It is said there is nothing new under the sun. Yet America's industrial pioneers time after time took discarded ideas and made them work. Crude hand-powered elevators had existed for centuries before Elisha Otis designed the safety elevator. Isaac Singer and Christopher Sholes were not the first to think of sewing machines and typewriters but they were the first to make them practical.

Success for some pioneers meant battling against firmly-entrenched customs. Having fun was a sin before that fabulous showman, P. T. Barnum, came along with his circuses. Proper women didn't paint their faces before Elizabeth Arden made the use of cosmetics widespread. Just about the most unsavory business you could name in the 1860's was advertising. It took the efforts of F. W. Ayer and J. Walter Thompson to make it respectable.

Many pioneers amassed fantastic fortunes — Cyrus McCormick, Henry Ford, John D. Rockefeller. Some disdained wealth and gave their money away: Thomas Cook donated his fortune to the temperance movement and George Eastman endowed schools, hospitals, and symphonies. Others like labor leader Samuel Gompers led modest lives and died with no wealth to show for their rewarding careers.

But rich or poor, bitter or satisfied, these fifty pioneers had two things in common: determination and courage. They used it to change the face of America.

THE STORIES OF ROCKEFELLER, SWIFT, EDISON, WOOLWORTH, SQUIBB, PROCTOR, SEARS, OTIS, SINGER, CARRIER AND 40 OTHER BUSINESS LEADERS AND COURAGEOUS INNOVATORS WHOSE ACTIVITIES FOUNDED MAJOR INDUSTRIES, AND SHAPED TODAY'S ECONOMY.

the 50 great PIONEERS of

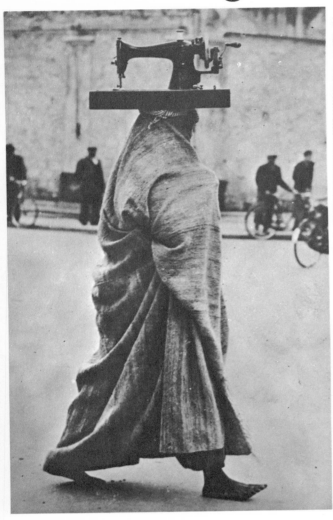

AMERICAN INDUSTRY

by the editors of **News Front YEAR**

News front.

The fifty great pioneers of
American industry

EDITOR'S NOTE

The U. S. economy is the largest, most successful and the most widely beneficial of all mankind's collective achievements. It has brought more real benefits, to more people, than any previous human effort.

Yet its foundations, its roots, are stubbornly and sturdily individual. They must remain so if the U.S. is to continue its advance, to continue to lead forward in genuine individual freedom and ever more abundant and ever more widely distributed prosperity of its own people and, by aid and example, all the rest of unenslaved mankind.

The men who laid the basis, charted the direction and directed the shape of U.S. industry, and the thriving economy which it sustains, were above all individuals. They chose their own paths, blazed their own trails, set their sights on their own particular stars. While other pioneers were continually pushing back the frontiers of physical environment, conquering the rivers and forests, the plains and the mountains, these pioneers were expanding the frontiers of enterprise and opportunity, each in his own way, in his own time, of his own volition.

They saw, where lesser men were blind, needs to be filled, opportunities which were open. But they did more. Not only did they recognize opportunity, they seized it, mastered it—even created it, so strong were the fires burning within each.

And in doing so—each in his own way and in his own field—they were the pioneers who created today's America.

They differed widely among themselves. Some, essentially, were inventors, like Otis, Carrier, the little known Hughes and Richardson. Still more were organizers, like Rockefeller and Vail. Others were the creators of modern business methods and techniques, like Patterson and Procter. Still others were production geniuses, like Ford.

But they had several fundamental characteristics in common. They were not afraid to be innovators. They had no reverence for tradition—what was done simply because it always had been done that way. And, above all, they simply could not be discouraged; they were almost incredibly persistent. Failure the first time or, for that matter, the third or even the fifth, was not a deterrent, but a challenge. They never lost heart. And they always followed through. They were not content to prove something *could* be done. They were never satisfied until it *was* being done, practically and successfully, in the practical world.

The stories of these Pioneers of American Industry constitute one of the most successful and widely reprinted of the regular series featured in NEWS FRONT, Management's News Magazine.

To help keep you abreast of the world of today, which these pioneers helped shape, NEWS FRONT's editors call your attention to: INDUSTRY IN THE FREE WORLD, an analysis of the economies of 26 nations and the opportunities they offer U.S. industry, which includes a ranking of the 1500 leading corporations outside the U.S.; the NEWS FRONT DIRECTORY OF 7500 LEADING U.S. MANUFACTURERS, an exhaustive analysis of the top U.S. manufacturing corporations; and NEWS FRONT's other companion book publications—YEAR, the Picture News Annual, and the YEAR Pictorial History Series.

BALDWIN H. WARD

YEAR Picture News and Picture History Books by the Editors of NEWS FRONT

| YEAR | TURBULENT | PICTORIAL HISTORY | PICTORIAL HISTORY | BIBLE & | SCIENCE & | FLIGHT |
| The Picture News Annual | 20TH CENTURY | OF AMERICA | OF THE WORLD | CHRISTIANITY | ENGINEERING | |

FOREWORD

Change . . . Courage . . . Progress . . . three inseparable ideas that men throughout history have forged into action.

Acting on new ideas takes courage, since men are not always sure that change will bring progress. But they are sure that progress comes only through change.

Progress in one generation has not often been enough for the next. Changing needs make it necessary to go beyond past conventions, and those men who, without prejudice, participate in change, create the history of progress.

Even more than in the past, progress through courage and change is a part of modern civilization. The challenge of progress confronts our society . . . but this challenge should never be a problem to the American businessman. For years he has participated in major changes and has faced problems of advocating innovation.

In the 1880s, Gustavus Swift shipped dressed meats to the Eastern market, instead of live steers. There was strong opposition to this new idea from Eastern butchers and consumers. But he finally overcame their fears of beef dressed a thousand miles away. How would you have reacted to these changes in meat processing and distribution? During the 1880s, would you have seen this as progress?

Another example of a businessman who advocated change is Rowland H. Macy. His merchandising ideas failed four times. But his successful fifth store created a sales pattern for the future. His new concepts included: fixed prices . . . cash only . . . fresh stock weekly . . . clearance sales . . . and weekly newspaper advertisements. How would you have reacted to Macy's merchandising concepts?

In the last two decades you have been asked many times to change your ideas about products and services.

In the early '50s, what did you think of George Romney's compact car? Did you reject Land's Polaroid camera as a gimmick? Was your door open? . . . was your mind open? . . . to the IBM or Remington Rand salesman who showed you the benefits of data processing?

These pioneers ask you to use individual judgment . . . to depart from conformity if logic dictates. They ask of you the courage and will to take the initiative . . . to support progress.

In perfecting new products and services during the years ahead, the continuing mission of The Pioneer is to seek out those men of personal courage and individual judgment, whose decisions are based on logic . . . not tradition . . . who regard change . . . not as a problem . . . but as an opportunity for progress.

The Pioneer counts on you to be in this vanguard.

CONTENTS

6

INDEX

BY INDUSTRY

BY PERSONALITY

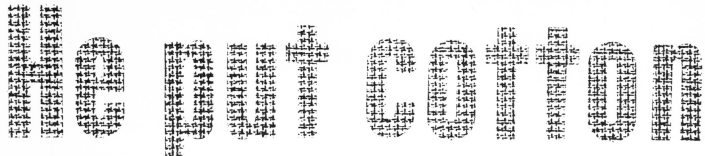

He put cotton

Samuel Slater ⧗ sparked U.S. Industrial Revolution with first mechanized

Samuel Slater

A YOUNG 18th century Englishman with a photographic memory was not only the pioneer of today's multi-billion-dollar U.S. textile industry, but also—in the words of President Andrew Jackson—the "father of American manufacturing."

He was Samuel Slater, who arrived in New York in 1789 with the plans for a cotton mill in his head.

Slater was born in 1768, just a year before Richard Arkwright patented the unified system of machine carding, spinning, and weaving that took textile manufacture out of the home and into the factory, and launched the industrial revolution.

By the time Slater was 14, water-powered cotton mills were prospering all over England. One of the largest —founded by Arkwright himself, in partnership with a stocking manufacturer named Jedediah Strutt—was near the Slater family home, on the Derwent River in Belden, Derbyshire.

Slater's father, a well-to-do farmer,

was a friend of Strutt's. And when the manufacturer suggested that one of the Slater boys might like to come into the Belden mill as an apprentice, he recommended young Samuel—a bright boy who liked mathematics and machinery.

After some talk with Strutt about the future of the textile industry, Samuel decided to take up the offer.

In 1782, he signed the form of indenture—unchanged since the passage of the British Statute of Apprentices in 1532—that bound him to serve Strutt for the next seven years, and to stay away from women, gambling houses, taverns, theaters, and just about anything else that might distract him from his duties.

Fourteen-year-old Samuel would probably not have been easily distracted in any case.

He was so fascinated by the mill that for the first six months of his apprenticeship, he spent all his Sundays there studying the machinery, instead of making the short trip home to the family farm.

When his apprenticeship ended, he spent an extra year working for

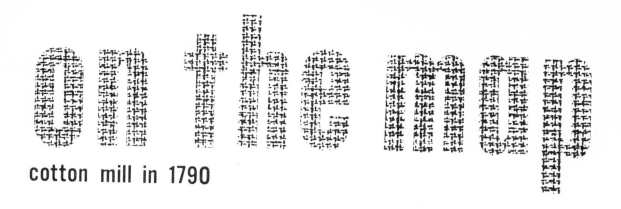

Strutt, supervising the construction of equipment at one of the manufacturer's newer mills. Then, in 1789, he decided to go to America.

The newly independent U.S. had barely begun its industrialization, and offered magnificent opportunities for young men trained in English factories.

The only problem was getting out of England. England at that time had a virtual monopoly on textile production—and wished to keep it.

Export of machinery or plans for construction of machinery was strictly prohibited, and trained mechanics were forbidden to emigrate.

Carder was hardest to perfect

Slater, however, managed to keep the dark secret of his apprenticeship in a textile mill, and was allowed to sail for America as the son of a farmer, and, presumably, a farmer himself.

He hid his indenture papers from Strutt in the bottom of his trunk, but did not run the risk of trying to smuggle out plans of the Arkwright machines.

Arriving in New York, he found that the U.S. textile industry was, indeed, 20 years behind England's.

First spinning frame had 48 spindles

The British government had performed a feat that today's security-conscious governments might well envy—not a single set of mechanical drawings had crossed the Atlantic.

American textile manufacturers had tried to build crude machinery of their own, based largely on imagination and rumors of English mills. Some of them had been fleeced by English immigrants who pretended to know all about the Arkwright machines. Several states of the new Union had offered rewards as high as $200 (in a day when $100 a year in cash was a substantial family income) for workable machinery.

SLATER FOUNDED
A DOZEN FIRMS

Slater was sure that he could build a textile mill from memory. And he lost no time in beginning the search for a backer.

He took a stopgap job with a New York company and wrote to Moses Brown, Providence Quaker businessman who was a partner in the machine-spinning firm of Almy & Brown.

"I have had opportunity, and oversight, of Sir Richard Arkwright's works in Mr. Strutt's mill for upwards of eight years.

"If you are not provided for, I should be glad to service you."
Moses Brown wrote back:

"We are destitute of a person acquainted with waterframe spinning. As the frame we have is the first attempt of the kind that has been made in America, it is too imperfect to afford much encouragement. We hardly know what to say to thee . . ."

Offered Partnership

An offer of a partnership followed, and young Slater was off to Pawtucket, R.I., where the Almy & Brown plant was located.

It took him a year to put Arkwright's machinery together from scratch—the carders that prepared the raw cotton for spinning, the complex waterframe spinners that Moses Brown had despaired of perfecting and the looms. He even had to make the tools for the mechanics who assisted him.

But his only serious difficulty came when his carder refused to card; the cotton, instead of passing out as thin fleece, ready to be twisted and spun, jammed up against the teeth of the machine.

He was so afraid that his backers would take him for just another English imposter that he almost ran away. But Sylvanus Brown, Moses Brown's brother and plant manager, helped him solve the problem.

Brown noticed that the teeth of his wife's home carding equipment lay at a different angle from those of Slater's unsuccessful prototype.

And the two men then realized that, although Slater had originally specified the correct slant for his carder's teeth, the machine had not been built sturdily enough to hold them in position.

When the teeth were bent back to the proper angle, the cotton went through.

On Dec. 20, 1790, the first practical U.S. cotton mill went into operation in Pawtucket.

Slater himself was in charge of the manufacturing end at Almy, Brown & Slater; Almy and Brown took care of purchasing and sales, and they soon found that they could hardly work fast enough to keep up with their energetic young partner.

Cotton Supply

Slater's letters to the Providence office are full of complaints like: "A number of frames are stopped for want of rollers. . ." "Please give me a little advice concerning the candles, shall I leave off work every night or buy them by the pound here?" . . .

"I wish there might be a little more attention paid to this business —we shall lose 13 or 14 dollars this week by shortness of cotton."

(Quality and quantity of cotton supply was a serious problem for the first three years. Eli Whitney's cotton gin, which made possible rapid, thorough processing of the raw fiber, was not invented until 1793.)

Nevertheless, the partners did good business. By 1793, they were ready to open their second Pawtucket mill. (Known today as the Slater Mill, it was opened to the public as a museum in 1955.)

By the end of the 1790s, Slater decided to branch out. S. Slater & Co. opened its first mill in Rehoboth, Mass., in 1802. However, he kept his interest in Almy, Brown & Slater.

If Slater had been born 74 years later, he would probably have become the head of a giant textile trust.

In the business world of the early 19th century, where things were done on a smaller scale, he simply founded one company after another, with a dozen different partners, and kept them all going.

Branching Out

Between 1802 and 1828 he organied 12 companies, and sold out his interest in only one of them.

He successfully weathered the two severe textile industry depressions in 1815 and 1829.

And he was an enthusiastic industry promoter, generously giving advice—and often financial backing to younger men entering the business.

In the years before his death in 1835, he was recognized as the founder of an industry that had been vital to the economic development of the young American republic, and as one of his adopted country's leading manufacturers.

One of his business contemporaries wrote in 1831 that "few have done more to bring young and enterprising men into business than Samuel Slater. He has, probably, now a larger amount employed in manufacturing than any other single individual in the U.S."

And the Providence Journal, in his obituary, paid a tribute that was impressive even in those days of flowery journalistic eloquence:

"It has rarely fallen to the lot of any individual to be made an instrument, under Providence, of so much and such widely diffused benefit to his fellow men."

Slater's second mill, now a museum, is industry shrine

BALTIMORE celebrated laying of B&O cornerstone on July 4, 1828. First spade of earth was dug by 92-year-old Charles Carroll of Carrollton, Md., last surviving signer of the Decla-ration of Independence, who said that he considered his honorary task to be "among the most important acts of my life," second only to his signing of the Declaration, if even to that.

ALL ABOARD!

Philip Thomas founded Baltimore and Ohio, first U.S. railroad, opened the way to the Middle West

THE 220,000-MILE network of railroads that crisscrosses the U.S. today began to grow in 1827, when a group of Baltimore businessmen decided to do something to boost their town's sagging share of commerce with the fast-growing pioneer West.

What they did was to charter the nation's first railroad, the Baltimore & Ohio—now 6000 miles long and sixth among U.S. railroads in revenue, with income of $389.4 million at the start of the Sixties.

The leader of the group, and the man who guided the B&O through its first nine years, was a Quaker banker, Philip E. Thomas.

The U.S. in 1827 had a population of just over 12 million, and Baltimore, with 80,000 inhabitants, was its third largest city.

The great surge of growth that was to carry the nation to the Pacific by mid-century had already begun.

The toll roads and turnpikes that were the only links between the coastal cities and the pioneer country West of the Alleghenies were overcrowded and inadequate.

A new form of transportation was clearly needed, and most Eastern businessmen were betting on canals.

New York's Erie Canal had opened in 1823; construction of the land-and-water Pennsylvania System of Public Works had begun in 1824.

Canal transportation was proving itself to be fast and cheap, and as "canal fever" mounted, Baltimore's trade—still dependent on the old National Road to Wheeling on the Ohio River—declined.

Work on the Chesapeake and Ohio Canal was under way at Georgetown, but, by 1826, Baltimore businessmen had decided that this new southern waterway, which would bypass their city, would do them no good at all. (Philip Thomas, then a Chesapeake and Ohio project commissioner, resigned his post in indignation.)

Baltimore's future looked so dark that several leading families had already moved away.

Then, in the fall of 1826, Philip Thomas began to listen to his brother, Evan, talk about railroads.

Evan had just returned from a visit to England, and had been dazzled by the newly completed Darlington & Stockton line.

Philip Thomas was 50 years old in 1826. He had begun his career in the hardware business, had risen to the presidency of the National Mechanics Bank and was one of Baltimore's most respected citizens.

According to John H. B. Latrobe, another of the B&O's founders, "his

11

Thomas' persistence overcame difficulties early

persuasiveness was remarkable. Never thrown off his balance, quiet in his speech, laborious in his search for the facts, and, above all, eminently successful in his own business, people listened to him with conviction."

Philip Thomas spent the last months of 1826 searching for the facts about railroads.

He was joined in his research by George Brown, a director of the National Mechanics Bank, who had also been receiving glowing accounts from a brother in England.

By February, 1827, the two men were convinced that a railroad was just what Baltimore needed, and on Feb. 12 they invited 27 Baltimore business leaders to a meeting at Brown's home to discuss the project.

A few days later, the group met again to listen to a highly favorable report by a subcommittee it had appointed to investigate details.

The report concluded, "it is the opinion of many judicious and practical men that these roads will, for heavy transportation, supersede canals as effectually as canals have superseded the turnpike roads."

For 1827, such a statement was little short of revolutionary.

The world's first known "rail road" had been built in England in 1602, for horsedrawn carts traveling from a mine to a nearby canal.

It had consisted of parallel strips of wood, laid on wooden crossties, which reduced friction so effectively that horses and mules could pull two-and-one-half times as much weight as before.

The wooden tracks were soon overlaid with iron, and by the early 19th

century the basic principles of railroad construction, still in use today, had all been developed.

However, the only "rail roads" in the U.S. were short, privately owned colliery lines. Even in Great Britain, where 2000 miles of track had been laid, railroads were just beginning to be thought of as a general, public means of transportation for people and freight.

The cars were still all horsedrawn, although scientists and inventors had been experimenting with steam power for almost 200 years.

Once the Baltimore businessmen had decided on their daring project, they moved fast.

The Baltimore and Ohio Railroad's charter, which was to serve as a model for dozens of railroad charters in the years to come, passed the Maryland state legislature on Feb. 28. (One of its notable provisions was exemption of the railroad from state taxes.)

With Thomas as president and Brown as treasurer, the new company began to sell stock.

The idea of a railroad had aroused so much popular enthusiasm that the initial offering of $3 million was soon oversubscribed.

Practically every citizen of Baltimore with any cash to spare owned a piece of the B&O, and the laying of the railroad's cornerstone, on July 4, 1828, was the occasion for a giant civic celebration.

Army engineers had surveyed the route from Baltimore to the Ohio River, and work on the first 13-mile line of track began in October.

The B&O began carrying passengers on a 13-mile run early in 1830.

Later the same year, the U.S.'s first steam engine — Peter Cooper's tiny *Tom Thumb* — puffed triumphantly down the B&O's track, and the B&O began switching to steam power as fast as it could commission the design and manufacture of engines. Within four years, seven locomotives were hauling the railroad's 44 passenger and 1078 freight cars.

By 1834, rails were running to Harper's Ferry, and in 1835 passenger service between Baltimore and Washington began.

In 1836, Philip Thomas retired. Every mile of B&O track had meant exhausting challenges—technical and administrative, financial and political —for the company's first president.

The $3 million stock issue of 1827 had been woefully inadequate as construction costs—over $4000 per mile of track—had mounted, and, in the depression years of the 1830s, capital was hard to come by.

The B&O's political troubles stemmed from its rivalry with the Chesapeake and Ohio Canal Co., whose president also happened to be chairman of the Roads and Canals Committee of the U.S. House of Representatives.

It was not until 1852 that the line finally reached its original goal—the Ohio River at Wheeling.

But it pushed on to reach St. Louis in 1857, Chicago in 1874.

Almost half a century after the pioneer railroad's birth, the great days of railroading in the United States were just beginning.

HISTORIC *Tom Thumb*, first U.S. locomotive, made trial run out of B&O's Baltimore station on Aug. 25, 1830, reached hitherto undreamed of speed of 18 miles per hour.

HORSEDRAWN RAILROAD CARS PROVIDED SERVICE DURING FIRST MONTHS OF B&O OPERATION, WERE SOON REPLACED BY STEAM.

PHILIP E. THOMAS, first president of B&O. was born in 1776, son of a prosperous Maryland planter, lived to see B&O carry Lincoln to first inaugural *(r.).* Thomas died in 1861, as Civil War, in which B&O played a vital role as supply lifeline of North, was beginning.

SURVEYING, construction of pioneer railroad's route across Alleghenies, was for 1830s, a stupendous engineering feat.

HIGHLIGHTS OF U.S. RAILROADING

1825—First steam locomotive operated experimentally.
1828—Construction of Baltimore & Ohio begun.
1830—Scheduled steam service begun on South Carolina Rail Road (now part of Southern Railway).
1831—First U.S. mails carried.
1837—World's first sleeping car service.
1840—Total track miles 2808.
1853—Chicago linked by rail with East.
1854—Rails from East reach the Mississippi.
1856—California's first railroad opened.
1859—Rails from East reach the Missouri.
1860—Track miles pass 30,000.
1862—President Lincoln signs bill authorizing transcontinental lines.

1869—First transcontinental rail link completed.
1883—Standard time adopted.
1886—Standard gauge adopted throughout U.S.
1893—Locomotive reaches 100 miles per hour.
1900—Total railroad investment passes $10 billion.
1917—Federal Government takes over rails during World War I.
1920—Trackage reaches all-time high—230,000 miles.
1934—First Diesel streamliner in service.
1952—More Diesel-electric than steam locomotives.
1960—Total rail investment reaches $35.5 billion

13

HARVESTER OF THE

McCormick's reaper opened up wheat wealth of the West, began transformation, mechanization of agriculture throughout world. U.S. spent $3.3 billion on farm machinery by 1960; company he began, International Harvester, has sales over $1.68 billion

ON A HOT Virginia afternoon in 1831, a 22-year-old farmer gave the first public demonstration of a mechanical reaper that could harvest grain four times as fast as a man with a cradle and scythe.

The young farmer was Cyrus McCormick; his invention was to revolutionize agriculture and lay the foundations for today's multi-billion-dollar agricultural equipment industry and one of its major corporations, International Harvester Co.

In 1831, farmers in the U.S.—and all over the world—were still harvesting grain with hand tools that had hardly changed since the days of the ancient Egyptians.

A strong man could cut only two acres of grain in a day of backbreaking labor.

Most farms in the North, worked by their owners with a hired hand or two, were necessarily small; in the South, operation of huge plantations was made possible only by slave labor. The great plains of the West were still waiting to be settled and sown with grain, and it is difficult to imagine how they could have been conquered if mechanized harvesting had not become a reality when it did.

Dozens of inventors before Cyrus McCormick had tried to produce a mechanical reaper and failed.

One of these inventors, in fact, was Cyrus' own father, Robert McCormick, a well-educated, well-to-do farmer of Scotch-Irish descent who also operated grist mills, sawmills, a smelter and a smithy in Rockbridge County, Va.

Robert McCormick began working on his reaper in 1816, when his eldest son was seven years old, and he did not give up until May of 1831.

By then, Cyrus had already shown considerable mechanical ability. When he was 15, he had built himself a lightweight cradle that enabled him to do the harvesting work of a grown man; a few years later, he invented a hillside plow. He had spent hours on end in the family blacksmith shop, watching his father tinker with reaper models—and when Robert McCormick decided to give the reaper up as a bad job, Cyrus took it over.

By mid-July, he had a reaper that worked.

He had abandoned the principles of his father's machine, which was pushed into the grain by two horses while the wheat was pressed against stationary convex sickles by rapidly revolving beaters, and developed a set of principles of his own—principles which lie behind every piece of grain cutting machinery at work today.

Basically, the first horsedrawn McCormick reaper had seven essential elements: a straight knife with a serrated edge and reciprocal or vibrating motion; a platform behind the knife to receive the cut grain; fingers or guards extending from the platform to keep the grain from slipping sideways; a revolving reel to hold the grain against the knife and lay the cut stalks on the platform; forward draft from the right or stubble side by means of shafts attached in front to the master wheel; a divider on the

Modern McCormick reapers are power-driven, vastly faster and more efficient than 1831 model; but, like all other grain cutting machinery in use today, they incorporate the seven basic elements first combined by Cyrus McCormick.

CYRUS McCORMICK

PRAIRIES

left side to separate the grain to be cut from that to be left standing; and a master wheel to carry most of the weight of the machine and furnish power.

McCormick had originated all seven of these elements independently; as far as he knew, no one but his father and himself had ever even thought of a mechanical reaper.

Actually, six of the seven had already been developed by other inventors; only the master wheel was his alone. But he first combined them into a working machine.

He first discovered that other inventors were interested in the reaper, too, in 1834, when he read in *Mechanics' Magazine* a description of a reaper just invented by a Cincinnati candlestick maker named Obed Hussey, based on principles similar to his. (Hussey was later to be one of his many competitors.)

He immediately sent a description of his own machine to the magazine's editor, explaining that it was three years old, and filed a patent claim in Washington.

However, he went on improving the reaper for six years more, selling only an occasional machine to a friend or neighbor. In 1840, he finally decided that it was good enough to be marketed on a broader scale.

He could hardly have picked a worse time to go into business. The McCormick enterprises had been hit hard by the panic of 1837; in 1841, he and his father had to sell their iron furnace and plunge deep into debt to keep the little plant in the black smith shop in operation.

Blacksmith shop on Walnut Grove Farm where McCormick invented the reaper also served as his first manufacturing plant

Moreover, he found out almost immediately that the reaper was not as thoroughly perfected as he had believed; the first two sold to customers outside Rockbridge County broke down in heavy grain in 1841 harvest.

Another winter of work eliminated the flaw that had produced the clogging, and, in 1842, for the first time, the reaper was offered with a money-back guarantee.

The small business began to grow. Seven reapers were sold in 1842, 23 in 1843, 50 in 1844, at $100 each.

During the next year or two, he began licensing Western manufacturers to produce McCormick reapers.

But, both because he was dissatisfied with the quality of the work turned out by his franchise holders and because he was so sure that the real future of the agricultural equipment industry lay in the West, he became more and more anxious to move his plant westward.

In 1847, he went to Chicago, built a factory there, and manufactured and sold 500 reapers.

During the 1850s, sales soared into the thousands.

However, competition in the infant industry was getting tough. Both McCormick and Hussey had applied for extensions of their 1834 patents in 1848; both had been refused, and the field was thrown open to dozens of rivals.

If McCormick's talents for sales, advertising and mar-

keting had not been as great as his inventive genius, his company could never have held its own.

He began to establish a chain of sales agencies throughout the grain-growing areas of the nation almost as soon as he moved to Chicago.

In the early '50s, he became the first major manufacturer to introduce consumer credit. A farmer could buy a McCormick reaper—then priced at $125—for $35 down at harvest time and the balance on December 1.

McCormick had begun advertising in the 1840s, and his ad budget grew as fast as his competition. (Early ads for the "Patent Virginia Reaper" usually showed a reaper being pulled at a trot by a pair of high-stepping horses, with a man dressed in his Sunday best raking the platform.)

He was one of the first advertisers to make use of testimonials—usually from socially or politically prominent men who had never seen a reaper, much less operated one, but who could be persuaded that the machine was a boon to the hard-working farmer—and one of the first to use direct mail campaigns.

The Civil War brought the agricultural equipment industry into its own once and for all.

"The reaper is to the North what slavery is to the

First McCormick reaper (l.) made a hit with local farmers at Steele's Tavern, Va., in July of 1831. Competitive field trials with other manufacturer's machines were later a favorite McCormick publicity stunt.

McCormick's first Chicago factory (r.) was destroyed by fire in 1851, rebuilt on same site. After great Chicago Fire of 1871, a giant new plant was built on a new site, today the location of International Harvester's McCormick Works.

MECHANIZATION OF THE U.S. FARM ($ million)

	1929	1937	1941	1950	1960
Farmers' Expenditures (machinery, trucks, tractors, etc.)	445*	461*	680	3014	3300
International Harvester Sales (Consolidated before 1941, parent company later)	337	352	365	943	1683

* Five-year average

APPEARED ABOUT 1900

South," declared Secretary of War Edwin M. Stanton, "and without McCormick's invention, I feel the North could not have won and the Union would have been dismembered."

McCormick himself, as a Southerner by birth and a Midwesterner by adoption, had hated to see war come.

In 1860, he founded the *Expositor*, a religious periodical, bought the Chicago *Times*, and published both until April, 1861, using them to urge preservation of the Union.

A big man with seemingly inexhaustible energy, he was constantly on the move; he often held conferences in his hotel bedrooms while he shaved.

He was considered cold and aloof by most of those who knew him. In September of 1857, however, he met a pretty girl from upstate New York, Nancy Fowler, and four months later he married her.

By 1874, he was the father of five children; in 1879, the McCormick family moved into a lavish Chicago mansion, and there, five years later, Cyrus McCormick died.

His eldest son, Cyrus H. McCormick, succeeded him as president of McCormick Reaper Works.

By then, the company was producing a harvester, mowers, reaper-mowers and binders as well as reapers; sales passed the 50,000-unit mark the year of Cyrus' death.

McCormick reapers had won top honors at a dozen international expositions, and were selling briskly in Europe as well as in the U.S.; in 1879, Cyrus had been elected to the French Academy of Sciences as "having done more for agriculture than any other living man."

International Harvester Co., today the giant of the industry (its 1959 sales were $1.36 billion), was formed in 1902—at just about the time when the first power-driven reapers were going on the market—by a merger of McCormick Reaper Works with six competitors. Cyrus H. McCormick became the new company's first president, and his grandson, Brooks McCormick, is now its executive vice president.

The giant strides that mechanized agriculture has made since the invention of the original McCormick reaper can perhaps be best summed up by a single set of statistics: harvesting one acre of wheat, a job that took 46 hours in 1829, takes less than half an hour today.

McCormick's sales strategy matched his inventive genius

Before Cyrus McCormick's reaper appeared in 1831, farmers used the cradle to harvest grain. This tool enabled men to cut two acres a day.

By 1858, harvesting machinery used canvas aprons to raise the grain to a table where two men riding on the reaper bound it as fast as collected and tossed the bundles overboard.

18

"READ ALL ABOUT IT!"

NEWSPAPERS WERE A LUXURY ITEM UNTIL BEN DAY PRINTED THE NEW YORK *SUN* — A "PENNY DAILY" THAT ANYONE COULD BUY AND JUST ABOUT EVERYONE WANTED TO READ.

ON SEPTEMBER 3, 1833, a new newspaper appeared on the streets of New York City.

It was a small paper, even for that day, with its four business-stationery-size pages divided into three columns each. But it was the most revolutionary venture in the colorful, controversy-packed, often rowdy 129-year history of American journalism.

The paper was the New York *Sun,* and its editor and publisher was a 23-year-old printer named Benjamin H. Day.

It was revolutionary because it sold for only a penny; because it was hawked on the street by newsboys; and because it recognized that the average reader was more interested in news from the police courts than from the royal courts of Europe.

In short, it was the first of the mass-circulation dailies.

Ben Day (his son was later to invent the engraving process that bears the family name) was the son of a Springfield, Mass., hat maker.

He entered the printing trade as an apprentice on the Springfield *Republican* in 1824, and moved on to New York in 1830.

Within two years, he had opened his own small print shop.

He began publishing the *Sun* as a

potentially profitable, if highly speculative, sideline to his printing business —but he must have realized that a successful "penny daily" would make newspaper history as well as profits.

In 1833, the U.S. newspaper business was growing as fast as the young nation itself.

The first American newspaper, a weekly called the Boston *News Letter,* had been founded in 1704.

The colonial period had produced scores of small papers, and a few remarkable editors like Benjamin Franklin and John Peter Zenger. But the quality of colonial journalism had, on the whole, been low, and publishers had been hamstrung by censorship and taxation.

NEWSPAPER BOOM

After the Revolutionary War, with freedom of the press guaranteed by the new Constitution and politics in a healthy ferment, newspapers began to boom.

In 1801, there were 200 papers in the country; in 1833, there were 1200. This spurt of growth was like no other in the history of journalism, and the U.S., by the end of the first quarter of the 19th century, had more newspapers with a higher total circulation than any other nation.

HIGHBROW

Nevertheless, newspapers were still a luxury item, and most of their readers were businessmen, politicians, intellectuals, and gentlemen of leisure.

Sold largely by subscription at $10 a year, with a single copy price of 6¢, they were simply too expensive for the man in the street—and they weren't edited for him, anyway.

Their contents were overwhelmingly either political or commercial.

The commercial papers ran shipping news, column upon column of wholesaler's advertising, and very little else.

The political papers were livelier reading—for politically minded readers. Republican and Federalist editors lambasted opposition policies, office holders and candidates (and, sometimes, each other) in terms that would make today's most partisan newsman blanch.

(One Republican organ asserted, the day after George Washington's retirement from the Presidency, that "the man who is the source of all the mis-

fortune of our country is . . . no longer possessed of power to multiply evils upon the United States. This day ought to be a jubilee.")

Six-weeks-old news from Europe got more space than local events, and feature material was decidedly highbrow.

In the early 1830s, several successful $4-a-year dailies (notably, the lively, non-partisan *Transcript*) sprang up in Boston and began attracting a larger and less exclusive audience.

But the real mass market was still untapped. Hopeful publishers in Boston and New York (one of them was

Printing shop (arrow) at 222 William St. where Ben Day's penny daily was born.

Tammany Hall, left, and building farther up Nassau St. were later homes of paper.

a young printer named Horace Greeley) began launching "penny dailies" to be sold on the street by the single copy, but they all failed within days or months.

And then came the *Sun*, with Ben Day as publisher, editor, pressman, and one-man reportorial staff.

Its first issue was a hodgepodge of local news items, out-of-town news culled from out-of-town papers, and ads that were copied straight from the pages of the $10-a-year journals. But several hundred curious citizens grab-

bed up copies at the phenomenal price of one cent.

NEWSBOYS

The second issue was much the same, with one important addition—a small ad from the publisher himself: "TO THE UNEMPLOYED: A number of men can find employment by vending this paper. A liberal discount is allowed to those who buy to sell again."

Ben Day was taking his first step toward success, setting up a distribution system that would make mass circulation possible.

No U.S. paper had ever been sold on the street; none had ever even tried to achieve a large single copy circulation, although a few copies of the six-penny dailies had been sold over the counter. Distribution by newsboys was called the "London Plan," because a few London dailies were the only ones to use it.

Would-be newsboys flocked to the *Sun's* office to answer the ad, and on the third day of the paper's life, it was peddled to surprised New Yorkers on street corners throughout the city.

(Pleasant September weather was on Ben Day's side—Greeley, who might have made a success of the London Plan, had launched his ill-fated *Morning Post* in the middle of a January snowstorm.)

But the *Sun* not only had to be available to everybody; it also had to be a paper that everybody would want to read.

And by the time it was two weeks old it had begun to be that.

A young unemployed printer named George Wisner, who, as Day recalled years later, "had a knack for writing," came around looking for a job, and Day hired him (at $4 a week) to cover the city police courts.

LOCAL COLOR

Wisner's police reporting was soon filling two columns a day.

It was full of items like: "William Luvoy got drunk yesterday because it was so devilishly warm. Drank nine glasses of brandy and water, and said he would be cursed if he wouldn't drink nine more as quick as he could raise the money to buy it with. Fined $1—forgot his pocketbook, and was sent over to Bridewell . . . Bridget Mc-

Nunn got drunk and threw a pitcher at Mr. Ellis of 53 Ludlow St. . . . Patrick Ludwick was sent up by his wife, who testified that she had supported him for several years in drunkenness and idleness."

The public found this sort of thing vastly more entertaining than politics and shipping news, and circulation began to soar.

By the end of the year, the *Sun* was selling 4000 copies a day—more than any of the six-penny political and mercantile journals with one exception, the *Morning Courier*, which boasted a circulation of 4500.

Its news coverage had expanded by this time, of course.

Local events, both serious and trivial, got the lion's share of the news columns, but readers were kept up to date on national and world affairs with short, no-nonsense paragraphs like: "The *Globe* of Monday (a six-penny competitor) contains in six columns the reasons which prompted the President to remove public deposits from the United States Bank, which were read to his assembled cabinet on the 18th inst."

MORE SOPHISTICATION

It ran theater and book reviews, the poems of Sir Walter Scott and the serialized memoirs of Davy Crockett.

It gave moderate editorial support to President Andrew Jackson and the Democrats, campaigned for better fire fighting apparatus, and cheered the abolition of slavery in the British West Indies.

And its circulation kept climbing, to reach the unbelievable figure of 10,000 in November, 1834, with advertising gains keeping pace.

In the summer of 1835, a new reporter named Richard Adams Locke joined the *Sun* staff.

Then, on August 25, the paper broke what appeared to be the news story of the century:

SCOOP

"GREAT ASTRONOMICAL DISCOVERIES MADE BY SIR JOHN HERSCHEL, LLD., FRS., ETC., AT THE CAPE OF GOOD HOPE."

According to the story, Sir John, an eminent British astronomer (who, safely down at the tip of Africa, was

extremely unlikely to see a copy of the *Sun*), had developed a telescope "of vast dimensions and an entirely new principle" that gave him a perfect view of everything that occurred on the moon.

For the next three days, *Sun* readers were regaled with detailed descriptions of lunar flora and fauna—and on Friday, August 28, the paper proudly announced that it had achieved the highest circulation of any newspaper in the world—19,360. The presses were running ten hours a day to satisfy the moon-struck public.

The "Sun" issued an extra July 28, 1839, when a new steamship arrived in N. Y.

Ben Day, at 23, launched first successful street corner penny daily in New York.

The series reached its climax in the Friday issue, with a report on the moon's "man-bats," apparently intelligent beings who were "covered, except on the face, with short and glossy copper-colored hair, and had wings . . . lying snugly upon their backs."

"The face, which was a yellowish flesh-color, was a slight improvement upon that of the large orang-utang," Sir John Herschel (presumably) went on. "In general symmetry of body and limbs, they were infinitely superior to the orang-utang, so much so that but

for their long wings, they would look as well on a parade ground as some of the old Cockney militia. They are doubtless innocent creatures, notwithstanding that some of their amusements would ill comport with our terrestrial notions of decorum."

The series ran through August 31, complete with illustrations; it was picked up by the *Sun's* New York competitors and by papers in Paris and London.

HOAX

Then Locke confided to a brother reporter from a rival journal (after several drinks) that he had written the whole thing himself. Naturally, the hoax was exposed in his drinking companion's paper the next day.

The *Sun*, of course, defended the series as a "satire" that shouldn't have been believed in the first place.

But nobody cared. *Sun* readers, including the thousands of new ones, had had their fun, and the paper was even more popular.

SUCCESS

The next year, it doubled in size, and its circulation grew to 30,000. Advertising occupied up to three-quarters of its space.

Rival penny dailies had begun to spring up, but the *Sun* was to keep its circulation lead until the late 1850s.

He dabbled in magazine publishing for a few years, and then retired comfortably.

Ben Day was by no means the greatest newspaperman of the 19th century.

Ben Day sold the paper to his brother-in-law, Moses Beach, for $40,000 in 1837—"The silliest thing I ever did," he claimed.

American journalism came of age, and newspapers reached the height of power, popularity, and distinction, under men like James Gordon Bennett of the *World*, Horace Greeley, who reappeared on the scene with the *Tribune* in 1841, Raymond of the *Times*, Pulitzer of the *World*, and Charles A. Dana, who re-won the New York circulation lead for the *Sun* in the 1870s.

But before the mass circulation daily could achieve greatness, somebody had to invent and pioneer it.

Ben Day did.

THE PRINCE OF HUMBUGS

Phineas T. Barnum exposed a staid and sober world to the joys of light-hearted fun and entertainment

ON A SULTRY AUGUST DAY in 1835, New York's quarter-of-a-million inhabitants were roused out of their summer lethargy by a sensational announcement.

Amid sobering newspaper headlines about Van Buren's nomination and child labor abuses, they read that a 161-year old woman who had been George Washington's nurse was to be placed on public exhibition.

"The Greatest Natural & National Curiosity in the World! JOICE HETH, nurse to General George Washington (the Father of our Country)....unquestionably the most astonishing and interesting curiosity in the World!" So went the ads.

Sponsor of the startling relic was one Phineas T. Barnum. And who was this Barnum? No one knew. But it would be the last time in his long

Today the names Barnum & Bailey are still synonymous with entertainment. Although Barnum did not develop interest in the big top until late in life, he is best remembered for his association with Bailey and sawdust.

and spectacular life that the name of P. T. Barnum would go unrecognized. He became a household word in America and a legend throughout the world. In so doing he amassed a personal fortune of $4 million, a considerable sum in those days. Among his friends were Queen Victoria and Abraham Lincoln.

Most significant, he pioneered a new age—an age of showmanship and popular entertainment for the masses.

Life in the United States before Barnum held little frivolity. Most cities had rigidly-enforced blue laws. A favorite sermon topic was the vice to be found in theaters, circuses, and in other public entertainment.

The little existing theater at this time was concentrated in New York, Boston, and Philadelphia. Its patrons came from opposite ends of the social spectrum: the very wealthy who sat in the orchestra and boxes and ladies of the night who plied their wares in the balcony.

Theater understandably held very little profit for a businessman. The few entertainment entrepreneurs made little impression on their times and were not able to modify public scorn and change a nation's habits.

Crashing through the puritan barriers, with his own dynamic personality, Barnum paved the way for popular entertainment — vaudeville and later motion pictures and television. He introduced the modern public museum, the popular concert, and the three-ring circus. He successfully popularized play-going by injecting elements of history, religion, and patriotism into his productions.

Barnum was the first to use advertising and publicity on a grand scale to make people aware of his attractions. He left a legacy of hokum and ballyhoo which still clings to U.S. advertising.

His heirs have been legion and read like a roll call of entertainment greats: Florenz Ziegfeld, the Shubert brothers, John Ringling, Sol Hurok, Billy Rose, and Mike Todd.

The remark he is best remembered for was, "There's a sucker born every minute." However, there is no record he ever uttered it and speech experts say the word "sucker" was not in use then.

Barnum's favorite expression was "the American people like to be hum-bugged," and he proudly referred to himself as the Prince of Humbugs.

Humbug or not, he provided people with a way to have fun without fear of fire and brimstone.

Phineas Taylor Barnum was born July 5, 1810 in Bethel, Connecticut. His life-long regret was that he had not arrived on the Fourth. (His name, Phineas, means "brazen mouth.")

His father Philo was at various times farmer, tailor, and tavern owner. But the biggest influence on Barnum's early life came from his grandfather. The old man was an incorrigible practical joker. Barnum delighted in his grandfather's harmless hoaxes—just about the only legal amusement in those days of stifling solemnity—and tried to emulate him all his life.

When he was 15, Barnum's father died and he became the sole support of the family. For the next ten years he tried one trade after another:

clerk, newspaper editor, hat salesman and, finally, owner of a small grocery store in New York City.

One day in 1835, as 25-year-old Barnum was minding his store, a customer told him about Joice Heth. The old slave woman belonged to a friend in Philadelphia, he said, who was anxious to sell her. Would Barnum be interested?

He was off to Philadelphia by stage the next day. As proof that Joice Heth was not a fake, the owner showed Barnum a yellowing bill of sale dated 1727, specifying that the woman was then 54 years old. Barnum was satisfied. Overnight he found himself in show business.

He barraged New York with publicity and, by the time his exhibit opened a few weeks later at Niblo's Garden, the public came in droves to view the patriotic crone.

Little more than an animated

Although some criticized the flamboyant Phineas T. Barnum for his "Humbugs," he educated a puritanical America to the art of enjoying itself.

Barnum, the master showman, taught America to laugh

mummy, Joice Heth answered questions about the youth of Washington and sang hymns. She was widely written about in the papers and became a great favorite with the public. When interest in New York fell off, Barnum took Joice on the road and added a juggler to the act.

A year later she died, putting Barnum out of business. Far more disturbing than her death, however, were the results of an autopsy. The old woman, doctors said, was not more than 80.

An astounded Barnum (or so he always maintained) insisted that "I had hired Joice in perfect good faith."

Barnum was exposed in the press as a fake, but the public did not seem to care. Indeed, the prevailing opinion was one of admiration.

Thus Barnum was launched on a career of notoriety. He now wanted to be a showman but he needed a showplace. When he learned that Scudder's Museum on lower Broadway was for sale, he finally succeeded in buying it.

The re-christened American Museum opened on New Year's Day 1842. At first Barnum had to be satisfied with the musty old exhibits he had inherited with the building: a waxworks, a glass-blowing exhibit, robots, and various animals. His own touch soon became evident, however, with authentic Indian war dances, baby contests, and his spectacular Feejee Mermaid, one of the most carefully plotted hoaxes in the annals of show business.

The mermaid, a shriveled baboon face with a fish body, was first discovered by a ship captain in Calcutta. Although Barnum suspected the mermaid had been manufactured, he had no idea how and would not admit the hoax until 30 years later. Resulting publicity catapulted the American Museum into a national institution.

Not all of Barnum's attractions were freakish. He was the first to stage "The Drunkard," a melodrama which is still being produced in "Little Theaters" today. Spectacular pageants dramatized subjects like the Christian Martyrs and Moses in Egypt.

He even did Shakespeare, after

cleaning up objectionable passages. Vaudeville acts were presented also.

On a visit to see his brother in Bridgeport, Conn., Barnum discovered the exhibit that gave him international fame.

He met a five-year-old local boy named Charles S. Stratton. Incredibly, the child stood 25 inches high and weighed 15 pounds.

The Strattons, a poor family, were more than happy to allow Barnum to exhibit the boy.

Barnum re-named his midget protege General Tom Thumb, updated his age to 11, and taught him to be impudent and autocratic.

Tom Thumb's debut, in which he cunningly portrayed Cupid, a Revolutionary War soldier, and the Biblical David, was greeted with delight. He soon became the talk of New York

but Barnum had his sights on Europe.

Arriving in London with Tom, he rented a fashionable mansion, hired a liveried butler and sent out invitations to prominent people to have tea.

By the time the midget made his first public appearance, the response was overwhelming. Queen Victoria requested a command performance and, as the tour progressed across Europe, Tom entertained the royalty of many nations.

"The General," wrote Barnum, "left America three years before a diffident, uncultivated little boy; he came back an educated, accomplished little man. He went abroad poor, and he came home rich."

The last words applied equally to Barnum.

By 1849, Barnum was the world's

"Advertise, advertise, advertise" was Barnum's business motto. His use of the medium has left its imprint upon advertising techniques to this day.

foremost showman. But one of his ungratified ambitions was to be not only a promoter of freaks but an impresario of the arts. In short, he wanted refinement and culture.

In Europe, Barnum had heard about a Swedish soprano who was taking the Continent by storm. He had never seen or heard Jenny Lind but, to Barnum, she spelled culture. He decided to bring her to America at any cost.

How to get her posed a problem. He decided to send a representative with the following terms: a percentage of the box office or $1,000 a night for a minimum of 150 concerts, an unheard of proposition in those days. Barnum also promised to pay for three musical assistants and a maid. The full sum would be deposited in advance in a London bank.

Barnum's emissary arrived at a fortunate time. Miss Lind was recovering from an unhappy romance and anxious for a change of scene. She was also eager to acquire $150,000.

Now that Barnum had captured the Swedish Nightingale, he discovered the toast of Europe was virtually unknown in the U.S. He casually asked a train conductor what he thought of Jenny Lind.

"Jenny Lind?" inquired the conductor. "Is she a dancer?"

The answer, Barnum recalled, "chilled me as if his words were ice." Yet in the next eight months he "educated" the public so well that they talked of nothing but her arrival. He conducted a song contest for a composition which Miss Lind would sing at her debut. He emphasized her great contributions to charity. He publicly auctioned opening night tickets; highest bid was $225.

When she arrived on August 21, 1850, Barnum was surprised to see she was no beauty. The 30-year old brunette was short and had a plain face. But when she sang, Jenny Lind was transformed into an angel.

After her breathlessly-awaited debut at Castle Garden, the *New York Tribune* proclaimed, "She is the greatest singer we have ever heard."

Lindomania hit the U.S. Songs and poems were dedicated to her. Jenny Lind cigars, pianos, bonnets and whisky appeared on the market.

The tour began with extreme good

Barnum's sponsorship of the Swedish Nightingale Jenny Lind paved the way for a stream of foreign artists to the U.S. such as Nellie Melba, Caruso.

will on both sides. Temper and tension, however, eventually created conflicts. After 93 concerts Miss Lind bought up her contract and proceeded alone.

For Barnum the partnership had been successful beyond his wildest dreams. His gamble on Jenny Lind, a talent almost unknown in a country that had never before accepted a foreigner in such an enthusiastic way, had grossed $176,000 for the singer and $535,000 for Barnum.

Because of his risk the path was now open for Melba, Paderewski, Caruso and Kreisler.

Sitting back to enjoy the fruits of his labors, Barnum built a palatial Oriental mansion in Bridgeport, Conn. "Iranistan" was half-Byzantine, half-Moorish and a wonder of the American countryside.

In 1855, after 20 years of success, disaster descended upon Barnum. During the next decade he was to suffer a series of misfortunes which would leave him practically penniless and his reputation in shambles.

The first setback was of his own

making. He wrote his autobiography, in which he told all. For the first time, he let his admiring public backstage to see how he carried out his humbugs and hoaxes.

Result was that he made people feel foolish. Overnight he became a rascal. He was called a swindler and villain whose career was "a living libel upon all that is manly in humanity" and his book was termed "trashy and offensive."

Before he could recover from this blow, "the great swindler" himself became the victim of a swindle. One of Barnum's most beloved projects was the fledgling community of East Bridgeport, Conn. In 1855 a seemingly reputable firm, the Jerome Clock Company, offered to move its factory to East Bridgeport if Barnum would extend them a temporary loan of $110,000.

Barnum signed a series of notes but during the complex financial transactions he kept poor track of how much he actually signed. After three months Jerome Clock went bankrupt and he discovered he had

Tom Thumb, most famous of Barnum's freaks, was favorite of Queen Victoria. His wedding to Lavinia Bumpus was highlight of social season.

endorsed them to the tune of a half million dollars.

Barnum, too, was bankrupt.

Two years later his palatial Iranistan burned to the ground. Because of his financial difficulties he had allowed most of the insurance to lapse. The meager sum he did collect was quickly swallowed by creditors.

While struggling to pay off monumental debts, the final blow struck. Sparks from machinery in the engine room of the American Museum started a fire, soon turning the building into a holocaust. Lions and bears leapt from windows. Firemen were able to rescue the freaks but by night the Museum was in ashen ruins.

Advised by his friend Horace Greeley to "go a-fishing," Barnum rejected the idea of retirement and plunged into new projects to eliminate his indebtedness.

He sailed for Europe with a company of actors in a dramatized version of "Uncle Tom's Cabin." Welcomed with enthusiasm, his tour was so successful he returned with Tom Thumb and, finally, exhibited himself in a series of lectures titled "The Art of Money-Getting." (He ruefully commented the lecture should be called "The Art of Money-Losing.")

In a few years Barnum had recouped many of his losses and had time for a political career. Back in 1852 he had refused the Democratic nomination for Governor of Connecticut. Now he ran and was elected to the State Legislature. After two terms, in which he vigorously crusaded against the railroad lobby, he ran for Congress but was defeated. Later he served as mayor of Bridgeport.

In 1868, his newly-rebuilt American Museum burned and Barnum, 58 and a millionaire again, decided to retire for good.

But two years later he suddenly bounded back into the public eye in a business with which he would ever after be associated—the circus.

Barnum did not invent circuses. They had existed since ancient Greece and Rome but he did give the circus its size, its memorable attractions and its popularity.

"Barnum's Own Greatest Show on Earth" opened for the first time in 1871 beneath three acres of canvas tent in Brooklyn. Tens of thousands of spectators peered at the freaks, clowns, and animals under flickering gaslights.

At the end of the first season his receipts totaled nearly a half million dollars; in the second year, one million.

To give his circus a permanent New York home, he built the block-long Great Roman Hippodrome which later became the first Madison Square Garden.

For nine years Barnum poured millions into securing the most unique acts he could find. Then, in 1880, he discovered that he had serious competition. The rival was a circus called International Allied Shows and its guiding genius was a retiring young man named James A. Bailey.

He persuaded Bailey to merge the two circuses. The result was a successful partnership until Barnum's death.

Bailey was as unlike Barnum as any man could be. He avoided publicity and, when reporters appeared, he would hide in his tent. Nevertheless, the two men got along well.

As the partnership saw one successful season after another, Barnum explained the secret: "As long as there's babies there'll be circuses."

Barnum's greatest circus attraction was the elephant Jumbo. Sold by the London Zoo because he was thought to be mad, Jumbo was transported to New York amid characteristic Barnum publicity. Ridden by over one million children for three years, Jumbo enriched the lives of the children and the coffers of Barnum. (He was killed in 1855 in a train accident.)

By 1891, Barnum was 81 years old and his health was failing. He had become an institution and received childish enjoyment when a letter from India, addressed to "Mr. Barnum, America," arrived safely.

He wondered what the newspapers would say of him after his death. Obligingly the *New York Sun* ran his obituary on March 24, 1891.

Two weeks later the great showman was dead.

He would have been pleased by these words in the *London Times:* "Barnum is gone...That fine flower of Western civilization ... gave a lustre to America."

CHARLES A. GOODYEAR

RUBBER FOR INDUSTRY

Charles Goodyear turned the impractical novelty called "India rubber" into a vital raw material with hundreds of industrial applications

Goodyear was born in 1800 in New Haven, Conn., the son of a small manufacturer and inventor.

He would have liked to study for the Congregational ministry, but family finances kept him from going beyond high school — and anyway,

his father, Amasa, who had decided to go into hardware sales, had the mistaken notion that young Charles would make a good merchant.

The hardware business, at that time, consisted entirely of manufacturer-wholesalers who sold to travel-

ing peddlers. A. Goodyear & Sons, which Charles joined after an apprenticeship with a Philadelphia firm, also had a retail store—probably the first in the U.S.

It did fairly well for a few years, but went under, like hundreds of other small businesses, in the depression that hit the nation at the end of the 1820s.

And Charles, who had assumed the responsibility for his elderly father's debts, began making the trips to debtors' prison that punctuated most of the rest of his life.

Seldom in all business history has one man's devotion to a product borne such amazing fruits as the devotion of Charles Goodyear to the sticky, temperamental material that his generation called India rubber.

Early in the 1830s, when Goodyear first noticed a line of rubber goods in a Manhattan store window, rubber was hardly more than a curiosity. When he died in 1860, it was the basis of a flourishing industry— an industry that owed its very existence to Goodyear's process of vulcanization, and its rapid growth, in large part, to his enthusiasm.

Charles Goodyear was a spectacularly unsuccessful businessman. But he deserves to be remembered as the pioneer of the rubber business not only because he turned rubber into a versatile, reliable, all-weather material with hundreds of industrial applications, but also because he saw its potentialities and devoted all his time and energy — and a small fortune—to developing and promoting them during the last 15 years of his life.

The Goodyears were stubbornly determined not to declare themselves bankrupt; Charles was in New York trying to raise yet another loan on the day in the early '30s when he saw a rubber life preserver in the Roxbury India Rubber Company's show window.

The near-bankrupt young hardware merchant walked into the company's showroom—and into history.

Rubber had been discovered by the Western world when Columbus came back from Santo Domingo with some of the odd little bouncing balls that the natives there played games with.

But it was given no practical application whatsoever until late in the 18th century, when somebody noticed that the stuff could rub out pencil marks.

This fact gave it its name, and a small market as an artists' supply;

but it was still so little in demand that ships were carrying it as ballast early in the 19th century.

Scientists and manufacturers alike were beginning to get curious about it, though.

In 1823, a Scotsman named Charles Mackintosh developed a solution of rubber and benzene that could be spread between two layers of cloth. He began manufacturing waterproof coats that gave commercially processed rubber its first toehold in the consumer market — and added a new word to the language.

The only trouble with Mackintosh's macintoshes was that they turned sticky and odoriferous when the wearer stood near a hot stove, and got as hard as boards in extreme cold.

But even this partial success stimulated enough excitement about rubber's potentialities to start dozens of experimenters on the search for the perfect rubber compound — a search that was to end almost two decades later with Goodyear's discovery of vulcanization.

French manufacturers began using rubber in garters and suspenders.

And the material made its first major appearance on the U.S. market when an enterprising importer began selling rubber shoes handmade by South American Indians. The shoes were a luxury item at $5 a pair, and an impractical one at that, since they too turned sticky in heat and rigid in cold; but they caught the popular fancy.

Then, late in the '20s, a Boston factory foreman named E. M. Chaffee came up with a rubber-turpentine compound that looked better than any of its predecessors. He also invented a spreading machine, and, with the backing of a group of local financiers, founded Roxbury India Rubber in 1828.

Rubber coats, hats, and shoes were soon flooding the market; in fact, just about anything that could be rubberized was. Other small companies followed Roxbury into the field, and for about five years, the industry enjoyed a small boom.

The boom was still on when Charles Goodyear saw the life preserver in the Roxbury display window. Intrigued by the device itself as well as by the new material, he went in to see how it worked, and decided when it was demonstrated to him that the valve was extremely inefficient.

He bought the life preserver, took it home and, in the little spare time that staving off his creditors allowed him, began developing a better valve.

A few months later, when he took the perfected valve back to the Roxbury Co., the rubber bubble had burst.

Toward the end of his life, in his two-volume treatise on rubber production, *Gum Elastic*, Goodyear listed the defects of rubber in its natural state:

"1. It becomes rigid and inflexible in cold weather.

"2. It is softened and decomposed in the sun and hot temperatures.

"3. It is very soluble and quickly dissolved when brought into contact with grease, essential or common oils, and though more slowly, yet as surely dissolved by perspiration.

"4. It is in its nature so very adhesive that when any two surfaces are brought into contact, they become by slight pressure one mass that cannot be separated.

"5. It loses its elasticity by continued tension or constant use.

"6. It has a very unpleasant odor."

And none of this formidable array of flaws had been more than partially or temporarily corrected by Chaffee's compound. It was hardly surprising that once the novelty appeal of the rubber goods made from it had worn off, their sales collapsed like a rubber coat in a heatwave.

But Goodyear, completely lacking as he was in both financial resources and scientific training, decided that a better compound could be found and that he was the man to find it.

Roxbury India Rubber, impressed by his new valve, encouraged him to try, but was in no financial position to offer him a retainer.

At least, he discovered when he began his work in 1834, rubber was an inexpensive subject for experimentation; its market price had plummeted to about five cents a pound.

Working in the kitchen of his New Haven home, with only small loans from friends to buy his rubber—and pay the family grocery bills—Goodyear began developing new compounds.

In 1835, he went alone to New York and persuaded friends there to set him up in a tiny laboratory and supply him with chemicals. Within a few months, he had developed a rubber-magnesia-lime compound that looked good enough to win medals at two trade fairs that fall.

He brought his family down from New Haven, launched a small manufacturing firm, and enjoyed a short period of relative prosperity.

The birth of the automobile industry in the 1890s (below, Frank and Charles Duryea in their first auto) created vast market for rubber products

Rubber
plus sulphur
plus heat

But he soon found out that the magnesia-lime coating was neutralized by the slightest touch of acid, leaving the rubber as sticky, adhesive, and temperature-sensitive as ever.

Out of business and back in debt, he began experimenting again.

The second apparently successful compound was the result of an accident. Trying to remove the color from a piece of rubber fabric that he had embossed, he used nitric acid—and saw that where the acid fell, the material turned black, lost its stickiness, and acquired a perfect finish.

If Goodyear had had enough chemistry to know that nitric acid is largely composed of sulphuric acid, he might have hit upon the secret of vulcanization then and there.

As it was, he decided that the nitric acid coating was the answer to the problem.

He began manufacturing again. In 1837, he was granted a patent for the process, and soon found a wealthy backer to help him expand the manufacturing operation.

When the panic of 1837 hit the nation a few months later, the new business was wiped out. But Goodyear was able to move on, with his patent, to his old friends from Roxbury India Rubber.

In 1838, the revitalized Roxbury Co. received a sizeable government contract for mail bags—and disaster struck again.

After a month in storage, the mail bags were found to have disintegrated into the old, familiar, sticky mess.

The trouble was — as Goodyear realized too late—that the nitric acid process worked successfully only on very thin rubber sheet.

The unfavorable publicity resulting from the mailbag fiasco, only three years after the failure of the magnesia-lime compound, was a near death blow to the infant rubber industry — and Goodyear's reputation.

He was already considered something of a crank; it was a standing joke among businessmen that "if you meet a man who has on an India rubber cap, stock, coat, vest and shoes, with an India rubber money purse without a cent in it, that is Charles Goodyear."

And now his hopes for the financial backing he would need to try again appeared so slim that he was almost ready to go back to the hardware business.

But this time, the real breakthrough was only months away.

It came when he found his assistant in the Roxbury plant experimenting with a sulphur coating that seemed to give excellent results when dried in the sun.

Sulphur might be the magic ingredient—but how to make it permeate not just sheets, but solid masses of rubber?

The final discovery, when it came, was another happy accident; Goodyear dropped a lump of sulphur-treated rubber on a hot stove and saw that although it charred on the surface, it did not melt.

He left the accidentally heat-treated lump outdoors overnight and found that it also resisted cold. The search was over.

However, although he now believed that rubber plus sulphur plus heat produced the perfect compound, he still had to develop an exact formula; and for that, he needed better equipment than a kitchen stove.

Close to 40 years old, in failing health, and still thoroughly discredited in the business community, he somehow scraped up the money to build a small test plant at Woburn, Mass., and there, with the help of his father and brothers, he experimented for four more years.

He finally applied for a patent on the vulcanization process in 1843, and received it in 1844.

He likened vulcanization to the tanning of hide or the conversion of iron to steel, and said of his invention: "While the inventor admits

that these discoveries were not the result of *scientific* chemical observation, he is not willing to admit that they were the result of what is commonly termed accident; he claims them to be the result of the closest application and observation."

Goodyear never went back to manufacturing; he devoted the rest of his life to experimenting with, writing about, and promoting rubber.

Licensing rights and royalties earned him close to $200,000, a sizeable fortune for the mid-19th century; but he poured most of it right back into the industry.

He spent $30,000 on "Goodyear's Vulcanite Palace" at the Great Exposition of 1851 in London, and $50,000 on an even more ambitious display at the Paris Exposition Universelle in 1855.

In *Gum Elastic*, he detailed close to 1000 applications for his favorite substance, virtually all of which have proved to be practical.

The rubber industry's great spurt of growth did not come until the end of the century, when the developing automotive and electrical industries created vast new demands for the material that not even Goodyear could have foreseen.

But it was solidly established, with capital investment of $7 million and annual sales of $4-5 million, well before Goodyear's death in 1860.

"If the search had failed," one of Goodyear's biographers has written of his discovery of vulcanization, "he would have been remembered, if at all, as a ruthless, crazy eccentric who sacrificed all the ordinary comforts of life in pursuing a shadow. The search succeeded, and laid the foundations for a great industry. The eccentric became the genius."

Small rubber companies of 1850s turned out products from combs and corset stays to furniture like that displayed by Goodyear at London Exposition.

English tourists in the 1890s were conducted along Paris boulevards in horse-drawn carriages from Cook's.

THE MAN FROM COOK'S

**Thomas Cook, crusading for the temperance cause,
accidentally launched the multi-billion dollar travel industry**

Thos. Cook & Son had become a household word by the turn of the century. In 1898 a musical comedy, "A Runaway Girl," opened at London's Gaiety Theater, featuring a song called "Follow the Man from Cook's:"
*"Oh, follow the man from Cook's,
The wonderful man from Cook's;
And whether your stay be short or long,*

*He'll show you the sights.
He can't go wrong:
Oh, follow the man from Cook's,
The wonderful man from Cook's.
It's twenty to one
You've plenty of fun,
So follow the man from Cook's!"*
Punch Magazine, in a less friendly gesture to Cook's, quickly countered with a parody:
"Oh bother the man from Cook's!

*The worrying man from Cook's!
For whether he's booked by week or day,
He'll tire you to death and call it play,
Oh, bother the man from Cook's!
The worrying man from Cook's!
It's twenty to one you say when he's done:
Oh, murder the man from Cook's!"*

DURING THE COMING YEAR, over 50 million tourists from over the world will pack their bags and passports, leave home and set out in pursuit of business or pleasure.

It may come as a surprise to the teacher from Ohio sipping an aperitif in a cafe along the Champs Elysées or to the businessman ordering a martini from his jet flight hostess that the man responsible for their present ease of travel

30

was violently opposed to spirits.

Thomas Cook, the pioneer who opened the world to the common man and made travel safe, comfortable and cheap, was an ardent crusader against liquor. Today, the offices of Thos. Cook & Son girdle the globe and the name Cook's is synonymous with international travel; yet Cook's Tours began accidentally as an adjunct to the temperance movement.

Thomas Cook was born in Melbourne, Derbyshire, England, in 1808 — four years before the first steam locomotive puffed its way along a railroad track. The son of poor parents, he was forced to leave school at the age of 10 and work as a gardener's assistant for a penny a day.

At 14 he was apprenticed to his uncle, a cabinet maker who spent more time in the alehouse than in his shop. The uncle's continual drunkeness was the determining factor in causing young Thomas to sign the pledge.

In the next few years he opened his own carpentering business, married and moved to Leicestershire, a town he came to regard as his home.

Somehow, Cook managed to acquire an education on his own and when he was 20 years old he gave up cabinet making and went to work for the General Baptist Association as a "Village Missionary." He walked two to three thousand miles a year delivering temperance tracts and organizing meetings to bring abstainers together.

In 1841, while walking to a temperance rally 15 miles away, he read a newspaper account about the opening of a railway in the district. It occurred to him that the steam engine could be harnessed to the temperance cause. Perhaps a large number of people going to the same destination — namely a temperance meeting—could, as a group, obtain cheaper fares and still provide the railway with an adequate profit.

Cook persuaded the Midland Railroad to put a special train at his disposal and give him round trip tickets for the price of one-way fares.

On July 5, 1841, some 570 teetotalers and reformed drunks crowded into the open carriages to travel 24 miles to the meeting. They played cricket, drank tea and returned home without any mishaps. It was the first successful excursion run and the "tourists" were hailed as daring adventurers.

Cook's fame as a travel impresario soon spread throughout the Midlands and he found other organizations asking him to arrange excursions.

For the next 50 years he would have the infant travel industry to himself as no competition rose to challenge him until nearly the turn of the century.

The world's first travel agents were traders who journeyed from country to country peddling their wares. They shared their experiences and hardships with other fellow travelers.

But the Romans invented tourism. For roughly five centuries—1 A.D. to 500 A.D. — the Roman Empire fostered the biggest tourist movement in history up to that time. It was not equalled again until the 19th century.

Many factors made travel easy. The Empire stretched from the Atlantic Ocean on the west to the Arabian Desert on the east, one million square miles with no foreign frontiers to cross. Rome had a magnificent highway system and her slave-driven galleys sailed the seas to the limits of the then-known world.

Roman legions enforced peace throughout the far-flung domain and a single currency was in use from Spain to Syria.

Citizens of Rome escaped the summer heat by fleeing to nearby seashores. Julius Caesar maintained a villa at Baiae, a popular resort near Naples. Nero poisoned his aunt to gain possession of her summer home there.

Thomas Cook gave almost every penny he made to aid temperance cause.

Cook opened the doors to the world and made travel cheap and safe

Just as Americans today now flock to Paris to saunter down the Rue de Rivoli or view the art treasures in the Louvre, the Romans traveled to Greece to gaze at the splendor of the Parthenon and the Acropolis. Another favorite travel spot of the Romans was the site of ancient Troy on the coast of Asia Minor.

There were no travel agents but government officials rendered many tourist services. They sold tickets entitling travelers to transportation and a change of horses en route. The wealthy rode in carriages equipped with sleeping quarters and cooking facilities.

Sea voyages were more rigorous. Huge galleys could transport 1200 passengers but a ticket bought only deck space. Meals were not included.

While sophisticated Roman citizens traveled to the far corners of the realm, provincials from Gaul, Britain and Spain trooped into Rome to gaze at the Colosseum and gape at the villas of Augustus and Pompey much as today's visitors to Hollywood stare at the homes of movie stars.

When Rome crumbled before the invading Visigoths in 500 A.D., the era of free travel and tourism came to an end. Countries were overrun by bands of roving bandits, highways fell into ruin and trade and travel were almost extinguished.

Fourteen centuries later the Industrial Revolution, the invention of the railroad and steamship and the appearance of Thomas Cook all combined to form the beginning of modern travel.

Cook's success as a travel promoter was not due entirely to his low-price excursions. He also taught people how to travel. He made extensive preparations for passengers' comfort, saw they were fed adequately and gave them advice about places to see along the way.

He convinced popular hotels to give special rates to his clients. In turn, he transformed unknown spots into fashionable resorts.

During Cook's early years as a travel agent, railroads were still in their infancy. The idea of making a sea voyage for pleasure was denounced as sheer lunacy. Sir Samuel Cunard's new paddle wheel steamers carried sails just in case.

In 1845, Cook organized his first pleasure cruise, taking a party to the Isle of Man by chartered steamer. One year later, he combined rail and steamer transportation to guide 350 on a tour of Scotland then considered a remote and somewhat dangerous land.

Soon he was able to make special arrangements with the British railways. They agreed to pay him a fixed commission on all tickets he sold. (Reputable travel agencies have operated in this manner ever since.)

In 1851, Cook conducted 165,000 tourists to the first World's Fair at London's Crystal Palace. The following year he moved his headquarters to London where his son John took charge.

At this time the now-famous Cook's tours sprouted international wings although the outlook was less than bright for traveling on the Continent. Low wages and widespread poverty existed at home while across the Channel the Crimean War and various insurrections and minor wars created an atmosphere of international tension.

Undaunted, Cook sold 400,000 tickets to the Paris Exhibition of 1855. He began to issue international travel tickets and hotel coupons providing for accommodations and meals at preset prices. (Prior to this, there were no international railway tickets or timetables. The independent traveler was at the mercy of any unscrupulous innkeeper.)

Cook continued to make travel history. In June, 1863, he left London with 64 eager companions for the first conducted tour of Switzerland. For 21 days the hardy tourist band traveled by mule and sedan chair up and down the Alps, bemoaning the absence of English tea every mile of the way. Cost per person: $100.

(The celebrated tour was re-enacted 100 years later with Cook's 26 year-old great, great grandson, a gentleman farmer, as guide.)

Cook's reputation may have been slightly marred by critics from London's snobbish Mayfair set who objected to the common man viewing sights once available only to the landed gentry.

One writer referred to Cook as "the Continental Bear-Leader who conducts tribes of unlettered British over the cities of Europe and amuses the foreigner with . . . our national oddities."

1909 Cook's travel poster advertised package tours of Europe for as little as $150. Cook also provided sightseers with numerous tips on food, hotels.

Still a missionary at heart, Cook dreamed of opening up the religious shrines of Palestine to tourists. In 1868, he negotiated with the Bedouin chiefs who agreed to allow "infidels" to use their caravan trails unmolested. The Cooks—father and son—then extended their travel operations into Egypt. Later they built their own ships in Cairo to provide navigation up and down the Nile.

1872 was a memorable year for Thomas Cook. He invaded the U.S. and with the completion of the first trans-continental railroad here, he was able to undertake a great ambition—a round-the-world tour.

America had been on Cook's agenda since 1861 but the Civil War had forced postponement. In 1866, he escorted the first group of tourists, having negotiated a uniform fare of two cents a mile over a 4000 mile network of U.S. railroads. High point of the tour were trips to Revolutionary and Civil War battlefields.

But not until 1872 did Cook open his first permanent U.S. office on lower Broadway in New York City from which he embarked with a party of nine on a globe-circling tour. The feat inspired Jules Verne to publish "Around the World in 80 Days," although Cook's tour lasted 222 days.

In the U.S. the teetotaling Cook was impressed by pitchers of ice water on hotel dining tables but shocked by the primitive sleeping arrangements in railway cars where privacy was almost nonexistant.

Thos. Cook & Son had been firmly implanted as the colossus of U.S. travel services for 15 years when local competition sprang up. The first home-grown U.S. travel service was Ask Mr. Foster followed a few years later by American Express.

Wells-Fargo, the forerunner of today's American Express Company, began in 1850 as an express company, shipping everything from gold bullion to plowshares.

Early in its history the company entered the travel business for four months but retreated after J. C. Fargo uttered these words, "There is no profit in the tourist business, and even if there were, this company wouldn't undertake it." Later, in 1915, American Express. officially opened a travel department catering to the needs of tourists.

Thomas Cook died in 1892 at the age of 84. Almost every penny he made during his lifetime had gone to fight the demon drink. The business was passed on to his son, John, who survived him by only seven years, and then to John's two sons.

In the first three decades of the 20th century, Thos. Cook & Son pioneered a series of tourist booms. The company originated the Bermuda honeymoon and vacation trade and launched pleasure cruises to the Caribbean. In the Twenties it lured tourists to Bali, the islands of the South Pacific and the jungles of Africa.

In 1927, Cook's conducted the first air excursion, a trip to the Dempsey-Tunney fight in Chicago.

Today, Thos. Cook & Son has 400 offices in 68 countries. The 40 outlets in the U.S. and Canada generate a substantial portion of the company's annual business.

Services for Cook's 10 million clients each year range from the ordinary to the bizarre. An escorted tour around New York's Radio City costs $1.75. For the more adventurous, Cook's will arrange a Cairo-to-Capetown safari costing $6200. Points of interest included in this tour are a visit to a pygmy village and an exhibition of tribal dances. A big game hunting expedition in Africa may run as high as $35,000 with professional guides, native porters and a doctor.

Cook's once supplied Richard Halliburton, U.S. author and traveler, with an elephant on which he retraced Hannibal's path across the Alps. The company also transported an entire British army and its supplies into battle in the Sudan.

In the days before maharajahs went out of style, the company maintained an Indian Princes Department whose sole function was to handle travel arrangements for the potentates and their large retinues.

Additional Cook's services include selection of a school abroad for one's children and escorting them home at vacation time, furniture storage, home delivery of 32 varieties of South African snakes, selling insurance.

The company's transportation facilities in remote corners of the world include local carriers such as camels, rickshaws, sampans, spitting llamas and donkeys.

Clients vary from the world's

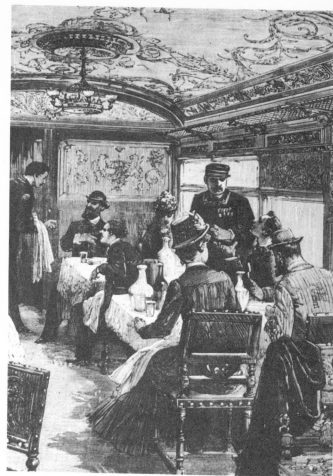

Luxurious interiors enhanced popularity of early train travel. Dining on wheels amid Victorian décor was elegant pastime in late 1800s.

royal and celebrated personages to high school students on their first trip to Washington, D.C.

Thos. Cook & Son was sold to Wagon-Lits in 1927 because the founder's grandsons left no male heirs. During World War II, the company's stock was purchased by four British railways. When the railroads nationalized in 1948, the company became, in effect, the property of the British people.

Travel is the single biggest item in international trade each year — an estimated $8 billion. Some nine million U.S. tourists spent about $3 billion on traveling overseas. And six million foreigners visit in the U.S. The April 1964 opening of the World's Fair in New York helped establish new records for domestic and foreign travel.

Thos. Cook & Son, pioneer travel service, is looking to the future. The company has announced it is ready to accept applications for trips to the moon and will provide guided tours as soon as transportation can be arranged. A number of deposits have already been made.

HE KEPT THE WORLD "IN STITCHES"

Singer's global empire spans 67 nations, has sold over 100 million sewing machines

In 1850, a highly talented machinist and not-so-talented Shakespearean actor named Isaac Merritt Singer built a sewing machine that worked.

That original Singer machine was the first of 100 million that have stitched their way into every habitable corner of the globe over the past 110 years.

Today, Singer Manufacturing Co. has 5000 sales centers in 67 countries, hands out instruction booklets in 54 languages. Its sales volume exceeds a half billion dollars.

The firm has not had a major U.S. competitor since Civil War days, and a dozen years ago, two-thirds of all the sewing machines sold in the U.S. were Singers. (Singer's current share of the U.S. market has declined to a still respectable one-third. The Japanese have grabbed 56%, and European manufacturers account for the remaining 11%.)

When Isaac Singer perfected the sewing machine, he did what at least half a dozen other inventors had failed to do over the 60 years since the first crude stitching device was patented by Thomas Saint.

All the pre-Singer machines had serious mechanical defects, and none had achieved commercial success.

The first U.S. sewing machine patent went to Elias Howe, Jr., in 1846.

But Howe failed to launch his product successfully on the U.S. market. He departed for England to try there, failed again, and returned penniless in 1849 to discover that two new machines—each with some original features, but basically infringing his patent—had been patented in his absence and were being marketed.

He began legal proceedings against their inventors, and launched the "sewing machine war" that was to continue until 1854.

By 1850, the year Singer himself saw his first sewing machine, other manufacturers had entered the fray.

But to the public, the sewing machine was still an unreliable gadget.

No machine on the market could sew more than a few stitches before the operator had to remove the cloth and make a fresh start. None could keep the thread from breaking and tangling. None could sew on a curve.

Sales, accordingly, were very small —in spite of a huge potential market both in the garment and leather working industries and among housewives who did all their family sewing by hand and professional seamstresses who could barely eke out a living with 18-hour days of slow, laborious hand stitching.

Isaac Singer was, in a way, the last man on earth who should have been responsible for anything as innately respectable and domestic as the sewing machine.

He was a colorful, lusty adventurer whose ideas of domesticity were, to say the least, unconventional.

He produced 24 children by two wives and three mistresses.

And, after his sewing machines began to make money, he set the prim New York of the 1860s on its ear by his lavishly exuberant ways.

Singer was born in Pittston, N. Y., in 1811, the son of poor German im-

The partnership of rambunctious Isaac Singer (above) and staid Edward Clark (below) was as uncongenial— and as profitable—as any in business history.

migrants. His formal education ended at the age of 12, when he ran away from home and became an apprentice machinist in Rochester, N. Y.

He was soon a qualified journeyman, but he decided that the stage was more to his liking than the work bench.

Those were the days when the arrival of a barnstorming road company was a major event in small towns where any entertainment more daring than a church social was rare.

Practically any company, good, bad or indifferent, could play everything

from Shakespeare to *The Stumbling Block*, or *Why the Deacon Gave Up His Wine*, to packed houses nightly.

In 20 years, he held only three jobs outside the theater.

Early in the 1840s, stranded in Fredericksburg, Ohio, he went to work in a local woodworking plant.

He invented a carving maohine, patented it, and scraped up the money to go east and into business.

In New York, he teamed up with a printer named George Zieber, and the two of them moved on to Boston.

There they rented space to display the carving machine in the workroom of Orson C. Phelps, a struggling sewing machine manufacturer.

Nobody came to buy carving machines, so Singer had plenty of time to study Phelps' sewing machine, a model patented by John A. Lerow and S. C. Blodgett, and decide that he could make it work.

In 11 days, living on a $40 loan from Zieber, he did just that.

He replaced the circular shuttle that twisted the thread with a horizontal one, and designed a table to support the cloth and a presser foot to hold it down against the upward stroke of the needle, so that the machine would sew continuously on any kind of seam. He also replaced the cumbersome hand crank of all the sewing machines then in existence with a foot pedal.

Singer, Zieber and Phelps immediately went into partnership to manufacture the new machine.

Their first big order, for 30 machines at $100 each, came from a New Haven, Conn., shirt manufacturer before the end of 1850.

By summer of 1851, the small company was doing a brisk business —but, like every other firm in the sewing machine field, it was being sued by Elias Howe, Jr.

A well-to-do attorney named Edward Clark agreed to come into the business, advancing cash and guaranteeing legal counsel for 20 years, in exchange for the one-third interest of Phelps, who had dropped out.

In the fall, Zieber fell ill and sold his interest to Singer and Clark.

The resulting partnership was one of the oddest—and most successful— in the annals of business.

Flamboyant Singer found
staid Clark ideal partner,
business balance wheel

During the Civil War, proudest Singer boast was that "We clothe the Union Armies."

Singer Manufacturing began advertising early (first New York ad, 1853) and was first U.S. corporation to spend $1 million a year on promotion.

Clark was an ultra-conservative manufacturer's son, and a college graduate. He was distressed by his partner's cultural deficiencies (to the end of his days, Singer could barely spell) and shocked by his personal life.

But, fortunately for Singer Manufacturing Co., he was fascinated by sewing machines, and he had tremendous talents as executive, salesman and promoter.

Clark's first major contribution to the company—and to the industry—was the settlement, in 1854, of the legal battle with Elias Howe.

He set up a "patent pool," to be shared by Howe, Singer, and two other inventors whose machines had some claim to true originality.

All the remaining manufacturers agreed to pay a $15 fee, to be divided by the pool members, on each machine they produced until the patents expired.

Then Clark settled down to selling sewing machines.

In the first years, Singer sales were largely to industry—in part, because the price of the original Singer sewing machine, $125, was a major investment for a private owner at a time when average U.S. family income was $500 a year.

To boost sales of sewing machines for home use, Clark introduced trade-in allowances (on competitors' machines as well as Singer models) and installment buying. Singer Manufacturing was the first major U.S. corporation to adopt either of these practices.

He also developed the company's sales agency system, and—most important of all, perhaps—launched its foreign operations.

Isaac Singer, in the meantime, went on improving the machines themselves, swapping jokes with the boys in the machine shop, and making good copy for New York newspapers.

The most spectacular of his extravagances was a two-ton, 31-passenger traveling carriage, equipped with all comforts of home but a kitchen.

After 1860, he spent most of his time in Europe.

His last love and second wife was a young French girl, with whom he seems to have settled down at last.

He died, in 1875, in the $500,000 Greco-Roman-Renaissance palace he had built on the English coast and called The Wigwam.

Edward Clark was to remain at the helm of Singer Manufacturing, which had been incorporated in 1863, until his death in 1882.

By then, the company had assumed the dominant position in the U.S. sewing machine industry which it has never lost, and the machine Mahatma Gandhi was to call "one of the few useful things ever invented" was well launched on its world travels.

36

Florida's Seminole Indians dressed drably till Singer salesmen arrived late in 19th Century. Now the machines stitch elaborate, multi-colored costumes.

Singer lost $100 million in Russian Revolution (r., St. Petersburg headquarters of Czarist days). Soviet government returned $3 million in 1959.

Before World War II, Singer machines sold briskly in Japan (l.). Today, Japan's own sewing machine industry is Singer's main U.S. competitor.

BILLION DOLLAR BY-PRODUCT

Impurities, adulteration of mid-19th-Century drugs outraged young Navy Surgeon Squibb; unintended result of lifelong campaign was modern pharmaceutical industry, vast enterprise still bearing his name

TODAY's pharmaceutical industry in general, and E. R. Squibb & Sons in particular, was pioneered by a maverick. Dr. Edward Robinson Squibb was a crusading scientist rather than a business man, and vehemently distrusted such business staples as patents, salesmen, advertising, and even corporations themselves.

Squibb spent his life battling for the standardization and purity of drugs, laying the basis of modern pharmacy and launching the movement that produced the first Pure Food and Drug Act.

Squibb was just as stern a moralist away from his laboratory. He considered certain passages of the opera Lohengrin "offensive," and was horrified to learn once that his wife had had European earrings smuggled past customs for her. He brought the earrings back to customs, had them assessed and paid the duty.

His campaign against commercial

drug adulteration started during his years as a young assistant surgeon in the Navy in the 1840s and 50s. A self-administered dose of rhubarb made him violently ill; analysis revealed that it was worm-eaten and full of sand. Later examinations in the ship's dispensary disclosed many other medical supplies unfit for use. He promptly dumped half the supplies overboard.

Repeated discoveries of such flagrant impurities as 21 pounds of sand in the gum arabic, and rhubarb in the opium, added fuel to his obsession.

Determined to replace the adulterated drugs issued to the Navy, he wangled an assignment to the New York Shipyard (popularly known as the Brooklyn Navy Yard). There he obtained permission to set up a laboratory to make his own pure drugs.

When Squibb found that the existing supply of commercially made ether varied so much in strength that

its clinical effect was unpredictable, he manufactured his own.

He then went on to make chloroform, which had recently come into use as an anesthetic. In 1855 he successfully administered his first dose to a brother-in-law before extracting a decayed tooth with a pair of pliers.

Dedicated as he was, however, Squibb needed to earn more money than the $1800 a year which the Navy paid him. He had married soon after arriving at the Brooklyn Yard, and already had two sons, Charles and Edward, to support.

His young wife was rather extravagant and frivolous, insisting on expensive bedroom furniture, imported clothes and a summer house during the hardest times. And to add to his burdens, she was subject to epilepsy.

Squibb resigned from the Navy in 1857, worked for a year in a new commercial laboratory in Louisville, Kentucky, and then, on the strength

FIRST BROOKLYN laboratory *(above)* of E. R. Squibb & Son produced ether and other drugs of dependable purity, standard strength, established today's "ethical" industry.

MASKED TECHNICIANS *(below)* in modern New Brunswick, N.J., plant manufacture antibiotics, undreamed of in Dr. Squibb's day, under strictly controlled sterile conditions.

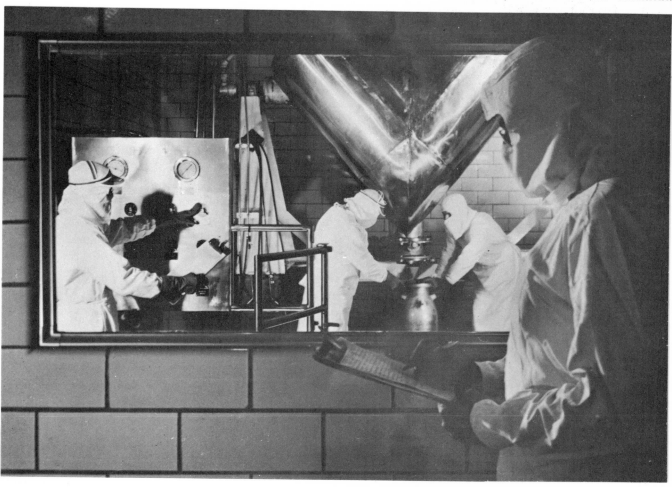

Fires, frustrations could not halt Squibb campaign, company progress

LEADING PHARMACEUTICAL COMPANIES
(in $ millions)

Company	1960 Sales	1960 Profits	1948 Sales	1948 Profits	1938 Sales	1938 Profits
Olin Mathieson*	$689.6	$34.7	$ 73.4	$ 3.6	n.a.	n.a.
			(Squibb)		(Squibb)	
American Cyanamid**	578.4	46.8	231.9	11.9	61.2	2.5
Charles Pfizer	269.4	26.2	47.7	9.4	5.6	.8
Merck***	218	27.8	35.2	3.9	8.9	.6
			(Sharp & Dohme)		(Sharp & Dohme)	
Sterling	218.5	22.2	134.2	12.7	35.6	8.7
Eli Lilly	178.5	18.8	n.a.	n.a.	n.a.	n.a.
Warner-Lambert	197.9	15.8	36.2	2.7	n.a.	n.a.
Parke-Davis	200.0	30.5	74.5	9.7	31.1	8.6
Upjohn	159.4	22.8	n.a.	n.a.	n.a.	n.a.
Smith Kline & French	148.0	24.4	37.0	4.5	n.a.	n.a.
Abbott Laboratories	126.0	12.4	66.9	11.1	9.7	1.6
Bristol-Myers	146.7	10.8	45.3	4.3	15.2	2.2
Vick Chemical	132.3	14.4	41.7	3.8	8.9	2.2

Note:
*Suby of Richardson Merrell Inc. sales and profit figures consolidated.
**Lederle, its pharmaceutical division, accounts for 30% of sales.
***Sharp & Dohme merged with Merck in 1953. Pharmaceuticals account for 52% of sales.

OLD BUILDING near entrance to Brooklyn Bridge housed first Squibb laboratory, started in 1858. A century later, Squibb's Brooklyn plant, whose gleaming lights welcome bridge traffic from Manhattan, fills 13 large buildings on the same spot.

of a promised army contract, borrowed $1300 and set up his own laboratory in Brooklyn Heights.

His only concession to advertising was the 320 circulars stating his qualifications which he sent to physicians and pharmacists.

In 1858 the firm of Edward R. Squibb, M.D., shipped its first order —18 pounds of chloroform. In less than six weeks more capital was needed for expansion.

Soon after, a young assistant, faint from ether fumes, dropped a bottle of it, thus starting the first of many fires which were to demolish Squibb's laboratories.

Squibb himself was severely burned but not beaten. He rebuilt the laboratory with $2100 raised by friends. Business recovered so quickly that the loan was repaid in three years.

Receipts from May to December, 1859, totalled over $5000. The Civil War broke out and the long-promised Army orders materialized. The firm was soon straining to keep up with production.

Concern for his private and business affairs never lessened his concern about drug adulteration. In 1860 he received an appointment to the Committee of Revision of the U.S. Pharmacopeia (the basic code of U.S. Pharmacy), where he began to take his first whacks at the quacks.

After melting down a cask of commercial aloes, from which he separated the debris, he mailed both to the Committee. The debris weighed half as much as the aloes.

During the War years Squibb petitioned Congress to enforce the Act of 1848, (which prohibited the import of adulterated drugs) by replacing politically appointed inspectors with those of scientific background. Congress took no action.

Some years before, he had petitioned Congress on quite a different matter. After flogging had been abolished in the Navy, he wrote a 2500-word demand for its restoration, which also went unheeded.

Just before the war ended Squibb

MASS ADVERTISING, started after death of Squibb, made firm's products household staples throughout entire nation.

MAJOR INTEREST of the young Dr. Squibb, shown here as assistant surgeon in the Navy, was production of pure, standard drugs, end to adulteration and quackery. Existing enormous industry was by-product of his lifelong, bitterly waged crusade.

expanded his laboratory to handle increased Army orders.

The timing was bad. Peacetime slowdown of orders, cost of expansion, and a general post-war depression left the company in a slump. Squibb was in debt for $6000—barely able even to renew a $25,000 mortgage on the laboratory.

The new structure remained almost idle for over five years while taxes and debts mounted. In 1867 alone, the loss was $8,000. The discouraged doctor began buying cemetery plots.

In 1871, despite another fire, the family finances took an upward swing. Squibb invested in and helped organize the National Chemical Wood Treatment Company to distil acetic acid from wood.

He took over personal management of the plant, and after five years the company was selling $33,000 worth of acid annually. The net earnings of the corporation in 1879 were over $10,000.

Meanwhile, business at Squibb's own laboratory had been improving. In 1873 sales were up 45%.

The problem of meeting debts and taxes reduced, Squibb once again turned his attention to the fight for pure drugs.

In 1876, convinced that the Pharmacopeia could never establish genuine standards until it was taken out of the hands of patent medicine profiteers, he asked the American Medical Association to take over control. The A.M.A. tabled the proposal.

Disgusted but not discouraged, he wrote a rough draft of a Pure Food and Drug Act, versions of which were enacted in 1880 by both the New York and New Jersey Legislatures. Powerful patent medicine lobbies stalled Federal passage, however, until six years after his death.

The A.M.A. had also rejected his plan to publish a periodical to keep the medical profession abreast of scientific development, so he founded his own publication, "An Ephemeris." It not only evaluated new medicines and techniques but also took a resounding whack at quacks and charlatans, as well as attacking Medical Journals for accepting advertising.

By this time he was in his 80s and not well. The business had prospered as his reputation for pure, ethical products grew—annual sales before his death came to $414,410. In 1882 he retired and his sons took over, but he refused to incorporate, feeling divided responsibility destroyed initiative.

Until his death in 1900 from a heart attack, he disapproved from the sidelines while his son Charles introduced modern business techniques such as the opening of a Manhattan showroom, enlarging the sales force from a counter attendant and stock man to 13 men.

In 1901, a year after the elder Squibb's death, the company was finally incorporated, and four years later control was sold to Lowell Palmer and Theodore Weicker. The business began to expand beyond the doctor's dreams.

In 1952 Mathieson Chemical Corp. purchased the company and two years later merged with Olin Industries to form Olin Mathieson Chemical Corp. Squibb sales today are in excess of $100 million. This corporate immensity would have surprised Dr. Squibb, who as a go-it-aloner, often said while fighting the whole world, "God and One is a Majority."

41

SELLING WAS NEVER THE SAME AGAIN

R. H. Macy combined old ideas into new, under-one-roof formula, created modern department store

R. H. Macy's 1858 New York store developed into first true department store, set merchandising pattern which quickly spread throughout U.S., world.

THE MAN who deserves most of the credit for the invention of that three-ring circus of the merchandising world, the department store, is Rowland Hussey Macy.

The founder of R. H. Macy & Co. had a big-league retailing career of only 19 years—from 1858, when he opened his New York store, to 1877, the year of his death.

But in those 19 years, he created a kind of store so new that nobody even had a name for it (the term "department store" did not come into use until the 1890s), and laid the foundation for one of today's great merchandising empires.

By 1960, the R. H. Macy department store chain's sales volume was $508.7 million; sales in the New York store alone reportedly ran well over $150 million a year.

Of all the new businesses started in New York in the year 1858, Rowland Macy's might easily have been voted least likely to succeed.

Its 36-year-old proprietor had already taken four unsuccessful flyers at storekeeping, the last of which had ended in bankruptcy.

Macy was born in 1822, the son of a Nantucket Island, Mass., sea captain. He grew up on the island, and when he was 15, he went to sea himself, on a whaling ship.

The voyage of the whaler, the Emily Morgan, to the South Pacific and back lasted four years; young Macy returned to Nantucket at 19 with a red star (later to become the trade mark of R. H. Macy & Co.) tattooed on his arm and a profit share of about $500 in his pocket.

He then moved to Boston, where he tried his hand at a variety of jobs, made friends with a dry goods retailer, George Houghton, and in 1844, married Houghton's sister.

It was probably his brother-in-law who set him up in his first store, a small needles-and-threads establishment in Boston.

The venture seems to have failed within a few months, and so, in 1846, did a small dry goods store.

Among the red-ink entries in one of his Boston ledgers appears the gloomy notation:

"I have worked Two Years for Nothing. Damn. Damn. damn. damn."

In 1849, Macy and one of his brothers joined the California Gold Rush, and with three other young men opened a general store near San Francisco. A year later, however, the brothers sold out—at a small profit, if any—and came back to New England.

Rowland Macy then opened his fourth store in Haverhill, Mass.

He stayed in Haverhill for the next four years, and it was there that he began to display his spectacular merchandising talents.

Still selling dry goods, he plunged gleefully into price wars with half a dozen competitors.

He advertised.

The Haverhill Cheap Store, as Macy's emporium was called, ran columns in the local newspapers to its competitors' inches; it advertised 52 weeks a year instead of only seasonally, as was the general rule, and, in another radical departure from common practice, it changed its advertising copy every week.

Macy wrote the copy himself, as he was to continue to do in New York. Usually written in the first person, it was lively, funny and opinionated, taking pokes at the Haverhill Cheap Store's competition and at Haverhill business in general. It also mentioned specific items in stock, quoted prices, and touted special sales—another new idea at a time when most retail advertising consisted of genteel generalities.

Macy brought in fresh stocks from New York and Boston every week, while most of his competition was contented with seasonal buying, and held frequent clearance sales for rapid turnover.

He kept a sharp eye open for novelty items on his buying trips, and soon expanded his store's line to include "notions and fancy goods"—shawls, bonnets, underwear, soap, perfume, fans, baskets, toys and parasols—as well as dry goods.

DEPARTMENT STORES

	1960		1940		1920		
	Sales ($ million)	Profits	Sales ($ million)	Profits	Sales ($ million)	Profits	When Inc.
Federated Dept. Stores (includes Filene's, Abraham & Straus, Bloomingdales')	$759.9	$33.9	110.1	3.6	......	......	1929
Allied Stores (includes Stern Bros.)	679.5	14.6	112.1	3.4	......	......	1928
May Dept. Stores	684.0	23.8	103.9	4.4	57.9	4.6	1910
R. H. Macy	508.7	8.7	84.9	3.9	35.8	2.7	1919
Gimbel Bros.	404.8	9.8	92.2	1.4	......	......	1922
City Stores (includes Franklin Simon, Oppenheim Collins)	274.6	2.8	45.2	1.0	......	......	1923
Associated Dry Goods (includes J. W. Robinson, (Sibley, Lindsay & Curr)	290.1	9.1	61.3	2.0	n.a.	1.8	1916
Marshall Field	234.3	9.2	89.9	5.7	n.a.	n.a.	1901
Broadway-Hale (includes Coulters)	179.8	6.3	15.9	0.2	n.a.	n.a.	1919
Mercantile Stores (includes Gayfera Co.)	167.8	5.0	29.5	0.6	n.a.	4.4	1919

Pioneer Macy (above) was succeeded after death by Isidore Straus (below), whose descendants still rule company.

Macy's moved uptown to present Herald Square main store site in 1902, when horsecar, El set transportation pace. Christmas windows have always been featured.

Innovator had four failures before spectacular New York success

It was also in Haverhill that he decided upon two business principles that were to guide him throughout the rest of his career.

The first was sale for cash only.

The second was fixed pricing.

Haggling was still the rule in most retail stores of the 1850s; it was taken for granted that more affluent or more gullible customers ought to pay more than the poorer or shrewder.

Macy was, in his adoption of all these principles and practices, in the forefront of a retailing revolution that was sweeping the country. And, although he was not the first to apply any one of them, he was among the first to put them all together. (His unique contribution, development of the full-fledged department store, was yet to come.)

It would be pleasant to report that Macy's aggressive salesmanship and sound business practices made the Haverhill Cheap Store a success.

In fact, he went bankrupt in 1855.

He had found his success formula, but it was not one that could be applied in a small town. Haverhill had more drygoods stores than it could

support, even without price wars, and too few customers to make Macy's kind of advertising pay.

After three years as a land speculator in Wisconsin, Macy moved on to New York.

The New York retailing world already had its giants—A. T. Stewart & Co., Arnold Constable, Lord & Taylor—all dignified establishments housed in marble palaces, catering largely to the carriage trade, and all specialty shops.

Macy, in his tiny store on 14th Street, began advertising to attract a mass market. As in Haverhill, his prices were rock bottom, his merchandising lively and all his sales at fixed price and for cash.

New York, a bustling, fast-growing city of close to 1 million inhabitants, was just the right place for him.

R. H. Macy & Co. grew until it occupied most of a city block. Sales soared from $90,000 in 1858 to $1.8 million in 1877. And, over these 19 years, it added new lines of merchandise so fast that by the founder's death it was undeniably the nation's first department store.

(A department store is defined to-

day as one selling at least ready-to-wear, dry goods and home furnishings, organized by departments but under a single management, with yearly sales of $100,000 or more; by the early 1870s, Macy's had amply met all these present requirements.)

Just why Macy decided to expand in this way, except out of sheer exuberance and optimism, nobody knows—but the idea was truly revolutionary; most stores of the day were so specialized that wags wanted to know when somebody was going to start selling nothing but pocket handkerchiefs.

It soon caught on. In 1876, a young Philadelphia clothing merchant named John Wanamaker opened his Grand Depot; in 1887, Adam Gimbel, a German-born former peddler, started a department store in Milwaukee.

Shortly after Macy's death on a buying trip to Europe, ownership of R. H. Macy & Co. passed into the hands of Isidore Straus and his sons, who had been running its china and glassware department. Their descendants are still minding what is today the world's biggest store.

Macy's-Roosevelt Field, on former air base site, typifies move of department stores to suburbs.

Gail Borden

Miracle Man Of Milk

Gail Borden's invention of pure, spoilage-free condensed milk opened a mass market for dairy products, launched today's $10 billion dairying industry

TODAY's multi-billion dollar dairy industry may well owe its existence to a single product — condensed milk.

The invention, just over 100 years ago, of a pure, spoilage-proof milk product that attracted a mass market and could be produced and distributed in quantity, launched the industry's first major firm, the Borden Co. The new milk thus laid the foundations of growth and product diversification for Borden and today's other dairying giants.

In the 1850s, when Gail Borden was battling to patent the milk condensation process he had just discovered, dairying was a small-scale, local industry.

For city-dwellers, dairy products in general were luxury items, and pure milk, in particular, was practically unobtainable. Milk for the cities came from cows kept in spectacularly unsanitary city barns and fed, as often as not, on mash from liquor distilleries.

Grownups drank practically no milk, and mothers fed "distillery milk" to their children with well-founded misgivings.

Last year, Americans—city and country dweller, grownups and children — drank $6.5 billion worth of milk alone and consumed just over $10 billion worth of all dairy products.

The Borden Co., second largest in the dairy industry, had sales of $956 million by 1960. (The industry leader, National Dairy, passed the $1.5 billion mark.

Many scientific and technological developments—notably, pasteurization and mechanical refrigeration—played important roles in the dairy-

ing revolution. But Gail Borden's condensed milk started it all.

(Sales of condensed and evaporated milk, which are still widely used for infants' formulas and in cooking, were $383 million in 1960.)

Gail Borden was already in his 50s when he went into the milk business.

He was born in 1801, the son of

an upstate New York farmer.

His family joined the first great wave of Westward migration in 1815, settling first in Kentucky and then in Indiana.

At 20, young Gail was a country schoolteacher—although he had had only a year and a half of formal schooling, himself — and a Hoosier militia captain.

But he and his younger brother, Tom, still had no wish to settle down.

Two years later, they navigated a flatboat down the Mississippi to New Orleans.

They found the city buzzing with talk of Texas; the vast territory to the West had just been opened to settlers from the U.S. by the Mexican government, and Stephen F. Austin was forming an expedition.

Within a few months, Tom Borden was heading for Texas with Austin's pioneer band of 300 families.

Gail, who had developed an alarming cough in the Indiana winters, had to stay behind to build up his health; he spent the next six years teaching school and surveying in Mississippi. But in 1829, with his father and two other brothers, he set out to join Tom.

The Bordens helped make Texas history in the colorful and tumultuous 1830s.

When war with Mexico broke out in 1835, three of the Borden brothers joined Austin's army, and Gail became editor of the rebels' newspaper, the *Telegraph and Texas Land Register*.

On March 2, 1836, he printed Texas' declaration of independence, under the headline, "Remember the

Alamo." (The words were Col. Sydney Sherman's, not Borden's — but the *Telegraph* helped make them a Texas rallying cry.)

When the war was over, Texas' President Sam Houston gave Borden the post of Collector of the Port of Galveston; a year later (he had a wife and six children, and needed more money than the fledgling Republic of Texas could pay), he joined a real estate firm, the Galveston City Co., as secretary and general agent.

He was still in the real estate business when he began experimenting—as a hobby, at first—with the condensation of food.

He started with fruits, moved on to meat, and, by the mid-1840s, had developed a meat "biscuit," similar to the Indians' pemmican but better-tasting, that seemed to have commercial potentialities.

A party of California-bound gold-seekers bought 600 pounds of Borden's biscuits; Dr. Elisha Kent Kane, the Arctic explorer, took a

supply on one of his expeditions.

Borden built a plant in Galveston and went into the meat biscuit business full-time in 1846.

However, although the product won scientific acclaim, it was a resounding commercial flop.

All Borden's efforts to sell it in quantity to steamship lines, hospitals, and the armed services met with failure, and in 1852, he lost the Texas plant.

"Don't infer I have given up, for I know that the meat biscuit is one of the discoveries of the age," he wrote to a friend.

During the next few years, the almost penniless Borden struggled to revive his meat biscuit business —and, at the same time, began venturing into a new line of research, the one that was to make his fortune.

He had tried unsuccessfully to condense milk during his first years of experimentation in Galveston, now he tried again.

(He became aware of the real need for a spoilage-proof milk prod-

uct in 1851, on a return voyage from England, when he discovered that babies on board ship were falling ill from the milk given by the two unhealthy cows that were kept in the hold.)

He first tried to condense milk simply by boiling it. The resulting product stayed fresh a little longer than whole milk, but it tasted decidedly burnt.

Then he remembered a colony of Shakers in upstate New York who used vacuum pans to condense sugar and fruit juices. He decided that, in the condensation of milk, vacuum equipment might serve a dual purpose; avoiding the burnt taste, because it would permit evaporation with less heat, and retarding spoilage by eliminating air during evaporation.

He had already moved his family back east; he made a trip to the Shaker colony to borrow some vacuum pans, and continued his experiments in a Brooklyn cellar "laboratory."

In 1853, he perfected his process and applied for a patent.

But for three long, hard years, the patent was refused. Other inventors had thought of ways to condense milk, although none of them had put a product on the market, and the patent office refused to be persuaded that the vacuum method of condensation was unique.

Finally, two scientist friends of Borden's (Robert McFarlane, editor of the *Scientific American*, and John H. Currie, head of a major research laboratory) came to his rescue. They tested every known method of milk condensation, and presented the patent office with evidence that Borden's was not only unique, but also superior.

Borden was in business again, with a small plant in Wolcottville, Conn., backed by another friend, a wealthy Washington lawyer named Thomas Green.

Within months, however, the Wolcottville venture had failed. It was under-financed; local farmers refused to extend credit for supplies of fresh milk, and the trickle

First successful Borden plant was set up in 1857 in Burrville, Conn.

46

UNION ARMY BECAME FIRST BULK CUSTOMER

Borden's condensed milk, made germ-free by vacuum heat processing, was first sold on city streets from open containers, later canned.

of condensed milk that reached New York sold poorly because housewives thought it tasted odd.

Green agreed to finance a second try, and Borden opened a new plant in Burrville, Conn., just as the financial panic of 1857 was striking the nation.

Soon he was deep in debt again, and, with money practically impossible to raise, the second plant seemed doomed to go the way of the first.

Then, on a train to New York, Borden met a New York banker named Jeremiah Milbank and sold him on the future of condensed milk.

A substantial loan from Milbank saved the day, and by February, 1858, production at the Burrville plant was in full swing.

A few months later, the New York Condensed Milk Company, as the Borden firm was first named, had its second stroke of luck.

Leslie's Illustrated Weekly, a popular New York paper, launched a campaign against "distillery milk." It praised the purity of Borden's milk, and sales began to rise.

In 1859, the Burrville plant, with 10 employes, grossed $48,000.

Then came the Civil War.

Borden received his first government order, for 500 pounds of condensed milk, in the fall of 1861, and, from then on, his problem was production, not sales. Eagle Brand Condensed Milk became part of the Union Army's field ration; the company's earnings for 1864 were over $145,000.

(Civilian sales during the war years got a boost when Mrs. Lincoln served condensed milk at a White House dinner.)

Borden himself was only partly aware of the reasons for his product's success.

He had proved that condensation of milk greatly retarded spoilage; and, in the Burrville plant and the other Borden plants that followed it as the company grew, he insisted on the most scrupulous sanitation.

But the most important reason for the fact that people who drank condensed milk stayed healthier

Elsie, the Cow, now blessed with husband, offspring, has symbolized pure milk products for generation.

than those who drank raw milk was that Borden's product was "pasteurized."

Borden had begun condensing milk long before Louis Pasteur's discoveries startled the scientific world. Since he had never heard of germs, he had no way of knowing that, by briefly heating his milk to a temperature of 190 degrees, he was destroying them. But he actually had by chance hit upon the principle of pasteurization.

Gail Borden retired in 1871, turning over the management of the company to one of his sons, John Gail.

Four years later, the New York Condensed Milk Company ("Borden" was not to enter the firm name until 1899) began its diversification by selling fresh milk, produced under the sanitary conditions that had made the company famous and ladled out from immaculate 10-gallon cans, on the streets of New York.

By the turn of the century, the company, under the presidency of a second Borden son, Henry Lee, had reached the $10 million annual sales mark.

Borden's had carried the dairying industry into the ranks of big business.

ELISHA G. OTIS

CHARLES R. OTIS

NORTON P. OTIS

GOING UP

Elisha Graves Otis' invention of safety elevator in 1853 started the rise of modern cities by making multi-story buildings practicable. Elevator industry sales volume today is over $500 million a year.

ELISHA GRAVES OTIS, inventor of the safety elevator, did more than pioneer an industry whose sales are now estimated at well over $500 million—he started the city skylines of the world soaring towards the clouds.

When it comes to elevators and skyscrapers, the question of the chicken and the egg is easy to answer.

Without a safe, rapid means of vertical transportation, office buildings and apartments more than five or six stories high simply could not have been built—too few people would want to live or work in them.

In the New York of 1853, the year Otis sold his first two elevators, the 280-foot spire of Trinity Church was a towering landmark. Most office buildings were only three or four stories high, hardly more than residential buildings on a larger scale, and even so, the top floor was usually given to the janitor to live in because no one would rent it.

By 1908, Old Trinity could no

longer be seen from New York harbor, and office workers were happily riding elevators to jobs in buildings that rose to the dizzying height of 20, 30 or even 40 stories.

Today, 50 story buildings are commonplace, and every day in New York, close to 50,000 elevators carry an estimated 20 million passengers a total distance of more than 125,000 miles—over half the distance to the moon.

Elisha Otis was born in 1811, the youngest son of a prosperous Vermont farmer.

He left the farm while he was still in his teens, and got a job with a construction firm in Troy, N. Y.

As a young man he seems to have been extremely enterprising and equally unlucky.

Before he was 40, he had tried his hand at four unsuccessful business ventures—a grist mill, a carriage shop, a saw mill and a machine shop.

Between the saw mill and the ma-

chine shop, he went to work as a master mechanic in an Albany, N. Y., bedstead factory. While there, he invented a machine that turned out bedstead parts four times as fast as had previously been possible, and also developed a number of other labor-saving devices.

One of the partners of the firm, Joseph Maise, was sufficiently impressed by Otis to offer him another job several years later, when the machine shop had failed.

So, in 1851, Elisha Otis came to Bergen, N. J., to work as the master mechanic of another Maise bedstead factory. A year later, the business moved to Yonkers, N. Y.

A mechanical hoist was needed in the plant, and Otis tackled the problem. He designed and installed the first elevator with an automatic safety device to keep it from falling.

Crude hand-powered elevators had existed for several centuries, but they were so unsafe that they had never

48

been used for passengers, and were used even for goods as little as possible.

Otis' design was truly revolutionary—but he apparently did not see its potentialities at first. His employer had needed an elevator, so he had designed one, and had made it as safe as possible—that was that.

In fact, he was on the point of packing up his family and leaving New York to join the California Gold Rush when, at the beginning of 1853, the bedstead plant received an unsolicited order for two safety elevators. They came from a Mr. Newhouse, a furniture manufacturer in whose New York City plant a serious accident had just occurred on a freight elevator.

Otis decided that if people wanted elevators, he would stay in New York and manufacture them.

At that point, the bedstead plant went out of business so Otis borrowed all the money he could, and set up his own small shop on the first floor of his former employer's plant.

By the end of 1853, sales had amounted to precisely $900, and the new company's total inventory was $122.71, including a second-hand lathe, two oil cans and the account book in which these figures were written.

When no more orders came in, he took his invention to the Crystal Palace Exhibition in New York City early in 1854.

The elevator was one of the hits of the show—largely because of Otis' showmanship in demonstrating it.

He stood on the platform, extolling the virtues of the equipment as it rose into the air—and then, when both oratory and elevator were at their height, he cut the rope which suspended the platform and stood, bowing, high above the crowd.

The *New York Tribune* gave him a good send-off in its story on the Crystal Palace Exhibition:

"We may commence by referring to an elevator or a machine for hoisting goods, exhibited by E. G. Otis of Yonkers — which attracts attention both by its prominent position and by the apparent daring of the inventor, who as he rides up and down the platform occasionally cuts the rope by which it is suspended."

ELEVATORLESS NEW YORK of 1798 *(above)* boasted few buildings of more than three or four stories; church spires still towered over city in mid-19th Century. By 1908 *(below)*, more than 21,000 elevators had created an entirely new city skyline.

ERA OF SKYSCRAPERS began for New Yorkers when famed Flatiron Building *(l.)* went up in 1902. Its original elevators are still in service. Today's skyline *(right)* of almost endless high buildings dwarfs most turn-of-the-century construction.

First of the firm's passenger elevators was installed in department store, cost just $300

Even after the Crystal Palace triumph, however, the world hardly beat a path to Otis' door in Yonkers.

Sales were only $2975 in 1854, and $5605 in 1855. In 1856, they climbed to $13,488 for 27 elevators.

All the elevators Otis sold in his first four years in business were for freight—using them for people must still have seemed risky. and as far as is known, he did nothing to promote this side of the business.

In 1857, however, he got his first order for a passenger elevator from a daring department store owner, E. V. Haughwort. The elevator he supplied was driven by belts from line shafting, had a speed of 40 feet per minute and cost $300. It made an immediate hit with the store's customers.

When Otis died in 1861, he left to his two sons, Charles and Norton, a small but growing business with an inventory of about $5000 and eight or ten employes.

Lean years were ahead during the Civil War period.

"If we could get more hands, we could go ahead," Charles wrote in the middle of the war. "But it requires money, and a good deal more than we have got."

In 1866, Charles thought things were looking up:

"The panic among businessmen seems to be over, and we hear less about the cholera. There is now beginning to be some inquiry about hoisting machinery. Money matters are easier, think we can get along pretty well now."

This proved to be the understatement of the decade.

Builders were about to discover that the elevator made it possible for them to build upward as high as brick bearing walls would go—and that, in an elevator building, upper floors were actually more valuable.

Soaring land values in every major U.S. city made construction of tall buildings on small plots a virtual economic necessity.

"They act about elevators as though they were some new discovery that had just come out," Norton Otis wrote in 1868, the year in which the company got contracts for New York's first three elevator office buildings—New York Life, Equitable Life and Park Bank.

Otis Bros. & Co. passed the $200,000 sales mark in 1870, and had its first $1 million year in 1889. In 1898, it merged with eight smaller elevator manufacturers to become Otis Elevator Co.

The first Otis hydraulic elevator, faster (up to 600 feet per minute) and safer than the old steam-powered models, was installed at 155 Broadway in 1878. The electric elevator made its appearance in the '90s.

By the turn of the century, steel frame construction—introduced first in Chicago in 1885 and later in New York—had revolutionized the building industry, making possible skyscrapers of practically any height.

From then on, the elevator—and the nation's cities— had no place to go but up.

OTIS DEMONSTRATED ELEVATOR'S SAFETY AT CRYSTAL PALACE BY CUTTING ROPES

50

ESCALATOR, an Otis Co. invention, was first used at 1900 Paris Exhibition, soon installed at New York "el" stations (*above*). Today, escalators are about 10% of industry's sales.

DEPARTMENT STORES (*above*, Lord & Taylor in 1873) were among first to install passenger elevators. Hotels, too, soon found that the new convenience boosted their business.

EARLY OTIS ADS emphasized use of the company's "patent hoisting machinery" for freight, and recommended it for "all places where it is desirable to use lofts and upper stories."

ADS OF 1890s urged installation of elevators in private homes. One claimed: "The day is not far distant when all houses of any pretension will be equipped with these elevators."

51

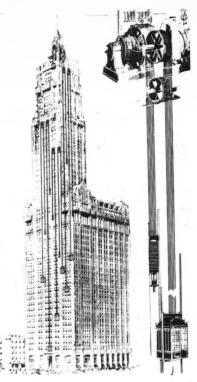

Original Otis factory (at top) at Yonkers, N.Y., 1853. In 1867, new $13,000 building was erected on site of present Yonkers Works (above).

Woolworth Building, N.Y., retains Otis' original gearless machines.

Otis elevators, operating at speeds up to 1200 feet per minute, were installed in United Nations building.

HE OPENED INDUSTRY'S BOOKS

Henry Varnum Poor, pioneer of financial research, defended the investor's right to know about his company in an era when the annual report was unknown

One hundred and two years ago, a middle-aged editor named Henry Varnum Poor published the first edition of his *Manual of Railroads.*

In the *Manual,* for the first time, basic facts about a major U.S. industry were made available to private investors and to the business community as a whole—a revolutionary idea in a day when most businessmen thought their business was their own and nobody else's.

Today, the compilation and interpretation of business statistics is a multi-million-dollar business in itself. (The leaders of the field are Standard & Poor's, direct descendants of Henry Varnum Poor's 19th century firm; Moody's, absorbed in March, 1962 by Dun & Bradstreet, which has itself been purveying information about business credit ratings since 1841; United Business Service and Value Line Survey) At least 100 smaller firms are also engaged in statistical research and analysis of investment opportunities; and the major financial publications, of course, offer similar services to their subscribers.

But business research is more than a business in its own right. It is the foundation of the whole incredibly complex structure of modern "people's capitalism."

Back in the 1850's, when Henry Varnum Poor was compiling his first *Manual,* the stockholder corporation was still a relatively new idea. But the great railroads that were beginning to roll toward the Pacific offered an excit-

HENRY VARNUM POOR

ing investment opportunity, and thousands of Americans were buying shares for the first time.

The New York Stock Exchange had had its dim beginnings more than half a century earlier, in 1792, when a group of gentleman traders began meeting every day under Manhattan's Buttonwood Tree (or at Tontine's Coffee House in bad weather). But they bought and sold only government bonds.

By the early 1800's, they were dealing in canal and toll road securities as well.

In 1829, the first corporation with stockholders—the Baltimore and Ohio Railroad — was born.

And over the next few decades, more and more businessmen found that the capital they needed could be raised only by selling stock to the public. U.S. industry was growing too fast for financing by the traditional means — partnerships and individual or family wealth.

The average mid-19th century investor, however, often had to buy a pig in a poke. It was almost impossible for him to find out what was what and who was who in the companies he was helping to finance.

Annual reports were almost unheard of; corporate records, if they were kept at all, were strictly confidential; the Federal and state governments required no accounting whatsoever.

Obviously, this situation made it difficult for the investor to choose his stocks wisely; and it made slipshod management or downright dishonesty much too easy to get away with.

Then Henry Varnum Poor began his fight for the investor's "right to know."

Poor was born in Andover, Maine, in 1812. He studied law under his uncle, and went through Bowdoin College, taking his BA degree in 1835 and his MA in 1838.

For the next ten years, he practiced law and dabbled in politics (he was a Whig, and campaigned for William Henry Harrison) in Bangor, Maine. He also took an interest in the building of the first Maine railroads.

Then, in 1849, he decided that he liked railroading—and writing—better than law, and came to New York to take a job as editor of the *American Railroad Journal*.

It wasn't long before the *Jour-*

lengthy and detailed report to its worried investors, shook up its management, and introduced other reforms.

Next, the *Journal* ran an article warning its readers against investing in seven shaky Midwestern and Southern railroads.

Poor's personal stock—among investors and railroad men alike —was beginning to soar.

Industry Refuses Information

It was at the same time, early in the 1850's, that the New York stock exchange began worrying about the dearth of information on securities, appointing a committee to remedy the situation.

But the committee had scant success. Few businesses were willing to tell anything; the secretary of one of the nation's largest corporations simply re-

POOR'S SURVIVED BUSINESS CRISES AND PANICS

RAILROADS WERE TOP 19TH CENTURY INVESTMENT BUY

nal, under Poor's talented direction (he was a gifted essayist, a sound economist, and a reporter with a nose for news), began asking the railroads embarrassing questions in print.

Putting the Brakes on Erie

In September, 1852, it sharply criticized the Erie Railroad which had just declared a seven per cent dividend.

Poor had analyzed the road's earnings and increases in construction, and had found that "instead of a dividend being earned, $1,642,492.80 has been borrowed, to pay the interest and dividend." He demanded additional figures and a breakdown of construction costs.

It may or may not have been a coincidence that, shortly thereafter, the company issued a

turned its letter with a succinct comment scribbled on the back:

"This company makes no reports and publishes no statements—and has not done anything of the kind for the last five years."

Poor Tackles U. S. Railroads

The *Railroad Journal*, noting the Stock Exchange's failure, embarked upon an editorial campaign for Federal and state legislation requiring corporations to issue regular, uniform reports. But it was too far ahead of its time—the idea met with massive resistance.

So, in 1854, Poor set out to compile his own report on the railroads, which he knew best.

He sent letters and questionnaires to every U.S. railroad, asking for, among other things, the names of their officers and directors; the first estimated cost of the road with the estimated amount of its income; construction dates; pattern and weight of rail used; physical features of the road; total costs of the road for each year of operation; total amount of stock; yearly mileage; costs per mile; gross receipts; current expenses; net receipts; dividends; receipts from passengers and from freight; and yearly earnings per mile.

The letter concluded with a disarming paragraph:

"I am aware that furnishing the information requested will impose a serious burden upon you. I hope it may be some compensation for your trouble that it will be the means of presenting the public a correct and satisfactory statement of the company with which you are associated."

And in 1860, the first *Poor's Manual* finally appeared; its full title was *History of the Railroad and the Canals of the United States.*

Poor's Manual Becomes Annual

The second edition of the *Manual* did not appear until 1868; Poor spent the Civil War years as an editorial writer on the *New York Times.*

But from 1868 on, it came out every year.

With the help of his scholarly son, Henry William (who read Greek, Latin, Sanskrit, Hebrew, Russian and Icelandic as easily as railroad reports), Poor began expanding his list of publications.

A Directory of American Officials first appeared in 1886, and a *Handbook of Investment Securities* in 1890.

BUSINESS RESEARCH THRIVED IN 1920'S INVESTMENT BOOM.

On the first round of replies, Poor received plenty of refusals as flat as those that had gone to the Stock Exchange.

Journal too Powerful to Ignore

But the railroads soon found out that the *Journal* was too powerful to ignore.

After a *Journal* article in July, 1855, commenting on the lack of information in the reports of the Michigan Central, the railroad's president, John Murray, sent a memo to his general manager:

"You must avoid cutting Poor's sensibilities, as we want to make a friend of him . . . There is no doubt that he cut our stock 5% by his confounded article."

For the next five years, Poor kept on crusading in the *Journal* for more and better corporate reports—and collecting statistics from the railroads.

Long before Poor's death in 1905, his manuals were an accepted and respected institution.

In 1900, a 32-year-old former newspaperman named John Moody published his first *Manual of Industrials and Miscellaneous Securities.*

Merger of Standard & Poor's

The financial research business was beginning to expand.

In 1914, another major firm, Standard Statistics, entered the field; in 1941, it merged with Poor's Publishing Co. to create the present Standard & Poor's.

Over the past 60 years the growth of business research has kept pace with—and contributed to—the growth of U.S. industry.

It has helped build the partnership that exists today between 12 million American stockholders and their companies.

Versatile engineer brought U.S. Bessemer process, laid foundation of world's largest steel industry

ALEXANDER LYMAN HOLLEY

A. L. HOLLEY, SIRE OF STEEL

TODAY'S $20 billion U.S. iron and steel industry was born in 1865, when the nation's first Bessemer steel plant opened in Troy, N. Y.

The Troy plant was designed and built by a young engineer, Alexander Lyman Holley, who deserves to be remembered as the technological father of the modern steel industry.

Alexander Holley possessed a rare blend of engineering genius and business acumen.

He used his combination of talents to introduce into the U.S. the steel conversion process developed by Great Britain's Sir Henry Bessemer—the process which was to make possible the mass production of steel, and thus open the way for the great industrial empire builders of the late 19th century.

Holley was born in 1832, the son of a wealthy Connecticut cutlery maker who later became governor.

By the time he was 17, he had fallen in love with locomotives.

He wrote to a friend that he had been spending all his spare time for two weeks "making sectional and perspective views of the internal works, machinery, steam works, etc., of the most improved locomotive engines, in some 17 different pictures, with explanations filling some ten pages."

Perhaps it was this treatise that persuaded his father to let him study mechanical engineering at Brown instead of classics at Yale, as the family had planned.

Holley graduated from Brown with honors in 1852; during his undergraduate years, he had begun contributing to scientific and technical magazines, and had invented a variable cutoff engine.

The engine was never patented, but it impressed a Providence, R.I., firm, Corliss & Nightingale, enough to induce them to hire the young inventor as a draughtsman and machinist in the locomotive department.

After three years, Holley left Corliss & Nightingale and took a brief, unsuccessful job hunting swing through the West.

"It is strange," he wrote home, "that when I have taken such pains to present myself modestly, and am willing to do anything; when I have got such strong letters, and know that I can build a better locomotive than all the rest of them put together —I cannot, in the whole Western country, get a place to earn my bread."

Back east late in 1855, the 23-year-old engineer decided to go into technical journalism.

He joined forces with a publisher named Zerah Colburn, and became co-proprietor and editor of the *Railroad Advocate*, and later of the *American Engineer*, with which the unsuccessful *Advocate* was merged.

The financial crash of 1857 interrupted publication of the second magazine, but by then, Holley and Colburn were well known and respected by U.S. railroad men, and they won a commission to go to Europe and study Continental railways.

In 1858, he began writing for the New York *Times*, on both technical and general news topics.

He contributed close to 200 articles to the *Times* in the next five years, and kept on making occasional contributions until 1875, to boost his total to 276.

In addition to his work for the *Times*, he became editor of the mechanical department of *American Railway Review*; wrote another book on railroading; contributed engineering articles and definitions to *Webster's Unabridged Dictionary*; and wrote for popular and scientific magazines on iron-clad ships and heavy ordnance, as well as on railroading.

Shortly after the Civil War broke out, he was commissioned to go to England and study armaments.

It was on this trip that he discovered Henry Bessemer's steel process.

The principal materials of construction in the 1860s were still wrought and cast iron, both of which had been produced in the U.S. since Colonial days.

However, cast iron was too brittle and wrought iron too soft for the increasingly difficult construction work of the industrial 19th century, and steel was in great demand.

It had been produced for centuries, largely in Great Britain, but only in small quantities and by slow and costly processes.

Then, in 1856, Bessemer discovered that oxygen for refining pig iron could be taken directly from the air (instead of from iron oxides, as in the older methods) if a blast were blown onto or through the melted pig iron. This method not only purified the iron, but also kept it hot enough to remain molten, so that an ingot of mill steel could be cast, ready for the forge or the rolling mill.

At the same time, an American inventor, William Kelly, was doing remarkably similar work.

Industrialists on both sides of the Atlantic were aware of the Bessemer and Kelly experiments, but were still not convinced that the new process was practical.

Holley returned to the U.S. sure that he could put Bessemer steelmaking on a mass production basis. He persuaded a Troy, N. Y., firm, Corning, Winslow & Co., to hire him and let him try.

In 1863, he made another trip to England and secured U.S. rights to the Bessemer patents for his firm.

Back in the U.S., he arranged for the purchase of William Kelly's conflicting patents, and went to work on the first U.S. Bessemer mill.

The first "blow" of the new steel was made in February, 1865, and two months later, the first ingot was shipped to the Baldwin Locomotive Works in Philadelphia.

Thirteen Bessemer steel mills were built in the U.S. between 1865 and 1880, and Alexander Holley designed 11 of them.

Late in the 1860s, a newly formed association of U.S. Bessemer steel manufacturers hired Holley as its

U.S. STEEL PRODUCTION
1870-1960
(millions of net tons)

Year	Open Hearth	Bessemer	Electric & Crucible	Basic Oxygen	Total
1870	.002	.042	.034		.077
1880	.113	1.2	.08		1.4
1890	.574	4.1	.08		4.8
1900	3.8	7.5	.118		11.4
1910	18.5	10.5	.198		29.2
1920	36.6	9.9	.6		47.2
1930	39.3	5.6	.7		45.6
1940	61.6	3.7	1.7		67.0
1950	86.3	4.5	6.0		96.8
1960	86.4	1.2	8.4	3.3	99.3

BY 1880s, U.S. BESSEMER STEEL PRODUCTION WAS IN FULL SWING (L., A PITTSBURGH MILL).

Troy, N.Y., steel mill (above), was first of 11 Bessemer plants Alexander Holley helped build in 1860s and 70s.

consulting engineer, and in this capacity, he made important technical contributions to the fast-growing industry's development.

Steel's pioneer chemist, Robert W. Hunt, wrote in 1882 that "the result of Holley's thought gave us the present accepted type of American Bessemer plant.

"He did away with the English deep pit, and raised the vessels so as to get working space under them. He substituted top-supported hydraulic cranes for the more expensive English ones, and put three ingot cranes around the pit instead of two, thereby obtaining greater area of power. He changed the location of the vessels as related to the pit and melting house. He modified the ladle crane, and worked all the cranes and vessels from a single point. He substituted cupolas for reverberatory furnaces; and last, but by no means least, he introduced the intermediate or accumulating ladle, which is placed on scales, thus ensuring econ-

omy of operation by rendering possible the weighing of each charge of melted iron before pouring into the converter.

"After building a plant, he began to meet the difficulties of details in manufacture, among the most serious of which was the short duration of the converter bottoms, and the time required to cool the whole vessel off to a point at which it was possible for workmen to enter and make new bottoms. After many experiments, the result was the Holley converter bottom, which has rendered possible, as much as any other one thing, the present immense production."

The Holley converter bottom was only one of 10 patents for improvements on the Bessemer process which Holley received.

He also made important contributions to the development of open hearth steel manufacturing, which was to overtake and pass Bessemer production in the 20th century.

And, until his death in 1882, he

wrote, lectured, and was active in the formation of technical and scientific societies.

Statistics tell the story of Holley's accomplishments: in 1867, the first year for which figures on Bessemer production are available, 3000 net tons were produced, and sold for $148.21 a ton. By 1882, production had risen to 1.7 million net tons; price per ton was down to $43.30.

A great industry had been launched by a pioneer industrial consultant who knew how to bridge the gap between the world of engineering research and the world of business.

In steel refining process invented by Sir Henry Bessemer (r.),

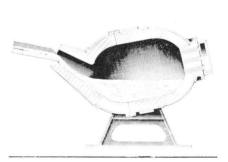

metal was poured into converter

purified by oxygen blast

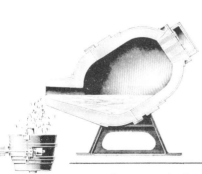

poured out ready for casting.

Harry Wright

BASEBALL'S FIRST PRO

Harry Wright and the Cincinnati Red Stockings of 1869 started baseball on the road to big time

CHANCES ARE that very few of the fans who pack the World Series ball parks in October could identify Harry Wright as the playing manager of the nation's first professional baseball team, the 1869 Cincinnati Red Stockings.

The fact is, though, that the story of baseball's development from amateur pastime to multi-million-dollar spectator sport began when the Red Stockings, under Wright's leadership, turned pro.

The pioneer of professionalism in the great American game was born in Sheffield, England, in 1835.

His father, a professional cricketer, moved the Wright family to the U.S. a few years later, and in the mid-1850s, young Harry began playing cricket for the St. George Club of Hoboken, N. J.

"Gentleman's game" for amateurs only

Unfortunately for the St. George Club, however, an amateur baseball club — the Knickerbockers — was playing in Hoboken, too. And after a summer of watching Knickerbocker games on his days off from the cricket field, Wright decided that he liked the new game better than the old one.

He began playing with the Knickerbockers in July of 1858; in his first game, he made three catches in the outfield but went 0 for 0 at the plate. (Twenty years later, he wrote to a friend, "Does not good fielding with low scores make a much more interesting game than the heavy batting and large score games?")

The game of baseball, a remote descendant of the old English game of rounders, was at least several decades old in 1858; in fact, the name "baseball" goes all the way back to 1700.

The diamond-shaped playing field was in use by the early 1800s.

Harvard men were playing baseball in the 1820s, according to Dr. Oliver Wendell Holmes, class of '29.

And the earliest known set of rules dates back to 1834.

The Knickerbockers, Harry Wright's first team, were founded in 1845 by Alexander Joy Cartwright, a pioneer baseball enthusiast who also deserves credit for elaborating and standardizing the rules.

(The legend that Civil War general Abner Doubleday "invented" baseball at Cooperstown, N. Y., in 1839 is just that. There's no evidence that he was even a fan.)

Baseball's popularity began to rise in the 1850s, and soared during the Civil War as teams were organized to entertain the troops. (On Christmas Day, 1862, two teams from the 165th New York Volunteer Infantry played a game before 40,000 soldiers—probably the best baseball crowd ever to be assembled up to that time.)

By 1865, the year in which Harry Wright moved from New Jersey to Cincinnati, the game was so popular that its very popularity was beginning to create problems for the ball clubs.

It was supposed to be a "gentleman's game," for amateurs only.

But the crowds that flocked to the ball fields were less concerned with the social status and amateur standing of the players than with seeing the home team win.

Profitable Venture

And civic pride—combined with the obvious fact that a successful ball club could be a very profitable proposition indeed—made the idea of hiring professional players an extremely tempting one to the men behind the clubs.

As early as 1860, a few top players had been paid, on the quiet, for their services to amateur teams; spectators were charged admission for the first time in Brooklyn in 1862.

Nevertheless, baseball was still officially an amateur sport when Harry Wright reached Cincinnati; and the gentleman ballplayers who dominated most of the clubs liked it that way.

Rather ironically, the ungentlemanly professional gamblers—who were moving in on the game in large numbers as its audiences grew—were also solidly anti-professional. They guessed that highly organized, money-making teams might be harder to manipulate than amateur ones with a sprinkling of surreptitiously paid pros.

But Harry Wright had his own ideas.

Since opportunities for earning a living as a baseball player were so limited, he had gone on playing professional cricket—and had worked as a jeweler — during the early 1860s. In fact, he came to Cincinnati with the idea of organizing a cricket club.

Amateurs vs. Professionals

But he soon found out that the citizens of Cincinnati shared his own preference for baseball, and in 1868, he became manager of the Red Stockings, one of the city's two ball clubs.

Four salaried players crept onto the Red Stockings' roster that season. And during the winter, Wright and his men decided that the whole pretense of amateurism had best be discarded, and that they would open the 1869 season with the best professional team they could put together.

The history-making Red Stockings (Harry Wright is shown in center, George behind him at left) posed for portrait at the end of 1869 season.

In comparison with today's major league ball clubs, the Red Stocking team that took the field in the spring of 1869 was barely a token skeleton force—it consisted of exactly nine regular players and one all-purpose substitute.

But all ten men were top-notch ball players. Wright had scoured the country to find them—only one was a native of Cincinnati.

Won 66, Lost One

And their salaries, although hardly enough to pay an instalment on a 1962 baseball star's income tax, were substantial for the 1860s. Harry Wright's 22-year-old brother, George, one of the greatest shortstops of the game's early years, drew $1400. Wright himself, as manager and center fielder, earned $1200, the pitcher $1100, the third baseman $1000, and the rest of the regulars $800 a piece, with $600 for the substitute.

With the exception of Wright himself, who was 35, the entire team was under 25.

At the start of the season, solid Cincinnati tended to look down its nose at the new professional team.

The *Cincinnati Enquirer's* coverage of its first game was hardly cordial: "The baseball season for 1869 opened yesterday . . . The playing on both sides was very poor. There was quite a large number of spectators present, but the enthusiasm of last summer was lacking."

It wasn't long, however, before Cincinnati changed its tune.

The Red Stockings were playing a brand of baseball that had never been seen before.

Of the 66 games they played that season, they won 65 and tied one.

Baseball Becomes Big Business

To rack up this almost unbelievable record, they traveled from Massachusetts to California, covering 12,000 miles by rail and boat and dazzling more than 200,000 spectators.

George Wright, the star of the team, ended the season with a batting average of .518, 339 runs scored, and 59 homers—an impressive record even in a day when hard hitting and high scoring were the rule.

The club's home run total was 169, or almost three per game.

Its proudest victory, however, was a hard-fought 4-2 win over the Mutuals of New York, who were generally considered to be by far the strongest of the amateur teams.

Horsedrawn buses carried turn-of-the-century baseball teams (above, the pennant-winning 1903 Pittsburgh Pirates) from their hotel to the ball park.

SERIES STATISTICS

COMPETITORS

Date	National	American	Attendance	Receipts
1903	Pittsburgh	Boston*	100,429	$ 55,500
1910	Chicago	Philadelphia*	124,222	173,980
1920	Brooklyn	Cleveland	178,737	564,800
1930	St. Louis	Philadelphia*	212,619	953,772
1940	Cincinnati*	Detroit	281,927	1,322,328
1950	Philadelphia	New York*	196,009	1,928,669
1960	Pittsburgh*	New York	349,813	2,230,627

* indicates winning team

Baseball first became a favorite GI sport in the Civil War (below). Union prisoners of war play while their Confederate captors look on.

Wright handled players with kid gloves

When the results of the game reached Cincinnati, the fans went wild; and when the Red Stockings came home a few weeks later, they were welcomed with brass bands and banquets.

During one of the celebrations, the team's president, Aaron Champion, declared: "Someone asked me today whom would I rather be, President Ulysses S. Grant or President Champion of the Cincinnati Baseball Club. I immediately answered that I would by far rather be president of the baseball club."

The amazing Red Stockings had brought baseball fever to a new high not only in Cincinnati, but throughout the country.

They had proved beyond any doubt that professional baseball could be big business as well as great sport.

And by the time the 1870 season rolled around, new professional teams were springing up by the dozen.

It was not until midsummer of 1870 that the Red Stockings met defeat — by an 8-7 score, at the hands of the Brooklyn Atlantics. (President Champion, who was traveling with the team, wired back to Cincinnati: "Our boys did nobly . . . though beaten, not disgraced.")

The 1870 season was the Red Stockings' last. The Cincinnati fans' enthusiasm had begun to cool, and the support for the team was falling off. So, when several Reds decided to accept spectacular offers from other cities (ball players were free agents in those days), there was nothing the Cincinnati organization could do but let the team disintegrate.

Cincinnati didn't become a baseball town again until 1876, when a new Red Stocking club joined the newly formed National League.

The forerunner of the National League, the National Association of Professional Baseball Clubs, was organized in 1871.

In that year, Harry Wright moved on to Boston, where he was to spend the next 11 seasons as playing manager. Then came two years with Providence, which was then in the National League, and 10 with Philadelphia.

Front Office Chores

No one has yet written a full scale biography of Wright, but his voluminous correspondence (couched in such elegant style as, to a fellow manager: "Allow me to congratulate you on the brilliant debut of your nine") gives a lively picture of his life as a pioneer baseball manager.

He was even busier than his modern counterparts, handling a great many chores that today would be taken care of by the front office —setting game dates, making hotel reservations, and handling team finances.

Game dates were rather casually arranged: "Your favor of the 5th received," runs a typical letter to a prospective opponent, in this case Brooklyn: "We will play your nine on the Union Grounds, Brooklyn, on the 28th, provided we receive a fair share of the gate money, say one third of the gross receipts. Would suggest that the admission fee be 50 cents. Will arrange about the umpire in N.Y."

Casual Arrangements

Once, at least, the opponents simply failed to show up for a home game at Boston: "We were very much disappointed at your not coming after agreeing to do so," Wright wrote the manager of the delinquent Hartford club, "as notices and advertisements of the game were in all the morning papers."

And occasionally a club conveniently forgot about financial arrangements, as New Bedford did in October, 1874: "I was surprised to learn from Mr. Shafer that you had refused to pay the sum of $100 when requested to do so by him at the close of our game with you on the 24th Inst. . . . I would respectfully call your attention to the fact that in one of your last letters in which terms were mentioned, you say 'of course we guarantee you

By the 1890s, baseball was well established as national pastime, and was so popular that even Victorian young ladies were tempted to play.

YOUNG LADIES' BASE BALL CLUB NO. 1.
(Copyrighted.)

...IE EARL, S. S.   EDITH MAYVES 3 B.   ALICE LEE. L. F.   ROSE MITCHELL, R. F.   ANGIE PARKER, 2 B.
MAY HOWARD, CAP AND P.   ANNIE GRANT. C. F.   KITTIE GRANT, 1 B.   NELLIE WILLIAMS, C.

$100'." (That afternoon in New Bedford must have been thoroughly disorganized—a P.S. to Wright's letter adds, "Will you please favor me with a copy of the score for my score book?")

Other letters reveal problems that would sound familiar to any present-day pilot—for instance, getting the team together for training.

Kid Gloves

"Dear Jim," Wright wrote to a Boston player in February, 1875: "Yours of the 17th duly rec'd. I am sorry that you should desire to be excused from being here on the 15th. Of course it is not of vital importance, but it would be pleasanter for us all to have every one of the players on hand on the morning of the 15th of March. It is none too soon for the boys to get together, to become acquainted, and to get in trim."

Apparently Wright liked to handle his players with kid gloves, but he did get results—four league championships during his 11 years in Boston.

There were sports writers to deal with, too: "Sir," runs a letter to the baseball editor of the *Chicago Field* written in April 1877, in answer to an inquiry about the Boston team's plans for the coming season: "I have delayed answering yours of the 15th inst. thinking I would be in a better position to do so by this time, by reason of outdoor practice. In this we have been disappointed, the weather preventing any such indulgence. Yesterday was pleasant and I had made all necessary arrangements for a good practice today on the grounds, and here it is snowing. Our list of players you well know; their positions for the season you don't, nor do I. Not until we have practiced a while ..."

Birth of World Series

When Harry Wright died in 1895, one of the best-loved men in the sporting world, baseball was just a few years from full maturity.

It had had a wild and woolly adolescence.

The 1871-76 National Association died largely because it couldn't keep its players out of bars and away from gamblers, or keep its administration honest (the owner of the New York Mutuals in the '70s was none other than Boss Tweed).

Modern Cincinnati Reds were National League champions in 1961, lost a hard-fought Series to Yankees. Above, Cincinnati first baseman Gordy Coleman slides into third base, is tagged out by Yanks' Clete Boyer.

Harry Wright, who was active in the affairs of the Association and later in those of the National League, seems to have been just about the only manager who succeeded in keeping his team on the straight and narrow path.

The National League, founded by William Hulbert of the Chicago White Sox, did a great deal to clean up the game and put it on a businesslike basis. But its first quarter century was marked by infighting, scandals, and constant conflict with would-be rival leagues: The American Association, nicknamed the "Beer and Whiskey Circuit" because, unlike the National League, it let fans buy drinks in the ball parks; the Brotherhood League, formed by players in revolt against National League club owners; and a number of others.

It was not until the turn of the century that today's American League arrived on the baseball scene to stay; the first World Series was played in 1903.

Baseball has had its full share of talented men, in front offices and league offices as well as on the diamond. But Harry Wright, an athlete who saw the business potential of the game he played, still deserves to be remembered as the father of big league ball.

Long neglected by most baseball historians, Harry Wright was finally elected to the Hall of Fame in 1953.

LET
THERE
BE
LIGHT

Edison's incandescent lamp lit up world

OF ALL THE GIANTS of late 19th century technology, Thomas Alva Edison was probably the greatest.

He was certainly the most prolific.

As every schoolchild knows, Edison invented the incandescent electric light; he also planned and put into operation the first complete electric lighting and power system.

But even before his spectacular triumph with the incandescent bulb, he had made contributions to the development of telegraphy and the telephone that established him as one of the greatest inventors of his day.

During the course of his long career, he also invented the phonograph, the motion picture camera, and the first practical electric storage battery.

Merely as a byproduct of his work on the electric light, he discovered an electrical phenomenon, the "Edison

Effect," that helped lay the foundations for 20th century electronics.

And, last but by no means least, while other 19th century inventors were tinkering in their basement or backyard workshops, Edison pioneered the development of the modern industrial research laboratory.

He was born on Feb. 11, 1847, in Milan, Ohio, the son of a lumber and feed dealer, and grew up in Port Huron, Mich.

Went to Work at 12

Until he was 12, he was educated at home by his mother, a former school teacher; then he went to work as a railroad newsboy and "candy butcher."

When he was 15, a friendly local stationmaster taught him telegraphy, and a year later, he began roaming the Middle West as a tramp telegraph operator.

In his spare time, he read all the scientific literature he could lay his hands on—as he had been doing ever since his newsboy days. And he experimented with the equipment in every Western Union office he worked in, often to his employers' dismay.

In Louisville, he recalled years later, "I went one night into the battery room to obtain some sulphuric acid. The carboy tipped over, the acid ran

out, went through the ceiling to the manager's room below, and ate up his desk and all the carpet. The next morning I was summoned before him and told that the company wanted operators, not experimenters."

By the time he was 18, he was seriously at work on his first great invention—the system of multiplex transmission that revolutionized telegraphy by making possible the sending of two or more messages along a single wire.

In 1867, he moved to Boston, then the center of electrical technology in the U.S.

At 21, "Full Time" Inventor

Just two years later, a notice appeared in a telegraphy trade journal, announcing that Thomas A. Edison, formerly a Western Union employee, would "hereafter devote his full time to bringing out his inventions."

At 21, Edison was in business as a freelance inventor.

His first patent was granted for a notably unsuccessful invention—electromagnetic "vote recorder" to speed the taking of roll call votes in Congress and the state legislatures. Each legislator would merely push a button on his desk to record his "aye" or "nay."

64

Edison was sure that the phonograph—
—his favorite invention—would
be used primarily for business dictation,
not for entertainment. By the
early 1900s, he knew he was wrong.

EDISON PUT RESEARCH
ON BIG BUSINESS BASIS

Not surprisingly, he was told in no uncertain terms—first by the Massachusetts legislature and then by Congress—that automated voting was the last thing any politician wanted; it would eliminate too many opportunities for speech-making.

Edison had his first stroke of luck in the middle of 1869, when he moved from Boston to New York and met Franklin Pope, an electrical engineer who worked for Gold Indicator, a wire service that supplied gold and stock quotations to half Wall St.

Coffee and Dumplings

Edison's funds had run out, and he was subsisting on a steady diet of coffee and apple dumplings; Pope was letting him sleep on a cot in the Gold Indicator Co. battery room.

Then, one day while Pope was showing him the mechanisms of the indicator, the whole transmitting apparatus came to a halt.

So did business in the Wall St. firms that were serviced by Gold Indicator; a few hours' delay in repairing the breakdown would have created enough ill will to send the company's customers running to a rival wire service.

Edison, who was working on a stock ticker of his own, quickly spotted the trouble and made the repair.

The next day, he was retained by Gold Indicator to work on improving the machine, and he was never out of work again.

$40,000 Fee

Over the next year, he patented his own stock ticker and took out seven other patents, covering a series of minor improvements in telegraphy, that earned him a $40,000 fee from his old employer, Western Union.

In 1871, he opened a small factory in Newark, N. J., and began turning out stock tickers and other electrical equipment for Western Union.

Over the next three years, while running his business and patenting scores of minor inventions, he returned to concentrated work on his multiplex telegraph.

66

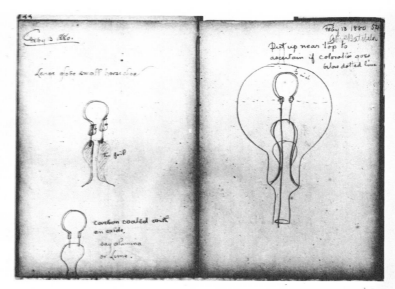

Edison's laboratory notebook for February, 1880, records his discovery of the "Edison Effect," related to the generation and movement of free electrons in space, vital to the development of modern electronics.

In 1874, the "quadruplex," which could send four messages on one wire (two in each direction) at a rate of 142 telegrams an hour, was finally perfected, and Edison's reputation as a major inventor was made.

Patent War

The quadruplex also triggered the first of many "patent wars" over Edison inventions—between Western Union, which had contracted for the system and then delayed in paying for it, and Jay Gould's Atlantic & Pacific Telegraph Co., which had taken the young inventor off the financial hook.

Shortly after the quadruplex was completed, Edison moved to Menlo Park, N. J.

The laboratory he built there was the first of its kind—virtually a pilot plant for the great industrial research laboratories of the 20th century.

Industrial R & D

It was an "invention factory," magnificiently equipped, staffed by the most talented mechanics and technicians from the Newark factory and also by several university-trained scientists—a radical departure in a day when practical technology and "pure" science were considered to be light years apart.

The first major invention to come out of Menlo Park was the carbon

telephone transmitter, patented in 1878.

Alexander Graham Bell had patented his telephone three years earlier but its transmitter was so weak that its users had to shout over the wire.

It was the combination of Bell's receiver and Edison's transmitter that made the telephone a success.

While he was working on the telephone, Edison noticed that the diaphragm of the receiver vibrated when the instrument was in use—and decided that these vibrations could be used to reproduce the human voice.

Edison regarded the research scientists on the staff of his Menlo Park, N. J., laboratory (below) with a

"Just tried experiment with a diaphragm having an embossing point and held against paraffin paper moving rapidly," he wrote in his laboratory notebook in July, 1877. "The speaking vibrations are indented nicely."

Four months later, the first phonograph played "Mary had a little lamb" to an astonished employee group. Early in 1878, it was patented.

The 1877 phonograph was extremely crude, however, and, although Edison always declared it was his favorite invention, he did not find time to perfect it until 1888.

The electric light came first.

Tired inventor posed with his improved phonograph in June, 1888, after 72 straight hours of work.

mixture of respect and friendly contempt. Edison said, "I can hire mathematicians, but they can't hire me."

Scientists had been learning how to turn electric power into light all through the 19th century.

In 1878, a few arc lights were already in use, but they were too large and glaring, and consumed too much current, for general use.

Half a dozen well-known inventors were already trying to develop a smaller light, and find a means of subdividing the current in an electric circuit so that a number of lights could be powered and turned on and off individually.

Enters Light Race

Edison entered the race in the fall of 1878, backed by a group of financiers headed by J. P. Morgan.

He announced to the press that he would have his light ready within six weeks—an estimate that was far too optimistic.

As he said in 1905, the electric light "caused me the greatest amount of study and required the most elaborate experiments" of any of his inventions. He was not ready to take it to the patent office until November, 1879.

The principle he worked on was that of the incandescent bulb, which earlier inventors had tried unsuccessfully to develop: a slender rod in a vacuum or near vacuum of glass, heated to incandescence by electric current and kept from burning out or melting by the absence of oxygen.

"Just consider this," he wrote while the work was in progress. "We have an almost infinitesimal filament heated to a degree which it is difficult to comprehend, and it is in a vacuum under conditions of which we are wholly ignorant. You cannot use your eyes to help you, and really know nothing of what is going on inside that tiny bulb."

Over the months, Edison made it his business to find out what was going on. He devoured all the available literature on high vacuums, an area in which research had only recently begun.

The bulb he finally produced was a vacuum of one-millionth part of an atmosphere, by far the highest ever produced in the U.S.

He tested hundreds of materials to find the right filament for the light, finally settling on a carbonized cellulose fiber.

On Oct. 20th, 1878, a lamp was turned on in the Menlo Park laboratory that burned for 13½ hours, according to laboratory records, 40 hours, according to tradition.

It would take only minor improvements, Edison knew, to make lights that would burn for hundreds of hours.

At 31, he had reached the pinnacle of his career.

During the year he spent on the light, he had also been studying the already successful gas distribution industry, and planning an electricity distribution system that, he believed, would put the gas companies out of business.

And he spent most of the next 10 years out of the laboratory, trying to put the system into operation.

His success was only moderate—partly because of financial conservatism of his backers, partly because of his own failing as a big businessman, and partly because he failed, astonishingly, to recognize the superiority of alternating current over direct current for large power installations. (The champion of A-C was George Westinghouse.)

By 1892, the Morgan group had formed the General Electric Co. (to engage in both power distribution and electrical manufacturing) and frozen Edison out of its active management.

After a brief and unsuccessful fling at mining, he returned to the laboratory.

He had patented his first motion picture camera in 1891, and its development occupied him during most of the decade.

In 1904 came his last major contribution to modern technology, the dry storage battery.

Although he had retired from the power industry, his days in the business world were by no means over. By the 1920s, his various manufacturing enterprises, combined into a single corporation as Thomas A. Edison, Inc., were grossing over $20 million a year.

Edison died in 1931, one of the most honored men of his generation.

The value of his gifts to the 20th century can hardly be calculated—even in billions of dollars or trillions of kilowatt hours.

FRANCIS WAYLAND AYER

JAMES WALTER THOMPSON

ARCHITECTS OF "MAD AVE"

The need to create mass demand for mass-produced goods
launched the multi-billion-dollar advertising industry

I N 1869, a 21-year-old Philadelphia schoolteacher decided to embark on a business career. He chose the infant and then not-too-respectable field of advertising and named the company in honor of his father — N. W. Ayer & Son.

Nine years later a 30-year-old bookkeeper and general factotum in a one-man advertising agency succeeded in buying out his boss before the firm went bankrupt. He named his company after himself — The J. Walter Thompson Company.

Francis Wayland Ayer developed his concept of service. He declared his loyalty to the advertiser rather than to the publisher and regarded his customers as clients. He was the first to start copy and plans departments, and he initiated market and product studies.

J. Walter Thompson pioneered magazine advertising. Recognizing the growing influence of household magazines, he became the first agent to sell advertising for a list of periodicals.

Between them they built the prototype of today's super-agency with emphasis on service, annual billings in the hundreds of millions of dollars, and diversification into such areas as product testing, psyche probing, television production and public relations.

Nearly a century later both companies still rank among the nation's top ten advertising agencies, with Thompson only now challenged by Interpublic for the distinction of being the largest agency.

Since the Civil War, U.S. advertising volume has multiplied 240 times, while Gross National Product has grown 85 times. Billings have mushroomed from $50,000 in 1865 to a recent $12.5 billion. $20 billion is forecast for 1970.

The industry's greatest periods of growth came after the Civil War when patent medicines flourished and advertising standards were notoriously low; in the 1920's when a new era of expansion helped agencies develop into big business; and after World War II when television and the marketing of hundreds of new products sent advertising volume to unprecedented highs.

Advertising is as old as history itself. In 3000 B.C., Babylonian bricks carried inscriptions which are thought to be the first advertisements. The British Museum displays a primitive want ad, written on papyrus, offering a reward for the return of a runaway slave to his Egyptian master.

68

Political ads, which go right to the point, have been uncovered on the walls of Pompeii:

"Make Publius Furius your Aedile, I beg of you. He's a good man.

"The sneak thieves request the election of Vatia as Aedile."

As late as the 17th Century, public criers and picture signboards identified tradesmen and told where goods and services were on sale. Such devices were the only practical method when most people could not read.

The turning point came with the widespread development of printing and the subsequent spread of literacy.

Printed handbills appeared first, followed by weekly newspapers. Ads, however, still were little more than announcements. The persuasive message, characteristic of 20th century advertising, was missing.

Modern advertising—and the advent of the advertising agency — is a product of the Industrial Revolution. Manufacturers suddenly were faced with the necessity of creating mass demand for mass-produced goods.

Until the 19th Century there were no advertising agents in either Europe or the U.S. A company wishing to advertise dealt directly with the newspaper. But by the early 1800's business had become so complex that a middleman was needed to purchase and sell space, relieving both the advertiser and publisher of this function.

Thus the cornerstone of Madison Avenue was laid.

The honor of being the first U.S. advertising agent usually falls upon Volney B. Palmer of Philadelphia. He started in 1841, dubbing himself "Agent for Country Newspapers."

Previously Palmer had been soliciting ads for his father's newspaper, the Mount Holly (N.J.) Mirror, and later for the Miner's Journal of Pottsville, Pa.

Palmer is said to have been pompous and irritable. His stout figure and florid face became a familiar sight to Philadelphia merchants and publishers. And his customary outfit — blue coat with brass buttons, gold spectacles, gold-headed walking cane, and a large bandanna handkerchief — usually were good for a few guffaws.

Palmer also conducted a real estate, firewood and coal business. He referred to himself as a "newspaper agent," and made it clear he was acting on behalf of the papers. He solicited ads, forwarded copy to the papers and collected payments. For his services he deducted 25% of the money paid by the advertiser.

(N. W. Ayer acquired what was left of the assets of Palmer's company in 1877.)

The second known agent was John L. Hooper, a solicitor for Horace Greeley's New York Tribune, who set out on his own in 1842. Hooper carried his office in his hat and won a reputation for honesty because he always paid the newspapers himself and collected from the advertisers later.

He eventually went into the lead pipe business, selling the remnants of his agency to George P. Rowell, the man who founded Printer's Ink and ushered in a new era in the slowly-evolving agency business.

This debonair Bostonian left his job on the Boston Post and became an agent in 1865. Rowell found advertising wallowing in a state of supreme confusion. Newspaper circulations were not verifiable. Advertising rates went as high as the traffic would bear and rate cards bore little resemblance to the actual price of space. Commissions ranged from zero from the metropolitan papers to 75% from a struggling country weekly.

Rowell first drew up a list of 100 newspapers and attached realistic circulation estimates. He assured advertisers their money would be well spent if they used his exclusive list. He offered "One inch of space a month in one hundred papers for one hundred dollars."

He then became a space wholesaler. He contracted to buy newspaper space in bulk and, in turn, retailed slices to advertisers. The practice soon spread.

When Rowell was asked in 1866 whom he represented, he replied, "Myself."

All agencies of that period were trying to serve two masters. They offered advice to both publisher and advertiser. It soon became evident they could not satisfy both.

Francis Ayer provided the solution. He adopted the principle that the agency should work for the advertiser, thereby setting a pattern for the industry's future. He also did much to improve the character and reputation of advertising.

Francis Wayland and his father Nathan Wheeler Ayer were New Englanders. The elder Ayer taught school in Massachusetts and finally settled in Philadelphia. At the age of 14, Francis followed in his father's footsteps, accepting a teaching position because the Civil War had taken most adult instructors to the front.

In his early years he developed two dominant characteristics: a deeply religious outlook, inherited from his soberly Puritan parents, and a serious view of life, largely because his father was not a financial success and the family lived sparsely.

Ayer made up his mind to make money as a businessman and, in 1868, took a job soliciting ads for a weekly religious paper, the National Baptist. Within a year the thrifty Yankee had saved $250 and gone into business for himself.

Although he named the company for his father (out of respect as well as a fear that his own youth might be held against him), the senior Ayer had no significant role in the company's history and he died a short time later.

For his first six years Ayer operated in the manner of all agencies at that time—as agent to publishers. Despite the fact that sharp practices of some agencies had given the field a bad name, Ayer appears to have given little thought to the situation.

But in 1875 he was offered a job in another field by a friend who declared he had no respect for the ad business.

"What is an advertising agent?" the friend demanded. "Nothing but a drummer and he never will be anything else."

The thought that his business was not respectable in the eyes of others came as an unpleasant shock to the high-principled Ayer.

"That was really for me the beginning of my business," recalled Ayer. He vowed, "I will not be an order taker any longer. I will mean something to somebody . . . and I will have clients."

Out of his chagrin came the decision to break with current practice and represent the advertiser.

He drew up an "Open Contract," in which he agreed to buy space to the best of his bargaining ability and to give the advertiser the low-

By the turn of the century
sophisticated slogans and emotional appeals
were tools of the trade

est possible rate. He would bill the client at this net rate, plus a fixed percentage for his services.

The first client to go along with Ayer's new plan was a firm of Pennsylvania rose growers. They agreed to a commission of 12½%.

This intimate relationship with the advertiser opened new directions for agency development. Buying space at the lowest cost for an advertiser meant buying wisely. This led to consideration of the client's product, his potential market, and the best means of reaching the people who might buy it.

In 1879, Ayer made the first market survey for a threshing machine manufacturer and this aspect of the business grew into the first plans department.

Ayer also was the first agency to establish a department to prepare copy for its customers. The earliest agents wrote no copy unless absolutely necessary. If an advertiser couldn't turn out his own purple prose, he had to hire a free lance "ad smith."

In many cases these were journalists or literary men who needed extra cash. One of the most influential was John Powers. He had a clean, lucid style but a fanatic passion for truth which often frightened his employers.

For the John Wanamaker department store he wrote, "We have a lot of rotten raincoats that we want to get rid of."

Powers developed the concept of "reason-why" copy, showing why it was in a reader's interest to buy the product. This idea dominated copywriting for several decades until advertising discovered the powers of hope and fear.

Many famous names studded Ayer's list of early clients: Montgomery Ward, John Wanamaker, Singer Sewing Machine, Pond's Cream in addition to many educational and religious groups.

But the backbone of his business — and the entire ad industry — was patent medicine. The tonics, laxatives and cancer cures of the late 1800's were as important as automo-

bile accounts are today, and as socially acceptable.

Agencies did not believe it was their business to check into the accuracy of claims to cure almost every human ailment.

Some of Ayer's nostrum clients were Kennedy's Ivory Tooth Cement which made "Everyone his own dentist," and the Pino-Palmine Mattress, "the very aroma of which medicates and tones the Florida air."

As competition increased so did flagrant claims to cure stuttering, worms, gout, and cholera, as well as restoratives for lost manhood and pills for venereal disease. Some cure-happy writers invented their own diseases: Sparks Before the Eyes, Dragging Sensation in the Groin, and Creeping Numbness.

A helpless medical profession was unable to keep the patent medicine boom under control. One reason: most contained enough alcohol or cocaine to induce a sense of well-being in the patient.

Francis Ayer dropped one of his most lucrative accounts, Dr. William's Pink Pills for Pale People, and refused to accept patent medicine ads.

"It reached the point where it became necessary to make or fake miracles," he said.

In 1906 passage of the first Pure Food and Drug Act acted as an effective brake.

In the 1880's the rise of such consumer magazines as Curtis' *Ladies Home Journal* sparked new growth in the advertising business. James Walter Thompson was the first to build an agency on magazines.

It was an uphill struggle against doubts of both advertisers and publishers. The great showman P. T. Barnum had aroused many merchants to the possibilities of publicity by his own successfully-advertised ventures. His advice: "Advertise or the chances are the sheriff will do it for you."

Still it was common to see commercial establishments sporting signs which stated: "No beggars, peddlers and advertising solicitors."

On the other hand, most magazine publishers of that period looked on advertising as a last resort when bankruptcy threatened. Some actively discouraged advertising. Others tolerated it but segregated ads in a special section so they would not deface editorial pages or distract readers. They were particularly testy about revealing circulation figures.

Thompson horrified the editors of *Harper's* by suggesting the back cover be used for an ad. He was told that would be an insult to the literary quality of their magazine. He finally convinced *Harper's* that from an economical standpoint it might be highly profitable. Back-cover ads date from his efforts.

He had difficulties with another high-tone periodical by supplying too much advertising in one month. The publishers complained because they had to print extra pages to fit in all the ads.

Thompson was born in Pittsfield, Mass. and grew up in Ohio. A poor youth, he secured a position in 1868 as bookkeeper and clerk to William J. Carlton, an advertising agent. Carlton was more interested in books than advertising and spent most of his time tracking down obscure old volumes.

Thompson is said to have been earnest, persistant, and a good salesman.

But George Rowell in his autobiography ruefully recalled his first impression of the young Thompson: "I had once an opportunity to engage this same clerk, Thompson, to work for me but, after a talk with him, concluded he would be too easily discouraged for an advertising man."

There is no question that Thompson was thrifty. Out of his $15 a week salary he managed to save enough to buy out Carlton before the agency went broke. Carlton became a bookseller and Thompson quickly changed the name of the agency, which was just about all he got for his money, to his own.

For many years Thompson had a near-monopoly on magazine advertising. As exclusive representative for over 100 magazines, he contracted for all the space in a publication and acted as wholesaler for both the advertiser and other agents.

On the letterhead of his stationary, he printed a list of 30 periodicals. Intense rivalry developed to be among "The Thirty." To be dropped from the list meant loss of prestige.

Thompson, like Ayer, was among the first agents to advise advertisers. For example, it was due to his ad campaigns that the Mennen Company successfully switched to cans for their talcum powder. The prod- uct had always been sold in cloth bags and consumers were reluctant to change.

By the turn of the century J. Walter Thompson was among the top three agencies in the U.S. and the only agency with a branch overseas.

In 1916, Thompson sold his com- pany to Stanley Resor, then head of his Cincinnati office. The be- whiskered Thompson, 69, bowed out with relief and confided to friends that the great days of advertising were over. His billings were $3 mil- lion and he felt an agency couldn't go much further. He died in 1928.

The last three decades of the 19th century saw advertising develop in- to a craft. Ads changed from prosaic announcements into sophisticated slogans, trademarks and emotional appeals. It soon became evident that a memorable slogan could catapult a company into a fortune.

An early notable example was a small Cincinnati soap company, Procter & Gamble. In 1874, it acci- dentally made a batch of soap which came out white (because it lacked expensive olive oil) and floated (because a workman went out to lunch without turning off the beat- ing machine.)

A lab report indicated the soap was 99 and 44/100ths per cent pure, although pure what was never speci- fied. The name Ivory came to Mr. Harley Procter in church one Sun- day morning during the reading of the Forty-fifth Psalm. These two elements, plus the soap's ability to float, created a lasting name and slogan.

N. W. Ayer & Son was adept at slogans which have stood the test of time. In 1898, a partner in the Ayer Co. came up with a pun for the National Biscuit Company: "Do you know Uneeda Biscuit?" At first Uneeda was ridiculed as an absurd name for a cracker. Heavy sales stopped the derision although today few recognize the pun involved.

A young executive in the Thomp- son Co. provided an enduring trade- mark for the Prudential Insurance Co. While riding a commuting train across the New Jersey meadows he passed a gigantic rock formation known as Snake Rock. It suggested a more impressive rock, Gibraltar, for his client who wanted a symbol of lasting strength.

Other slogans from the same era have persisted: "When it rains, it pours" (Morton Salt); "Milk from contented cows" (Carnation); and "That schoolgirl complexion" (Palm- olive).

Francis Ayer and J. Walter Thompson appear sober and con- servative from today's vantage point, but the revolution they started is still going strong.

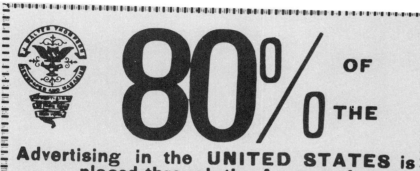

Thompson, representing over 100 publications, ran advertising monopoly.

SOAP'S
FIRST
BIG SPLASH

HARLEY T. PROCTER

When Harley Procter in 1878, used direct-to-consumer, large-scale advertising and merchandising to launch Ivory soap, he charted a new course for the entire soap industry. Today the combined advertising expenditures of the three leading soap firms have passed a new high of over $300 million

IN 1878 a far sighted young salesman took a bar of white soap and floated it across the nation.

In lifting his soap from the anonymity of the grocer's barrel and splashing it in front of the public, Harley Procter laid the groundwork for most of the direct-consumer advertising, merchandising and marketing techniques in use today.

Eighty-one years ago Procter and Gamble, a sound, ultra-conservative Cincinnati firm dealing in candles, lard and soap, brought out a new, hard, white soap that had all the qualities of the expensive castiles—it just needed to be put on the market.

And Harley Procter, a salesman for

the family business, had been waiting for this opportunity. He took over. First, he decided, the new product needed identity. Possibilities of "The White Soap," as it was called, had Harley's imagination working overtime. He actually christened Ivory in church while reading psalm 45:8— "All thy garments smell of myrrh, and aloes, and cassia, out of the *ivory* palaces. . . ."

Then, for added distinction, he designed (and patented) Ivory into a laundry size bar, notched in the middle for easy division into two toilet-sized cakes. A black and white checkered wrapper put finishing touches on the new-born Ivory's personality.

Now Harley wanted to advertise his soap and make it nationally known. Here his progressive ideas ran smack into the rock-bound conservatism of the firm, whose partners were so cautious they had each agreed not to draw more than $5000 a year out of the business. (Even Harley's use of the telegraph was considered extravagant.) To the partners, who had been accustomed to spending $3000-$4000 a year on business card advertising, Harley's request for a budget to cover full page magazine ads seemed outrageous.

Until then only a few patent medicines were national advertisers—primarily in religious weeklies and almanacs. Other magazines were only just beginning to accept ads. But Harley, looking into the future, insisted that the only way to reach consumer masses was through continuous periodical advertising. He kept up the fight. In 1882 the first Ivory ads appeared on the back page of *Harper's*, *The Century* and *The Ladies' Home Journal*. Even after that, rumor has it, he sometimes had to sign contracts without consulting the partners, borrowing the money from friends.

Advertising agencies at that time were essentially space brokers—clients had to write their own copy. Harley sent Ivory samples to chemistry professors at Yale, Michigan and Princeton for analysis. From their reports he worked out the now-familiar 99-44/100% pure (admission of even fractional impurity demonstrated his keen sense of human relations). His later use of the chemists' testimony on Ivory's purity is one of the earliest examples of endorsement advertising.

With purity established as a talking point, Harley went on to play up diversity—here was a soap safe enough for both laundry and personal use. Association with infants would dramatize its purity—thus the Ivory baby was born.

"It Floats"—Ivory's second classic slogan—was, like the quality of buoyancy itself, the result of an accident. A batch of Ivory was left unattended in the stirring vat while a negligent workman took an extra long lunch hour. It was shipped out anyway, and a delighted customer, to the surprise of the firm, ordered more of that "floating soap." The accident was reconstructed and the formula modified until "floating soap" was produced every time.

Harley, dissatisfied with the crude efforts of the commercial "artists" of the time, made another radical innovation by commissioning some of the leading magazine artists to illustrate his ads.

The tone of all the ads—whether an elephant that wanted to be white, a grinning cat floating on a cake of Ivory, or a young lady at a bubble blowing party—was always affectionate and humorous. Harley's aim was to create a warm bond between Ivory and its newly-created public.

FIRST INDUSTRIAL BILLBOARD showed factory workers washing up with Ivory soap. Harley used photographer's artists as models and superimposed print on painted background depicting foundry. Composite picture was then blown up to poster size.

SALES AND PROFITS OF LEADING SOAP MANUFACTURERS
(in $ millions)

COMPANY	1960		1950		1940		1930	
	Sales	Profits	Sales	Profits	Sales	Profits	Sales	Profits
Procter & Gamble	1441.5	98.1	632.9	61.1	205.0	28.6	192.4	25.0
Colgate Palmolive	576.3	21.2	312.0	21.0	96.1	4.2	98.6	8.6
Lever	388.6	11.4	n.a.	n.a.	n.a.	n.a.	n.a.	n.a.

EARLY IVORY SAMPLING CREW manned wagon bearing Ivory slogan. Lenox, P&G's brown soap, which made the firm strong in the laundry field, was, unlike Ivory, promoted through dealers with coupons, free merchandise, store streamers, etc.

However, P&G was not in business just for laughs. At one point the illustration was omitted and in its place was a pointed request—if the reader had been enjoying the series would he please "reciprocate" by buying a cake of Ivory .

Harley's energies extended beyond advertising. An incessant traveller—he kept galoshes and umbrellas on every Cincinnati sleeper on the Chicago run—he set up P&G's first national sales organization, consisting of three men.

While covering his own Western territory—mostly mining camps—he inadvertently became the firm's first market researcher. He could see that electric lights would soon snuff out candle sales. By convincing the partners to switch production emphasis to soap—originally only one-fourth of P&G's volume—he probably saved the firm from extinction.

Harley swept P&G into the big time in little more than 20 years, but then, largely because of differences with his older brother William, who had succeeded to the presidency on their father's death, withdrew almost completely from the company picture. (William was so conservative that, in later life, he refused to venture into the new-fangled automobile.)

William was particularly infuriated by Harley's announced intention to retire at 45 to "enjoy life," and when the company was incorporated in 1890, Harley, then 43, received only the title of second vice president.

Several years later, although in virtual retirement, Harley went abroad to buy Ivory's English trademark from a nimble preemptor. When, upon his return, he was criticized for

HARLEY OFFERED YOUNGSTERS free coloring books for 15 Ivory wrappers, then ran ad *(below l.)* showing eager children begging from door to door for them. The premium offer for 12 wrappers was an Ivory watch charm. Introductory ad *(below r.)*, inserted in a grocery trade paper in 1879, marked Harley's first effort to gain national distribution for Ivory.

The Children's Latest Craze.

BOY: "Please give me your Ivory Soap wrappers, I want to get fifteen to send to Procter & Gamble in Cincinnati, so they will send me one of their drawing books and a pad."

LADY: "I'm sorry I can not give you any, for my children are collecting them also for the same purpose."

A WORD OF WARNING.

There are many white soaps, each represented to be "just as good as the 'Ivory';" they ARE NOT, but like all counterfeits, lack the peculiar and remarkable qualities of the genuine. Ask for "Ivory" Soap and insist upon getting it.

Copyright, 1886, by Procter & Gamble.

THE "IVORY" is a Laundry Soap, with all the fine qualities of a choice Toilet Soap, and is 99 44-100 per cent. pure.

Ladies will find this Soap especially adapted for washing laces, infants' clothing, silk hose, cleaning gloves and all articles of fine texture and delicate color, and for the varied uses about the house that daily arise, requiring the use of soap that is above the ordinary in quality.

For the Bath, Toilet, or Nursery it is preferred to most of the Soaps sold for toilet use, being purer and much more pleasant and effective and possessing all the desirable properties of the finest unadultered White Castile Soap. The Ivory Soap will "float."

The cakes are so shaped that they may be used entire for general purposes or divided with a stout thread (as illustrated) into two perfectly formed cakes, of convenient size for toilet use.

The price, compared to the quality and the size of the cakes, makes it the cheapest Soap for everybody for every want. TRY IT.

SOLD EVERYWHERE.

having muffed what he considered to have been an eminently successful job, he resigned altogether.

Harley put as much imagination into "enjoying life" as he had put into his work. He sampled the continent with an apartment in Paris, a town house in London and four months in Egypt. Along the way he acquired a stable of horses and an estate in Massachusetts. He died in 1907 at the age of 73.

Harley Procter laid the cornerstone of P&G's present prosperity — 1960 sales reached an all time high of $1 44 billion. Traces of his influence can be found today in the firm's $125 million advertising budget—the second in the nation.

Harley's once revolutionary theories of advertising and merchandising *directly* to the consumer, instead of to the middleman or dealer, has been nowhere more faithfully followed than, appropriately enough, in the soap industry itself. Following fast on P&G's heels on the list of the ten top advertisers, Lever Brothers ranks fourth and Colgate-Palmolive sixth.

Although even Harley probably did not foresee the advent of radio and TV, he, nevertheless, is the grandfather of both radio's soap opera and the television spectacular.

BATHING BEAUTIES shampooing in the lake were grateful that Ivory floated in this 1909 ad. Other ads pointed out that Ivory's buoyance was helpful for careless servants, who left ordinary cakes at bottom of dish pan, and for workers, fishing for soap in factory wash sinks.

"USE IVORY SOAP—IT FLOATS!"

"One morning, last summer, at a Michigan resort, a party of girls went down to the lake in their bathing suits for the purpose of washing their hair. Each carried the necessary articles, including a cake of soap. One had a cake of _____'s soap; another, a cake of _____ soap. Several other varieties were represented.

The place selected was near the pier, and the implements for washing the hair were placed in the interstices of the logs supporting the pier. During the process of washing, the _____'s soap girl lost her soap and in the effort to recover it, the _____ soap girl lost her's, too. The girl with the Ivory Soap thereupon threw it far out into the lake, swam after it and, holding it aloft, cried: '*Use Ivory Soap—it floats!*'

In the end, all three girls used Ivory Soap—they had to!"

— [Extract from a Letter.]

Again we ask: Even if Ivory Soap were no better than other soaps, does not the fact that *it floats* make it better?

AFTER RETIRING, HARLEY, SHOWN (BELOW) IN COACH-AND-FOUR IN ENGLAND, ENJOYED LIFE BY COMBINING LOVE FOR HORSES, TRAVEL

John Dryden (at desk) launched Prudential Insurance from unpretentious basement office in 1874.

INSURANCE FOR EVERYBODY

John F. Dryden tapped the mass market for life insurance with low-cost, pay-by-the-week "industrial" policies

BEFORE THE 1870s, life insurance was a luxury item.

It was John F. Dryden, co-founder of the Prudential Insurance Co. of America, who broadened the base of the life insurance industry in 1874 by making small "industrial" policies available to factory workers for only pennies a week.

Today, life insurance is part of the financial planning of seven out of every 10 American adults, including two thirds of those with family incomes between $3000 and $5000 a year and half of those whose family incomes are under $3000.

(Some 78% of all U.S. families now own insurance, compared to 74% who own automobiles, 60% homes (non-farm families), 38% liquid assets of savings bonds, savings and other bank accounts, etc., and 14% corporate stocks).

These 132 million Americans were buying nearly $78 billion of new insurance by 1960, to bring total policies to almost $685 billion, and collected $8 billion in benefits.

As for John F. Dryden's Prudential Co., it is one of the giants of the industry, second only to Metropolitan Life in size. (It has 36 million policy holders with $90.4 billion worth of life insurance in force, and it is paying $1.7 billion, including $509 million in dividends, to policyholders and beneficiaries).

The story of insurance goes back almost to the dawn of civilization. The early maritime peoples of the Mediterranean had primitive forms of marine and other property insurance. The military and religious fraternal organizations of classical Rome paid death benefits to their members, and so did the guilds of medieval Europe and cooperatives in 16th century England.

76

The development of true life insurance began in the 17th century, when the foundations of actuarial science were laid by mathematicians. (It was Dr. Edmund Halley, discoverer of the comet that bears his name, who constructed the first scientific mortality table.)

From the late 17th century on, the life insurance business grew rapidly in England and more slowly on the European continent. (For a time, British gamblers considered it a sporting wager to take out a policy on the life of anyone from the King on down. Parliament stopped this practice in 1744 with the Gambling Act, which prohibited buying life insurance except where "the person insuring shall have an interest in the life or death of the person insured.")

Churchmen pioneered

The first American life insurance company was established in 1759 by the Presbyterian Synods of New York and Philadelphia. Its sonorous title was "Corporation for the Relief of Poor and Distressed Presbyterian Ministers and for the Poor and Distressed Widows and Orphans of Presbyterian Ministers," later shortened by just "Presbyterian Ministers' Fund."

The Episcopalians followed suit with a non-profit insurance company of their own in 1769. But after that, the business grew only slowly until the mid-19th century.

Twenty-four marine and property insurance companies were chartered in the 1790s, but only one of them, the Insurance Co. of North America, appears to have sold any life insurance. This kind of protection was little needed in a predominantly rural society where the sons of the family simply took over the farm when the breadwinner died.

The first profit-making life insurance company, the Pennsylvania Co. for Insurance on Lives and Granting Annuities, appeared in 1809.

A number of others followed, but they were all low-pressure concerns that did little advertising, hired few, if any, agents, and were content with a small volume of business.

These early 19th century insurance firms were ordinary stock companies, owned and controlled by their stockholders like any other corporation, although a few of them did pay special dividends to policyholders who did not own stock.

The first mutual companies, owned and controlled by policyholders who automatically earn dividends from their "participating" policies, appeared in 1843.

And for the next 25 years, the industry enjoyed rapid growth. By the end of the 1860s, $2 billion worth of life insurance was in force in the U.S., and the agency system was well established.

However, only the well-to-do could afford the high annual premiums of ordinary life insurance.

The factory workers whose numbers swelled as the Industrial Revolution gained momentum had virtually no way to protect their families.

All that was available to them were the death benefits provided for members by some lodges and fraternal organizations and the embryonic labor unions; and the "assessment insurance" offered by businesses known, as the 16th century English cooperatives had been, as "Friendly Societies."

A Friendly Society simply assessed its members for small fixed sums, either at regular intervals or only when somebody died, for a fund from which to pay benefits to deceased members' families.

At worst, the Friendly Societies were completely fraudulent; at best, they were inefficient and liable to collapse under the weight of claims, since they ignored actuarial tables and accumulated no substantial cash reserves.

The upshot of all this was, of course, that the families that needed life insurance most—accumulating a personal nest egg of any size on a 19th century factory worker's wage was very difficult indeed—were least likely to have any.

A huge mass market for life insurance was ready and waiting to be

In 1892, the flourishing Prudential Co. moved to new building, a turreted, gray stone structure inspired by French chateau.

Established insurance firms weren't interested in idea of pennies-a-week industrial policies

tapped when John F. Dryden went into the insurance business shortly after the Civil War.

Dryden understood this mass market for the very good reason that he came from a factory family.

He was born in 1839, the son of a mechanic who, after a brief fling at farming in Maine, returned to work in the mills of Worcester. Mass., and settled his family there.

John Dryden, Sr., died when young John was 10. He had been a skilled worker, undoubtedly earning good wages for the 1830s, and he left his family better off than most.

They owned their own home, and Mrs. Dryden took in roomers to help make ends meet. Nevertheless, young John Dryden's adolescence was hard. He worked as a bakery delivery boy in the early mornings and as a machinist's apprentice after school, putting a strain on his health from which he never entirely recovered.

After graduating from high school, he worked in a machine shop for several years. By 1861, he had saved enough to go on to Yale – a very unusual accomplishment for a 19th century workingman's son.

He spent four years in New Haven, married his landlady's daughter, and was prevented from earning a degree only by a complete physical breakdown his senior year.

He and his young wife moved to Ohio, where his married sister had settled – and where the climate was proverbially heathful. And it was there that his insurance career began.

Dryden had become interested in the insurance business—and particularly in the idea of low-cost policies for workingmen – while he was still in college. He had studied the growth of the Prudential Assurance Co. of London, which had been selling industrial insurance in England since 1854, and he was positive that the same type of business could succeed in the U.S.

To all the established U.S. insurance companies, however—including Dryden's first employer, Aetna Life Insurance Co. – the thought of selling small policies to factory workers for a few cents a week, collected weekly by agents from the policyholders' homes seemed completely unsound.

Dryden spent his first two years

in the business selling ordinary insurance for Aetna.

His Columbus, Ohio, agency failed, and in 1866 he brought his family back East (Forrest Dryden, a future president of Prudential, had been born at the end of 1864) and settled in Brooklyn, where he began selling insurance again.

The late 1860s were a boom time for the insurance business, but even so, it was not until the end of the decade that Dryden was able to interest anyone in expanding into the untried field of industrial insurance.

Then, when he did find a partner – a wealthy insurance man named H. H. Goodman – New York State refused to grant his projected industrial insurance company a charter, and the partnership collapsed.

So in 1873, Dryden moved on to Newark, N.J., and rented desk space in the office of a real estate man named Allen Bassett.

Family protection

In the meantime, the worst economic depression of the century had struck the nation. Insurance companies, like business of all kinds, were folding by the dozen, and conditions for launching a radically new venture could hardly have been less favorable.

On the other hand, however, the Panic of 1873 underscored the desperate need of industrial workers for some kind of family protection. With thousands thrown out of work, there

Prudential offered good jobs to "typewriter girls" of 1900; today, company has 55,000 employees

The Prudential Girl 1904

THE PRUDENTIAL
INSURANCE CO. OF AMERICA

"Prudential girls" enlivened company ads at turn of the century.

were more burials in pauper's graves —and more destitute families— than ever before.

And Dryden, who was more determined than ever to found his industrial insurance company, could hardly have chosen a better location than Newark.

Newark in 1873 was the third largest industrial city in the U.S. Its population was 115,000, swelled by 70,000 new arrivals in 15 years— most of them industrial workers, many Irish and German immigrants. The average Newark worker earned just $513 a year.

Dryden quickly made a convert of his well-to-do office mate, Bassett.

Next he approached Dr. Leslie Ward, a young Newark physician from a wealthy and prominent family. Dr. Ward's active social conscience had led him to hang out his shingle in a working class neighborhood, and he liked the idea of an insurance company that would help his patients and people like them.

Dryden still had to sell a number of hard-headed businessmen — enough to raise $30,000 of capital — on the idea that industrial insurance

could be not just another kind of charity, as many of them were inclined to believe, but a sound business proposition.

And even with two prominent citizens like Bassett and Ward as partners, the task of persuasion took many months.

But in February, 1875, the Prudential Friendly Society — named after its successful British counterpart — was finally chartered.

All through the spring and summer of 1875, Dryden labored over actuarial tables, figuring rates, costs and commissions.

The new company actually went into business in September, with only $5900 in the bank and the rest of its $30,000 capitalization pledged but still unreceived.

Shortly thereafter, a New Jersey state actuary was told by his supervisors to visit a "peculiar little company which is doing a novel kind of insurance business in Newark."

And, to any established insurance firm, the description would have seemed quite accurate.

On a shoestring

Prudential was operating on the thinnest of shoestrings. Bassett, as president, was paid $150 a month, Dryden, as secretary, $100. The only other employees were a $40-a-month bookkeeper and a $3-a-week office boy.

The company still used Bassett's basement real estate office, refurbished with $52.40 worth of second-hand furniture, and defrayed its $116.67 monthly rent by subletting a back room to a Penn Mutual Life Insurance agent and renting desk space to a representative of J. M. Bradstreet & Sons.

However, this "peculiar little company" did have the backing of leading businessmen. "No institution in Newark," wrote the conservative *Newark Register*, "has a board of directors that can more strongly claim the confidence of our people."

Dryden began advertising for agents in December, but he himself was the company's star salesman during its first months.

He visited factory after factory during lunch hours, and shocked the business community by staying open in the evening so that workers could

Life Insurance — 1895 to 1960
Figures from Institute of Life Insurance (millions)

	Ordinary Life		Industrial		Group Life	
	No. of Policies	Amount	No. of Policies	Amount	No. of Policies*	Amount
1895	2	$ 4170	7	$ 818	....	$........
1900	3	6124	11	1449	....	....
1905	5	9585	17	2278	....	....
1910	6	11783	23	3125	....	....
1915	9	16650	32	4279	.120	100
1920	16	32018	48	6948	2	1570
1925	23	52892	71	12318	3	4247
1930	32	78576	86	17963	6	9801
1935	33	70684	81	17471	6	10208
1940	37	79346	85	20866	9	14938
1945	48	101550	101	24874	11	22172
1950	64	149071	108	33415	19	47793
1955	80	216600	112	39682	32	101300
1960	95	340268	100	39563	44	175434

*Refers to number of individual policies, not "master certificates" held by organizations

New Prudential Co. was in the black by 1877

come in and talk insurance.

The first Prudential policies offered sickness benefits of $3 to $25 a week; $100 a year after age 65; $50 to $500 in death benefits for adults, and $10 to $50 for children.

This was minimal coverage, but it paid for funeral expenses, a crushing financial blow to an uninsured working class family, and could provide a small nest egg, too. (Five hundred dollars, after all, was almost a year's wages for an average worker.)

And all claims were paid within 24 hours.

By the end of 1875, Prudential had 279 policies in force. By November, 1876, the number had risen to 7000 — and claims came in so fast that the company was dangerously in the red. "I am afraid that we are likely to be swamped by this expensive kind of success," wrote one member of the board of directors.

Turn of the tide

At one point during the summer of 1876, it was only Dr. Ward's medical skill that kept Prudential in business. He saved the life of a dangerously ill patient who also happened to be the holder of a $500 policy; and just then, a $500 claim would have driven the company into bankruptcy.

By the end of the year, Prudential's directors were beginning to think that their investment in the company had been nothing but a charitable contribution, after all.

They agreed, however, to send Dryden to England, on a $250 expense account, for consultation with Prudential Assurance of London.

Rather to the disenchanted directors' surprise, the trip was a triumph. Dryden interviewed Henry Harben, head of the giant British enterprise, which by then was selling 1.5 million policies a year and collecting an annual $5 million in premiums, and won his enthusiastic support.

He got advice on every aspect of operation, from agent organization to bookkeeping, and a full set of the work-saving forms that Prudential of London had developed.

After two weeks in London, Dryden returned with a complete plan for reorganization of the U.S. Prudential—and for its eventual expansion from coast to coast.

Economy measures adopted immediately included—in addition to the streamlined bookkeeping with the new forms—the abandonment of sickness benefits and a slight rate increase; the actuarial tables that had been used for the company's original rates were based on the experience of ordinary insurance companies, whose customers were better heeled and healthier.

1877, the worst year of the depression, was the year the tide turned for Prudential.

With company finances on a sound footing, profits began to ap-

THE WORLD OF THRIFT.

Assets, : : : $15,780,000
Income, : : : 12,500,000
Surplus, : : : 3,300,000

A Life Insurance Policy issued by **The Prudential**
is vastly more important to the welfare of a family than is Gibraltar to the British Empire. The Prudential insures men, women and children. Write for descriptive literature.
THE PRUDENTIAL INSURANCE COMPANY OF AMERICA
JOHN F. DRYDEN, President.

J. Walter Thompson came up with Prudential "Rock" idea in 1895.

pear. The first branch office was opened in Paterson, N. J., in April.

Two years later, the company—whose name had been changed to The Prudential Insurance Co. of America—began to expand on a larger scale, with offices in New York and Philadelphia.

There was still some criticism of industrial insurance from conservative quarters; it was even said that the small policies on children's lives encouraged poor mothers to murder their babies. Less dramatic but no less ludicrous was the charge that Prudential agents deliberately let

policies lapse to reap bigger profits for their employers. Actually, the company did far better on policies that stayed in force.

When the first Prudential office opened in New York, the *Sunday Mercury* said, "It may be known to some of our readers that a small, one-horse insurance company with its headquarters in Newark, N. J., is actually endeavoring to scoop in a harvest of victims in this city and state... On the 31st day of July, its agents crossed the Hudson River and invaded this city like microscopic pestilence or an army of worms or hornets."

But none of this kept the people who needed them from buying Prudential policies. By the end of 1879, 43,715 were in force, amounting to $3,866,913.

And in the same year, two of the biggest ordinary insurance companies, Metropolitan and John Hancock, accorded Prudential the sincerest form of flattery by moving into the industrial insurance business.

Six years later, with one million industrial policies in force, Prudential returned the compliment by entering the rapidly growing ordinary insurance field.

John Dryden took over the presidency of his big company in 1881, and held the office until his death in 1911, when he was succeeded by his son Forrest.

During all those years, Prudential's spectacular growth continued—from the million policies of 1885 to 2.5 million in 1896, 10 million in 1911.

In this century, Prudential, like all major insurance companies, has derived more and more of its income from ordinary insurance, less and less from industrial.

With the steady rise in their living standards and aspirations, U.S. workers have tended to "move up" to ordinary insurance for more coverage and the convenience and lower cost of annual payments by mail.

And group insurance (introduced in 1911 by Equitable Life) has also risen in importance.

But industrial insurance, which contributed so much to the growth of the insurance business, is still very much alive. It is the sole source of protection for millions of low-income families. And although their dollar volume is far lower than that earned by either ordinary or group insurance, there are actually more industrial policies in force today than any other type.

HE STARTED SODA
SALES POPPING

CHARLES E. HIRES' ROOT BEER LAUNCHED IN 1876 SET PATTERN OF NATIONAL DISTRIBUTION

A LARGE, thirsty market was ready and waiting in 1876 when Charles E. Hires, a young Philadelphia druggist, began marketing a drink he called Root Beer.

Soft drinks were already a national habit. An infant bottling industry was turning out hundreds of variously flavored beverages. Many housewives concocted their own, and so did the proud proprietors of newfangled soda fountains.

But no one brand had won more than local popularity until Hires Root Beer came along.

It was Hires, with national advertising and distribution, that set the pace for the industry's phenomenal late 19th century growth—from 8.4 million cases of bottled drinks in 1869 to 38.8 million thirty years later.

(By 1960, over 1.5 billion cases were turned out in 5400 bottling plants; the industry's sales volume was over $1.5 billion. And per capita consumption of soft drinks was 205 bottles.)

Studied at night

Charles E. Hires was a farmer's son who began his career as an apothecary's apprentice in Millville, N. J.

In 1866, his apprenticeship over, he moved to Philadelphia, found a job as a pharmacist's clerk, and began attending night classes at the Philadelphia College of Pharmacy and the Jefferson Medical School.

When he had $400 in the bank, he rented a small drugstore of his own, outfitting it—on credit—with $3000 worth of the latest fixtures, including a soda fountain made of Tennessee marble.

He got himself out of debt by recognizing a good thing when he saw it—just as he was to do a few years later in the case of a farmer's wife's "herb tea."

He was walking to work one morning when he noticed a crew of men excavating reddish, claylike earth from a cellar near his store.

"Hires Special Cleaner"

He picked up a handful of the dirt, took it along to his laboratory for analysis, and discovered that it was, as he had suspected, Fuller's Earth—a substance then much in demand as a cleansing and filtering agent.

The young pharmacist went back to the excavation site, and asked the foreman how he was getting rid of all that dirt. Told that it was being carted off to a New Jersey dump, he asked if the foreman would not prefer to dump it in the cellar of the drugstore just down the block and be rid of it.

Naturally, the offer was accepted. And Hires went to work, molding the Fuller's Earth into cakes, stamping "Hires' Special Cleaner" on them,

Hires himself designed the first, cork-stopped bottle. The crown cap, introduced in 1910, has been twice redesigned by Norman Bel-Geddes.

FARM DRINK FORMS BASIS

wrapping them individually in tissue paper, and peddling them to wholesale drug houses.

Since Fuller's Earth had always been sold loose in barrels and was extremely messy stuff, the little cakes were a tremendous success. Hires was soon able to pay off his debts and begin accumulating a nest egg.

Early in the 1870s, he married and took his bride to a New Jersey farm boarding house for their honeymoon.

It was there that he discovered the "herb tea" that he was to make famous as Hires Root Beer.

The farmer's wife served her guests a drink made of 16 different wild roots and berries—including juniper, pipsissewa, spikenard, wintergreen, Sarsaparilla and hops.

Hires decided that it was too good to stay down on the farm, and when he started back to Philadelphia, the recipe was in his pocket.

Back in his drugstore, he began working on a packaged, water-soluble extract of the ingredients, and soon had samples ready for tasting.

One of the first tasters was his friend Dr. Russell Conwell, founder of Temple University. Dr. Conwell agreed that the drink was delicious, but suggested that more people—especially hard-drinking Pennsylvania coal miners—might buy it if it had a more stimulating name than Hires Herb Tea — say, Hires Root Beer, for instance.

Began advertising

So it was Hires Root Beer Extract that was launched at the Philadelphia Centennial Exposition in 1876.

The extract was sold in 25¢ packages, to which the housewife or soda fountain proprietor added five gallons of water, four pounds of sugar, and half a yeast cake — to make a drink that cost a little over a nickel a gallon.

In 1877, when the makings for an estimated 11,520 glasses of Root Beer had been sold, the publisher of the Philadelphia *Public Ledger* told Hires that he ought to begin advertising.

82

Hires agreed, but said he could not afford it; and the publisher, George W. Childs, offered to carry his account until he was ready to ask for a bill.

By the time $700 worth of one and two-inch Root Beer ads had run in the *Ledger* on credit, the drink was established as a Pennsylvania favorite.

In the 1880s, Hires began marketing a liquid concentrate as well as the packaged extract. He broadened his distribution and stepped up his advertising campaign, becoming one of the very earliest national advertisers.

He was the first manufacturer to take a full page of newspaper space —in the *Ledger*, in 1889—and later, the first to occupy the back cover of the *Ladies' Home Journal*.

"Temperance Drink"

By the mid-80s, over 1.5 million drinks of Root Beer had been sold, and the nation's first brand name soft drink was well on its way to becoming a household word.

In 1893, bottled Root Beer first went on the market.

Shortly thereafter, Hires ran afoul of the Women's Christian Temperance Union.

Root Beer had originally been promoted as a "temperance drink," and as a tonic to "purify the blood and make rosy cheeks." Hires himself a Quaker convert, was as scrupulous about his product's mildness as he was about the purity of its ingredients, steadfastly refusing to add even caffeine.

But the WCTU could not believe that any drink with the terrible word "beer" in its name was entirely innocent.

Between 1895 and 1898, it battled Root Beer in the press, claiming that the "fermentation of a sweet liquid in ordinary temperatures always produces alcohol."

The ladies were finally pacified when Hires published the results of an independent laboratory analysis of the drink, showing that the alcohol content of a bottle of Root Beer was less than half that of a homemade loaf of bread.

By the turn of the century, Root Beer was no longer alone in the brand name soft drink field.

Coca-Cola, invented by an Atlanta, Ga., druggist in 1886, began flowing into the national market early in the '90s. Pepsi-Cola, created by a druggist in Bern, N. C., in 1896, went national in 1903. (Dr. Pepper's first appeared in Texas in the late 1880s, but did not begin getting national distribution and advertising until 1922.)

The franchise system of soft drink production and distribution, under

Old and new in 1920s transportation meet outside of Philadelphia distribution point

Charles E. Hires was convinced by friend that Root Beer was more persuasive name than "herb tea."

Year	Sales ($ millions)	Total Cases* (millions)	Total Bottles (millions)	Per Capita (bottles)
1869	4.2	8.4	202	6.4
1879	4.7	9.5	227	4.5
1889	14.3	26.1	626	9.9
1899	23.3	38.8	930	12.2
1909	43.5	62.2	1491	16.2
1919	135.3	169.2	4060	38.4
1929	214.3	272.4	6538	53.1
1939	299.8	293.2	7037	54.9
1949	860.9	1012.9	24,309	162.0
1960**	1500.0	1536.5	36,976	205.0

THE SWELLING TIDE OF SOFT DRINKS

* 24 bottles to the case
** estimated

Summary: Since 1869, per capita consumption of soft drinks has multiplied 32 times, production 190 times and sales volume 360 times, to a staggering $1.5 billion in 1960.

which extract is supplied by the parent company to local bottlers, was well developed by the early 1900s.

Root Beer, the drink that started it all, accounts for a relatively small slice of today's soft drink sales.

The cola drinks are the national favorites by a wide margin, accounting for 64% of sales. Lemon and lime are second with 9%, orange third with 6%. Root Beer and ginger ale are tied for fourth place with 4% each.

The industry's five largest firms are, in order, Coca-Cola Co., Pepsi-Cola Co., Seven-Up Co., Nehi Corp., and Dr. Pepper Co. (Its diversity is indicated by the fact that these five giants, between them, control only slightly more than half of the nation's 5400 franchise bottling plants.)

The company, which remained under family ownership until last year, when Consolidated Foods Corp. acquired the Hires family stock, is still the largest root beer maker in the world. About 25% of the root beer sold in the U.S. is Hires; the rest comes from more than 1000 small companies.

The grand total of drinks of Hires Root Beer sold stands today at a thirst-quenching 11.5 billion—and is still climbing slowly but steadily up.

83

Woolworth opened his first five and ten in Lancaster, heart of Pennsylvania Dutch country, on June 21, 1879.

KING OF THE FIVE-AND-DIME

Nickels and dimes added up to a multi-million-dollar merchandising empire for Frank W. Woolworth

FRANK WINFIELD WOOLWORTH was a man obsessed with an idea. In the best Horatio Alger tradition, he clung tenaciously to his vision of becoming *somebody* throughout early years of poverty, depression and failure.

He pioneered the "five-and-ten" merchandising concept which was to become an integral part of American life just as the Sunday funnies or Little League baseball.

By creating a gold mine out of nickels and dimes, Woolworth

helped to develop mass production at low unit prices, and he brought thousands of items within reach of the lowest economic group. Ten-cent dentifrices and cosmetics put toothbrushes in every bathroom and cold cream on every woman's vanity.

When Woolworth started out in the decades after the Civil War, his idea of a small change store was looked down upon by established merchants. But the once-startling five-and-ten has blossomed into a billion dollar annual business.

Frank Woolworth was born in Jefferson County, upper New York State, in 1852. For generations the Woolworths had been tied to the soil, sometimes as tenant farmers, sometimes as landowners. Men of the family were trained for no other work. Woolworth's father owned 108 acres and eight cows. Principal crops were potatoes and dairy products.

At 16, when Woolworth finished his education, he went to work full time on the family farm. But he

84

hated the long winters and rough, monotonous work. He dreamed of escaping to a clerking job behind a store counter, but no one would hire the inexperienced youth. Business was slow and prices had skyrocketed after the Civil War.

At the age of 21 he landed a job of sorts with Augsbury & Moore, a leading drygoods store in Watertown, New York. He received no salary for the first three months. His tasks were sweeping the floor, delivering packages and dressing windows.

During the next six years Woolworth rose to the position of clerk at a weekly salary of $10, married a young Canadian girl named Jennie Creighton, bought a four-acre farm, and saw the birth of his first child. But the dream of making his mark in the world was nowhere in sight.

"No one thought Woolworth would rise higher than a clerkship," a friend recalled years later. But his mother had more confidence. "Someday, my son, you'll be a rich man."

A new merchandising craze — the five-cent counter — flared up briefly during these hard years. Merchants with superfluous stock dumped it on a "five cent counter" to get rid of it. Unwanted items quickly disappeared and customers usually bought some of the store's regular merchandise as well.

However, the boom in five-cent selling soon faded because goods were shoddy and merchandise lacked variety. Profits were small and experienced retailers dubbed the idea a passing fad.

But to Woolworth, another man's failure was his opportunity. His lifelong ambition to be somebody finally found a concrete objective — to open a store of his own stocked only with five-cent items.

In 1879, he borrowed $300 from his employer and set out to find a town where he could locate. He discovered that Utica, New York (35,000 population) had been untouched by the new merchandising strategy.

He rented a small store and distributed flyers announcing the grand opening of his "Great Five Cent Store". He stocked such items as candlesticks, biscuit cutters, pie plates, tin spoons, thread and handkerchiefs. (Woolworth's affinity for the color red showed itself in brilliant displays of red jewelry and turkey red napkins and later in the

60-story Woolworth Building, once world's tallest building, celebrated 50th anniversary in 1963. Company still maintains its headquarters here.

85

Woolworth's low prices brought many items within reach of the poor

now-familiar red store fronts.)

Trade was heavy during the first two weeks but customers soon lost interest and returned to higher-priced stores.

But Woolworth was convinced that failure was not due to his idea but to Utica. The biggest handicap was lack of sufficient five-cent merchandise so he decided to raise the figure to ten cents and look for another town.

One month later he opened the first five-and-ten in Lancaster, Pennsylvania. Years later one of the three women clerks in the store remarked that "Mr. Woolworth sat on a platform on a winding stairway at the back of the store, guarding the sales box and watching the clerks at work."

The store proved highly popular with the thrifty Pennsylvania Dutch housewives and soon Woolworth began to broaden his horizons. His next ventures were in Harrisburg and York, but they proved repetitions of the Utica experience and he was forced to close the stores.

Scranton was the next Keystone State city to feel the Woolworth touch. This time a brother, Charles, was brought into partnership and for the remainder of Woolworth's career, relatives and trusted friends were to fill key positions within the company. And nearly 100 employees — buyers, managers — were to become millionaires.

Early records show that Woolworth sales reached $18.000 in 1881 and climbed to $24.125 by 1882. Although three of his five early attempts ended in failure, Woolworth was now the proud proprietor of one flourishing and one fairly successful store.

Old dreams of expansion soon returned to haunt him. It was obvious that the five-and-dime business needed more outlets. A chain of stores would enable him to buy goods in quantity, to attract new kinds of merchandise, and to sell more cheaply.

To expand, he needed more capital. He searched for partners with cash who would share half the risk in opening each new store in return for half its profits. By 1886, Woolworth had seven stores in Pennsylvania, New York and New Jersey.

Annual sales climbed over the $100,000 mark.

Woolworth personally bought every item that appeared for sale on his counters. Profits depended upon intelligent buying and, since most jobbers were located in New York, he moved there in 1886.

Taking a $25-a-month room in Chambers Street and moving his family into a house in Brooklyn, he began a quest for low-priced articles. He soon learned that prices were kept high by jobbers who had the inside track with manfaucturers and they didn't want to be bothered by selling to him directly.

A Mother Hen

As he was walking along lower Broadway one day, he happened on a small candy shop whose proprietor was willing to supply him with candy at the low price of 20 cents a pound. Woolworth jubilantly ordered 100 pounds for his stores and thus began one of the most profitable dime store lines. Today Woolworth sells 250 million pounds of candy a year.

He tried the same tack with a small Christmas tree ornament factory and eventually built up a stable of suppliers.

In 1890, he made the first of many pilgrimages to Europe to buy toys and knickknacks directly from German and Austrian factories.

The dime store king watched over his business like a mother hen. He would send out memorandums to the effect: "Be sure and not have more clerks than you can use and don't turn all the gas burners on every night."

He also kept his employees alert with anonymous visits. His favorite trick was to stroll through a store and fill his pockets with postcards, rubber balls, etc. Then he would dump the lot on the manager's desk and remark acidly, "I could have filled a delivery truck."

Discovery of a wasted penny never failed to annoy Woolworth, even when he became fabulously rich. He was notorious for the low wages he paid his female clerks. He felt "when a clerk gets so good, she can get higher wages elsewhere . . ."

When labor troubles plagued him and clerks went on strike for higher wages, he instructed his managers to

---

SUPERMARKET OF MERCHANDISE

Sales of dime stores — or variety stores as they prefer to be called — totals about $1.1 billion, but only a small portion comes from five and ten cent items. (As far back as 1932, the limit jumped to 20 cents and a no-limit policy was established in 1935).

Even the name five-and-ten is no longer completely valid. Today, the dime or variety store rivals the big department store in merchandise and prices. One may buy a diamond ring for $99.95, caviar at $1.29 an ounce or a mynah bird for $44.95.

The modern Woolworth store resembles a supermarket. A 42nd Street outlet in New York City recently sprouted a fresh fruit and vegetable stand. Biggest similarity, however, stems from introduction of a self-service system. Over 75% of the 3607 Woolworth stores in the U.S. and overseas now have check-out counters.

Woolworth sells more dolls than any other retailer in the world. It is one of the leading sellers of brassieres — now about seven million — and also does brisk business in rose bushes and turtles.

Its restaurants are without peer in quantity of food served.

Nearly one million meals are prepared daily.

Recently Woolworth entered the discount race and opened the first of 18 self-service department stores under the name of Woolco in Columbus, Ohio. Woolco stores sell everything from clothing to furniture to major appliances. In addition, the discount shops offer specialized departments for auto service, drug prescriptions, beauty salons and portrait studios. Parking lots can accommodate 5000 cars.

In the present age of spiraling living costs and dim memories of nickel cups of coffee and five-cent subway rides, Woolworth remains a refreshing oasis for budget-minded Americans. It offers something no one can resist — a bargain.

Woolworth maintained his policy of "Nothing in this store over 10 cents" until 1930s. Today stores derive major business from $1-and-over items.

Woolworth entered mass merchandising field in 1962. Shoppers flocked to opening of the first Woolco discount department store in Columbus, Ohio.

Accordingly, in 1905, a $10 million stock corporation came into existence under the name F. W. Woolworth & Co. All stock was held within the company so the five-and-ten still remained a family affair.

By 1909, the dime store was firmly implanted on the American scene. Woolworth, now a portly 57, decided to invade England by opening a "three and sixpence" store in Liverpool. English newspapers quipped that he chose Liverpool to be near the boat when failure came.

Woolworth sank $64,000 into the venture and by 1962 there were 1078 "Wooly's" in Great Britain with net income of $46 million.

Soon Woolworth began to feel the pinch of competition. Names like Kresge Kress and McCrory began to crop up. Individually, they did not worry him but, collectively, he began to feel their mounting threat.

He also experienced friendly rivalry — his brother, Charles, a cousin and other early partners who had branched out on their own along the Pacific Coast and in Canada where Woolworth had no stores. They often purchased large quantities of items together and, as a group, controlled 276 stores in addition to Woolworth's 318.

In 1911, holdings were consolidated into one company to increase profits and ward off competition. A $65 million corporation was formed with F. W. Woolworth retaining 50% interest.

Although his commercial success was assured, Woolworth's last years were filled with poor health and tragedy. Nervous attacks of weeping and insomnia sent him in search of expensive cures at European spas. His closest aides, who had been with him since the beginning, began to die. His beloved daughter, Edna, passed away suddenly from an ear ailment and his wife, Jennie, whose mind had failed completely, retreated into the past.

As business flourished, Woolworth grew fatter and became more lackadaisical. He gorged on soft, rich foods, over-ripe bananas being a favorite, and he refused to exercise or even take short walks.

He died in April 1919 at the age of 66 from a combination of gallstones and uremic and septic poisoning. An editorial in the *New York Sun* summed up his life and labors: "He won a fortune, not in showing how little could be sold for much, but how much could be sold for little."

"remember all such girls and when the dull season comes give them the bounce."

The great tide of immigration was beginning to hit the U.S. and to Woolworth those millions of poor were ripe for his dime stores. In 1891 he astonished his managers with the grand pronouncement: "I have been looking over a census of the United States and I am convinced there are 100 cities and towns where we can locate five-and-ten cent stores and we can sell a million dollars of goods a year!"

If anything, his prediction was short-sighted. Sales for 59 stores in 1900 surpassed $5 million, and the modest Brooklyn brownstone was replaced by a 30-room mansion on fashionable Fifth Avenue.

Woolworth clearly saw that his business could not remain a one-man show. He was a victim of nervous attacks and constantly worried over the fate of his empire should he die.

HE BROUGHT ORDER TO TROUBLED OIL

Rockefeller ended industry chaos

In 1863, a 24-year-old Cleveland commission agent named John D. Rockefeller went into the oil business.

Edwin L. Drake had struck oil at Titusville, Pa., just four years earlier; the infant industry was chaotically competitive, with dozens of small producers and refiners jockeying for position.

Over the next 20 years, Rockefeller put an end to the chaos — and to most of the competition. By the 1880s, his Standard Oil Trust controlled 85% of all U.S. oil production and distribution.

He launched an industry whose total 1960 sales approximated $30 billion; even more importantly, he pioneered the development of modern, large-scale industrial organization.

The future Oil King was born in Richford, N. Y., in 1839.

His father, William Avery Rockefeller, was an intelligent, irrepressible and irresponsible salesman of patent medicines who was described by a reminiscing friend, after the family became famous, as having had "all

Structure of Rockefeller empire was completed before advent of automobile, which increased demand for petroleum tremendously.

the vices but one." (He was a tee-totaller.)

His mother, on the other hand, was frugal, strict and devoutly religious; and it was she who set the tone of family life, since William spent most of his time on the road.

The family drifted West, and settled in Cleveland when John was 15. A year later, he graduated from high school and began looking for work.

It took John D. Rockefeller six weeks to find his first job.

Business was bad in Cleveland, and the quiet, serious young man did not impress prospective employers as a "hustler."

As the weeks dragged on, his father began trying to persuade him to give up and come home to the rural community near Cleveland where the family was living.

"It makes a cold chill run down my spine when I think of it," he declared as an old man. "What would have become of me if I had gone to the country?" But he added hopefully, "Maybe I would have gotten a start in business later."

Before his father became adamant, however, he managed to find a bookkeeper's position, at $25 a month, with a firm of commission merchants called Hewitt & Tuttle.

All through his life, one of Rockefeller's most striking characteristics was the sheer fun he got from his work. He was drivingly ambitious, and the charges of money and power-madness that his enemies heaped upon him were, from one point of view, justified; but it is equally true that he loved business for its own sake.

He used to recall that from his first day, Hewitt & Tuttle was "delightful to me—all the method and system of the office."

Within a year or two, he had taken over most of Mr. Tuttle's work; his salary rose to $700 a year.

But the firm was doing poorly, and, early in 1859, he decided to begin working for himself. He and a young Englishman, Maurice B. Clark, went into business together as commission merchants in farm produce.

It was in that same year that the first U.S. oil well was drilled.

"Seneca Oil," as petroleum was called, had long been highly esteemed

Rockefeller, in heyday of power, dressed, looked like "richest man in world."

as a medicine; it was believed that, if it could be extracted in commercially profitable quantities, it would rival whale and other oils as an illuminating fluid.

The land of Western Pennsylvania was known to be oil-rich, and a development company, the Pennsylvania Rock Oil Co., had been at work there for two years.

Its agent, a former railroad man named Edwin L. Drake, had decided to try to get at the oil by drilling, using techniques similar to those of salt mining.

Battling rain, mud, and the jeers of his neighbors (the idea of pumping oil from the ground seemed so far fetched that he was hard put to find men willing to work for him), Drake brought in his first well at

Titusville in August, 1859.

Within 24 hours, oil fever set in. Land values skyrocketed as prospectors poured into the area.

In January, 1860, Luther Atwood obtained the first patent for "cracking" crude oil, thus making possible mass production of light illuminating oils; in November of the same year, the first refinery went into production.

News of each of these exciting events soon reached Cleveland, where Rockefeller and Clark were busily and successfully marketing produce.

The new industry seems to have attracted the two young men from the beginning; here was where fortunes could be made in the years ahead.

In the early 1860s, it was as easy to open a refinery as it is to start a gas station today; in 1863, Rockefeller and Clark opened theirs.

In 1865, Rockefeller bought out Clark and Clark's brother for $74,500, and entered a new partnership with his own brother, William, and Samuel Andrews, the technical expert of the firm. A fourth partner, Henry M. Flagler, soon joined them.

Later the same year, the new firm of Rockefeller, Andrews & Flagler opened its second refinery. In 1866, William, who had inherited his father's gregarious nature and talent for salesmanship, went to New York to open an office there and begin an export business.

By 1868, the Rockefeller firm was the nation's largest oil "manufacturer" and in 1870 it was reorganized as the Standard Oil Co. of Ohio.

It had already begun making the railroad rebate deals that were to help it grow to monolithic size and power—and contribute to its unsavory public reputation.

Hard bargaining between railroads and shippers was the rule in the 19th century, and rebates were often granted to favored customers in exchange for guarantees of business. Standard Oil simply bargained harder — and more successfully — than any of its competitors, and therefore came in for perhaps more than its share of public enmity when the rebate system began to be attacked and investigated later in the century.

Rockefeller had decided that, if the industry was to move ahead, its production and distribution facilities would have to be concentrated in one gigantic organization; and he wanted that organization to be his.

To some extent, at least, the state of the industry in the early 1870s bore him out.

Too many adventurers had rushed into the new field too fast; prices were dropping and small firms were going bankrupt.

If a business genius like Rockefeller had not come along, the industry probably would have consolidated itself into three or four large organizations instead of only one; but a high degree of consolidation was almost inevitable.

As the 1870s moved along, one Cleveland company after another was absorbed by Standard Oil. In all, over 20 were drawn in, some willingly, others unwillingly.

Absorption of oil interests in other states followed; and in 1882, the Standard Oil Trust was capitalized at $70 million.

By 1885, the structure of Standard Oil was complete, although its greatest years of growth lay ahead in the era of the automobile.

The company had acquired wells and potential oil producing land; it had taken over pipelines and built added ones to create a network worth $31.5 million; its 20 component companies operated at least 50 refineries.

Standard plants were producing a wide variety of products and by-products, and the trust's marketing department was wiping out independent distributors as efficiently as Standard of Ohio had absorbed independent refiners a decade earlier.

Poor boy who rose to millionaire through own efforts and luck was widespread American dream of the period. Rockefeller's oil career was outstanding inspiration.

Rockefeller's vast industrial empire could not have been built without the use of ruthless competitive tactics; but these tactics could not have succeeded if the company's internal organization had not been superb in every administrative and technical department, and the complex structure would have fallen apart if its efficiency had not increased in proportion to its size.

It was not to fall apart, of course, until 1911, when the trust was "busted" by the U.S. Supreme Court.

Rockefeller himself retired from the active management of his companies in 1896, the richest man in the U.S.—and one of the most unpopular.

His real contribution to U.S. business received little objective evaluation before the Standard Oil monopoly was destroyed.

Harvard president Charles W. Eliot wrote in 1915 that the "organization of the great business of taking petroleum out of the earth, piping the oil over great distances, distilling and refining it, and distributing it all over the earth, was an American invention."

It could almost be said to have been the invention of one American, John D. Rockefeller.

Horse-drawn Standard Oil tank wagon symbolizes past, future of transportation.

Cattle dealer Swift (1873)

Industry leader Swift (1900)

HOW TO BUILD
YOUR OWN BUSINESS

Gustavus Swift, at 16, borrowed $25 from his father, bought and butchered a heifer. When he died 58 years later his meat-packing firm was world's largest, with yearly sales today over $2.5 billion

TODAY'S staggeringly complex U.S. food industry, which currently can stock cupboards, refrigerators and freezers to the tune of $80 billion, was born in the last quarter of the 19th century.

It grew up to meet the needs of a fast-growing, increasingly urban and industrial nation, which could no longer depend for its food supplies on small farmers and local markets.

Among the men who saw the challenge—and the profit potential—of the new need for large scale food processing and distribution was Gustavus Franklin Swift, pioneer of the

meat industry and founder of its largest firm, Swift & Co.

G. F. Swift was born on a Cape Cod farm in 1839, the ninth child in a family of 12.

He left school at 14 to go to work in his brother Noble's butcher shop, and from then on, he was never to spend a day in any business but the meat business.

After two years with his brother, young Swift borrowed $25 from his father, bought a heifer from a neighbor for $19, slaughtered and dressed the animal in the family barn, and sold the meat at a profit.

Then, a few months later, he borrowed $400 from a prosperous uncle and hiked 60 miles to the Brighton, Mass., livestock market, where he bought several dozen hogs.

He was in business for himself, peddling beef and pork door-to door, at 16; he opened his first retail store at 20; and two years later, he entered the wholesale cattle dealing business on a small scale.

In 1869, Swift launched a substantial retail-wholesale business in Clinton, Mass. He had been giving some serious thought to merchandising, and he began putting his new ideas

91

In the 1880s, after his partner, cattle dealer J. A. Hathaway, pulled out of the business, G. F. Swift established Swift & Co., (above) in Chicago, nerve center of the nation's fast-growing meat processing industry. Swift's business acumen and ingenious marketing strategy for selling dressed beef in markets located 1000 miles away, had turned the company, incorporated in 1885 with $300,000, into a $200 million enterprise, below.

into practice in the Clinton market.

Most meat markets in the 1860s were dirty, dingy places. Their proprietors made no attempt at attractive display; when a customer asked for a steak or roast, it was brought out from an icebox in the rear of the shop.

But in Swift's market, the windows sparkled; the floors were covered with clean sawdust; the butcher's block was scrubbed, and tempting cuts of meat were laid out for customers' inspection on marble slabs.

A few years later, in Chicago, the same kind of merchandising was to boost sales for Swift & Co. The company's wholesale coolers were kept full not of whole carcasses, but of cuts of meat, dressed and invitingly displayed, on the theory that a buyer

would be more likely to remember that he was running low on chops if he saw chops before his eyes than if he was merely confronted with a side of beef.

The attractiveness of the Clinton market helped Swift "push" the cheaper cuts of meat. He had decided early in his peddling days that the way to earn the maximum profit on each animal was to sell the pot roast and chuck and let the steaks and prime ribs sell themselves—but this took real salesmanship in a day when a family could dine on the best cuts for 25 cents and most butchers threw in a pound of liver "for the cat."

Here, too, Swift & Co. was to excel in later years. In the 1890s, for instance, the company successfully changed the "image" of pork sausage,

which well-to-do housewives spurned because they thought it was made of unsavory scraps, by giving Swift sausages the impressive name of "Brookfield" and selling them in attractive paperboard boxes.

Swift's enterprises grew rapidly in the early 1870s.

He formed two partnerships—one with a wholesale slaughterer, D. M. Anthony, and the other with a leading cattle dealer, J. A. Hathaway. His own retail-wholesale business, with headquarters in Clinton, continued to thrive under the management of his youngest brother, Edwin.

Then, in 1875, he moved on to Chicago to open a buying office for the firm of Hathaway & Swift.

Chicago, midway between the cattle lands of the West and the fast-growing markets of the East, had been rising in importance as a live-stock center for 25 years.

Its great Union Stock Yards had been established in 1865.

The Chicago packing and processing firms concentrated on pork. Very small quantities of beef were beginning to be dressed in the Midwest, but most cattle were shipped out live for processing in the East.

Soon after the 35-year-old Swift reached Chicago, he had the idea that was to revolutionize the industry—he decided to find a way to ship dressed beef to Eastern markets on a grand scale.

His conservative partner, Hathaway, wanted no part of such a wild undertaking, and the firm of Hathaway & Swift was amicably dissolved.

Swift's half of the business came to $30,000, and with this meagre capital —barely enough to keep a small packing house running for a month—he launched Swift & Co.

The established Chicago cattle dealers and pork packers were positive that if the Yankee newcomer was given enough rope, the proverbial results could be expected.

However, Swift had a spectacular talent for borrowing money, paying it back promptly, and borrowing more, which he used to keep his business expanding at such a rapid rate that it outdistanced all its competitors in 15 years.

He began shipping fresh, dressed beef East in the winter of 1876.

It was a tricky business; meat that

Swift & Co. today has more than 500 processing plants and distributing units throughout U.S. and Canada, plus 115 in Europe and sales offices all over the Free World. The company markets grocery and dairy products, animal feed, chemicals, leather, adhesives and industrials oils, as well as a full line of meats and poultry.

left Chicago frozen solid in zero weather might run into a warm spell in Indiana, thaw, freeze and thaw again, and spoil before it reached New York or New England.

And even at best, without refrigeration, dressed meat shipping was a strictly seasonal business.

So Swift began looking for a practical refrigerator car.

Other meat packers were looking, too; and so were the fruit growers of the Pacific coast.

Half a dozen cars had been designed and patented, but none of them was completely satisfactory.

Swift combined their best features, and found a firm, the Michigan Car Co., that was willing to undertake the highly speculative job of building him 10 cars on credit.

Then he began negotiating with the railroads, which had no wish to ship dressed beef when live steers gave them double the tonnage.

The only line he could find to take his business at a reasonable rate was the Grand Trunk, which ran East by a devious route through Canada and got practically no livestock business. (It was not until 1887, when the Interstate Commerce Act curbed the railroads' rate fixing practices, that Swift & Co. was able to use a direct route East.)

The final hurdle that had to be overcome was the Eastern consumer's prejudice against beef that had been dressed 1000 miles away, and local butchers' unwillingness to handle it.

Here Swift used sheer stubbornness, and the willingness to sell at a loss rather than not at all.

He simply refused to let his sales representatives in Eastern cities take "no" for an answer.

"Sell it in Lowell," he telegraphed when his Lowell, Mass., sales agent reported a boycott by local meat markets and wanted to know where he should send his carload of beef.

The same four-word wire was repeated in response to all the agent's pleas for relief; and the meat was finally sold in Lowell. It was sold at a loss, but the boycott was broken.

With this technique, Swift broke down sales resistance in town after town throughout the East, and within two years, his 10-car fleet had grown to 200.

By the end of the 1870s, Swift &

94

G. F. Swift began his career in the meat business on a peddler's cart in 1850s, by 1880s, fleets of horsedrawn red wagons were carrying Swift meat to market.

Co. had branched out from beef into mutton, pork and processed meats. It was beginning to develop the business in by-products—hide, soap, glue, fertilizer, margarine and a dozen others—that led to the industry byword about using "everything from the pig but the squeal."

Swift & Co. was incorporated in 1885 with a capital of $300,000.

Just one year later, its capitalization was increased to $3 million, and in 1891, to $5 million.

New packing houses were opened in Kansas City in 1888, in Omaha in 1890, and St. Louis in 1892.

Exports of fresh dressed beef to Europe began in 1890.

Then came the Panic of 1893.

In May of the panic year, Swift & Co. owed $10 million in bank loans; its expansion had been, as Swift's eldest son, Louis, who succeeded him as company president, was to admit in the 1920s, "faster than was altogether conservative."

All through the summer, rumors of the company's impending collapse floated through the Chicago Board of Trade.

But in September, Swift was not only still in business; he had reduced his firm's indebtedness to banks to $1 million.

Most department heads—and many rank-and-file employes—had lent the company their life savings.

Warehouse shelves had been stripped bare of glue, hides, wool, smoked and pickled meats — everything that could be sold for cash.

And more than once, sheer luck had helped—as when Swift heard that another packer had suffered a disasterous warehouse fire and was due to collect $100,000 in insurance. The well-insured gentleman was invited to Swift's office and quickly persuaded that the best thing he could do with his money was to lend it to Swift & Co. at six per cent interest.

After the panic year, the company expanded faster than ever. Capitalization was increased to $15 million in 1896, and new plants opened in St. Paul, Minn., and St. Joseph, Mo., a year later.

When G. F. Swift died in 1903, six of his seven sons had already joined the company, and the seventh was getting ready to come in. Sales that year were over $200 million.

And over the past 50 years, under continued family management (today Swift's youngest son is still a director, and two grandsons and a great-grandson are vice presidents), Swift & Co. has kept right on expanding as the U.S. food budget has soared. Its 1960 sales were over $2.5 billion.

SOLD AMERICAN

Founder of American Tobacco Co., Buck Duke was first to mass-produce cigarettes, sparked revolution in U.S. smoking habits, laid foundations for today's $6.6 billion U.S. tobacco industry

James B. Duke

In 1881, a 24-year-old North Carolina tobacco man named James Buchanan ("Buck") Duke decided to go into the cigarette business.

He was backing a very dark horse indeed; late 19th-century Americans smoked pipes and cigars, chewed plug and sniffed snuff, but most of them scorned the cigarette as a dandified foreign invention.

Moreover, the machine that would make possible mass production of cigarettes for a mass market if one could be created was still in its inventor's workshop, completely untried.

In 1880, the year before Buck Duke made his decision, the U.S. tobacco industry had produced only 400 million cigarettes, all hand-rolled.

By 1889, nine years later, merchandising and mass production had boosted cigarette output to 2.2 billion.

The revolution that was to create the modern U.S. tobacco industry had begun, and most of the credit belonged to Buck Duke.

(In 1960, tobacco industry sales volume was $6.6 billion, over 90% of which came from cigarettes—more than 400 billion of them for an estimated 60 million U.S. cigarette smokers. And American Tobacco, the company Buck Duke founded in 1890, had a 1960 sales volume of $1.2 billion.)

Buck Duke's original tobacco business, W. B. Duke & Sons, was a small family firm, founded by his father, Washington Duke.

Before the Civil War, Washington Duke was a prosperous planter with a 300-acre estate.

He entered the Confederate Army in 1863, and was taken prisoner in the retreat from Richmond.

Released in 1865 with 50¢ in his

CIGARETTE SALES SOARED IN '80s

pocket (the proceeds of sale of a souvenir Confederate $5 bill to a Yankee soldier), he hiked 137 miles home to his neglected plantation.

Starting from scratch, Washington Duke and his three sons (Buck was the youngest) began farming again.

Their slaves were gone and there was no money for wages, so they concentrated on tobacco, which a four-man work force could grow, harvest and bag in quantity.

They soon found that the market for North Carolina's Bright Leaf was booming; soldiers of both armies had acquired a taste for it during the war.

They also found that the industry was dominated by a single brand—Bull Durham pipe tobacco.

Bull Durham was so unbeatably popular during the 1870s that the best its competitors could do was to market brands with names as similar as possible to the magic one: Sitting Bull Durham, Jersey Bull, Pride of Durham, Black Durham, Dime Durham were only a few; one manufacturer, deciding that all possible English variations on the theme had been exhausted, dubbed his product Los Toros Tabaco de Fumar.

The Duke family's two brands, Duke of Durham and Pro Bono Publico, were making money; but Buck Duke, who took charge of manufacturing early in the 1870s, was aim-

ing for industry leadership. And he saw no chance of getting to the top with pipe tobacco.

"My company is up against a stone wall," he told a friend. "It cannot compete with the Bull. Something has to be done, and that quick. I am going into the cigarette business."

The paper-rolled cigarette had been known in Europe ever since the 16th century; the Spanish conquerors of Mexico got the idea from the Aztecs, who rolled their smoking tobacco into small cylinders of corn husk.

It began gaining popularity in the 19th century, first in Turkey, then in France, where production began in the 1840s, then, in the 1860s, in England and the U.S.

The U.S. cigarette industry, such as it was, was centered in New York; when Buck Duke went into cigarette production in 1881, he had to go to New York to find a factory manager and skilled workers.

But, later in the same year, he found that a Virginian, James Bonsack, had invented a cigarette-rolling machine.

The Bonsack machine fed prepared tobacco onto a continuous strip of paper flowing into a tube. In the tube, a cylinder was formed and passed against a pasting brush, and a rotary cutting knife cut off ciga-

rettes of the proper length as they emerged from the tube.

Bonsack claimed that each machine could do the work of 50 hand workers and cut cost from 80¢ to 30¢ per thousand cigarettes.

None of the established cigarette manufacturers, satisfied with their hand-made luxury item, wanted to take a chance on the new machinery —but Duke did.

He ordered two machines, and the happy Bonsack gave him a favorable royalty rate that was to be a competitive advantage for years to come.

The machines did not work as well as their inventor had hoped; but Duke found a young mechanic, William O'Brian, who was able to improve them, and soon they were turning out 200 cigarettes a minute. (Today's machines have a top speed of 1600 and a "cruising speed" of about 1300).

Duke cut his profit margin to the bone to broaden his new product's market as fast as possible; 10 Duke of Durham cigarettes sold for a nickel, only half the standard price of the '80s.

Next, he launched a vigorous sales campaign, sparked by newspaper and billboard advertising and by the introduction of picture cards and premium coupons in cigarette boxes. (For 75 coupons, a Duke of Durham

AMERICA LIGHTS UP
(eight decades of tobacco consumption)

	1960	1950	1940	1930	1920	1910	1900	1890	1880
Cigarettes (billions)	468.6	355.1	177.7	119.9	50.4	7.9	2.6	2.2	0.4
Cigars, large (billions)	6.5	5.5	5.5	6.6	8.3	7.1	5.3	4.1	2.4
Cigars, small (billions)	0.1	0.08	0.1	0.4	0.7	1.1	0.6	n.a.	n.a.
Pipe Tobacco, Chewing Tobacco and Snuff (millions of lbs.)	171.0	235.9	339.8	375.7	453.5	468.6	293.9	238.3	136.3

Summary: Cigarette consumption has multiplied more than 1100 times since 1880, passed large cigars in 1910, now amounts to more than 2500 annually per capita.

THE INDUSTRY'S LEADERS
($ millions)

	1960		1950		1940		1930		1920	
	Sales	Profits	Sales	Profits	Sales	Profits	Sales	Profits	Sales	Profits
R. J. Reynolds	$1418.3	$105.3	$759.9	$40.3	$292.0	$35.5	n.a.	$34.3	n.a.	$10.7
American Tobacco	1215.0	62.5	841.6	41.7	285.8	28.3	n.a.	43.3	n.a.	20.1
Liggett & Myers	543.2	28.7	530.5	29.1	246.3	20.3	n.a.	25.7	n.a.	10.6
Philip Morris	506.4	21.0	255.8	15.3	73.2	7.4	n.a.	0.4	n.a.	0.2
P. Lorillard	487.3	27.4	167.9	6.7	78.9	3.8	n.a.	5.6	n.a.	7.8

Summary: American Tobacco, with **Pall Mall**, R. J. Reynolds, with **Camel**, are in a nip-and-tuck race for industry leadership.

Before 1884, cigarettes were hand-rolled (above) for a few city dwellers and immigrants from Southern Europe.

smoker could obtain a folding album of pin-up girls.)

The company moved to New York, where Duke supervised manufacturing and visited retailers by day and prowled the streets at night, counting discarded cigarette boxes to see how his brands were doing.

They were doing very well.

In 1880, the four top tobacco firms accounted for 80% of U.S. cigarette sales.

By 1889, Duke had moved into first place with 38%; the four firms he had overtaken divided most of the rest.

And, in 1890, Duke became president of the new American Tobacco Co., capitalized at $25 million, the result of a merger between his firm and its four rivals.

The cigarettes that had made Buck Duke's fortune were only a small part of the new company's output.

Cigarette consumption was climbing fast (it hit the 4 billion a year mark in 1895, suffered a baffling downturn between 1897 and 1902, then began to rise again), but cigars and pipe tobacco, chewing tobacco and snuff were still the choice of most Americans outside the big cities.

In 1904, 5¢ of the U.S. tobacco dollar went for cigarettes, 60¢ for cigars, 33¢ for pipe tobacco and plug, and 2¢ for snuff.

By then, American Tobacco had grown into a sprawling combine; Buck Duke was as powerful a figure in the tobacco industry as Rockefel-

ler in oil or Carnegie in steel.

He was a salesman and executive, not a financier. He never owned a controlling interest in his company; but he never needed it. On the single occasion when one of his wealthy backers began trying to run the business, Duke squelched him simply by threatening to resign and start a rival firm.

American Tobacco was reorganized in 1904, with capitalization of $235 million.

It controlled 88% of U.S. cigarette production, 80% of plug, 75% of pipe tobacco, over 90% of snuff, and 14% (the largest single share) of cigars.

It had three major subsidiaries (British-American Tobacco, American Cigar and American Snuff), and no less than 77 smaller ones.

In 1911, the American Tobacco trust was "busted" by the Supreme Court, and the "Big Four" of the tobacco industry—a somewhat smaller American Tobacco, Liggett & Myers, P. Lorillard and R. J. Reynolds —emerged.

Buck Duke retired from active industry leadership the next year.

He lived until 1925, however—long enough to see the fiercely competitive industry that had sprung from his tobacco empire turning out close to 100 billion cigarettes a year.

"Pro Bono Publico" pipe tobacco gave Washington Duke and his sons start in post-Civil War tobacco industry

Sweet Caporals (below) were one of American Tobacco's first brands. Duke himself invented - slide-and-shell box.

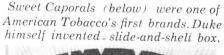

97

Christopher Latham Sholes was first to invent workable writing machine.

Oilman James Densmore financed and promoted Sholes' experiments.

Henry Benedict was a partner in the agency which popularized typewriters.

THE FABULOUS WRITING MACHINE

Christopher Sholes and the Remington Company revolutionized
U.S. business life with the first practical typewriter

IN JANUARY, 1866, three men huddled around a workbench in a Milwaukee machine shop appraising a machine for numbering pages of books. Its inventor, Christopher Latham Sholes, put finishing touches on his new device while Samuel Soule and Charles Glidden, his co-workers, kibitzed.

Offhandedly, Glidden suggested to Sholes, "If you can build a machine which will print figures like this, why can't you build a machine which will print words and letters the same way?"

Thus was triggered off the development of the first practical typewriter — a machine which would revolutionize business and communications, change the character of the labor force, influence language and education, and give birth to a new U.S. industry.

Christopher Sholes was born in 1819 in Pennsylvania. At 14 he was apprenticed to a printer and in the following years became an expert compositor, thoroughly familiar with the mechanics of printing and presses.

His first job was with an older brother, also a printer, who ran a newspaper in Wisconsin.

In 1866, at the age of 47 he already had a distinguished career behind him as newspaperman, printer, and politician. He had edited the Milwaukee Daily Sentinel and News, served in the Wisconsin legislature, had been Milwaukee's postmaster, and was then collector of customs.

Tall and thin with long flowing hair and sad eyes, he resembled a poet. As he was fond of tinkering with his hands, his hobby was carpentry and machine shop work.

Sholes was not the first to attempt a writing machine. He was actually the 52nd man to invent the typewriter.

In 1714, when reading and writing were accomplishments of the few, Queen Anne granted a patent on a writing machine to Henry Mill, an English engineer. No model or drawing exists, however, and for the rest of the 18th century the only other recorded effort was a machine for embossing printed characters for the blind.

First U.S. patent was granted by President Andrew Jackson to William Burt of Detroit in 1829. Burt called his table-sized machine a "Typographer" but could find no one interested enough to back him. Eventually he lost interest himself and went on to invent a successful surveyor's compass.

In 1843 Charles Thurber of Worcester, Mass. patented a machine important because it used the idea of a cylindrical roller to hold the paper. It was never produced.

Typewriter inventions began to pop up with greater frequency. They looked like pianos or permanent waving machines and were clumsy and complicated.

It remained for Sholes to translate the need for a writing machine into a practical device which could be manufactured in volume and sold at reasonable prices.

Sholes and his friends Soule and Glidden spent seven years building model after model, improving and refining until they had a working model.

At first they knew little of the

pioneering efforts of others. Then in 1867, Sholes read an article in the Scientific American magazine by editor Alfred E. Beach in which he described a machine then being exhibited in London. Beach predicted someday school children would be taught to write only their names with a pen, everything else would be written on the "literary piano," as he termed it.

Fired with new enthusiasm, Sholes and his partners finished a crude printing machine made from scraps of wood and iron. It printed only one letter—"W."

They immediately started another model, which was patented in 1868. This one looked like a combination piano and phonograph. It had two rows of black and white keys, an inked ribbon to make the impression, and it printed the entire alphabet but only in capital letters.

Up until now Sholes had called his invention "the machine." Searching for a more distinctive name, he finally arrived at the word "Type-Writer" with a hyphen.

Now his most pressing problem was to find money to continue his work. Sholes began to write letters—on the "Type-Writer" — to friends and acquaintances offering them a share in return for quick cash. One of the letters went to James Densmore, a loud, brassy businessman and promoter from Pennsylvania whom Sholes had met years before and taken an instant dislike to. But Sholes had heard that Densmore recently made a killing in oil.

Densmore promptly replied with an offer to pay Sholes' back bills—amounting to $600—and provide all future financing in return for 25% interest. What Sholes did not know was the $600 represented Densmore's total liquid assets at the moment.

During the next five years Densmore footed the bill for more than 50 typewriters at a cost of $250 each.

But his help was more than merely financial. He supplied tremendous optimism, while continually finding fault with each model. Partners Soule and Glidden discouragedly bowed out, but Densmore charged about the country like a high-powered Madison Avenue promoter and talked up the machine wherever he went.

Sholes was afraid that his invention would enjoy brief popularity and then "like any other novelty . . . be thrown aside."

By 1873 Sholes and Densmore

realized that more work of an exacting, technical nature had to be done on the machine. They looked around for a manufacturer familiar with the problems of making a product with many small, intricate parts.

A logical choice seemed to be E. Remington & Sons of Ilion, N. Y., a well-known manufacturer of firearms, sewing machines, and farm implements. Remington had a factory full of precision equipment, and excess capacity because the firearms business had slowed down considerably after the Civil War.

Eliphalet Remington, the company's founder had died in 1861 and passed the business on to his three sons. It was to son Philo Remington that Densmore and a persuasive salesman by the name of G. N. Yost presented Sholes' machine in 1873.

Remington offered to buy the patent rights rather than manufacture the machines for Sholes and Dens-

more. Sholes accepted $12,000 for his share of the patent; Densmore shrewdly chose a royalty basis, which was to bring him a million and a half dollars during his life.

Philo Remington agreed to devote one wing of his plant for typewriter production and the manufacture of 1000 machines. Densmore and Yost were to be the selling agents and the typewriter was to bear the famous Remington name.

Remington put to work William K. Jenne, head of his sewing machine division and a mechanical genius, on remodeling the machine for quantity production. Within a few months he solved dozens of the problems plaguing Sholes. Actual manufacture began in September, 1873, and the first shipments were made in early 1874.

Since Jenne was a sewing machine man, it's not surprising that "Model I Remington" looked much like a

Inventor's daughter, Lillian Sholes, operates the first working model. Unable to solve minor problems, Sholes sold to Remington & Sons in 1873.

Typewriter gave women first niche in business offices

sewing machine. On a stand, it had a foot treadle which operated the carriage return and delicate flowers stenciled on its black metal case.

As there was no shift key, it wrote only capital letters. The type bars struck upwards so the operator could not read what had been printed until four lines later.

One of the thorniest problems had been the keyboard. At first Remington arranged the keys in alphabetical order. But the most often used letters were not necessarily the most accessible and the type bars frequently collided.

Finally they adopted the printer's type case in which letters are arranged according to convenience. This system has remained virtually unchanged.

Now that the typewriter had become a reality, there was the task of selling it. Remington's first catalog shows how far off they were in estimating potential buyers. Main sales pitch was: "Persons traveling by sea can write with it when pen writing is impossible." The catalog also recommended the machine for court reporters, lawyers, editors, authors, and clergymen. In the last paragraphs, a vague reference was made to businessmen.

Progress was slow for the first few years. Mechanical difficulties sent many machines back to the Ilion plant. Few people were interested in paying $125 for the new-fangled gadget when a pen sold for a penny. Also nobody knew how to operate it.

Others objected to the all capitals it printed.

First big public viewing came at the Philadelphia Centennial Exposition in 1876. A pretty girl typed out notes for exposition-goers to mail back home, a feat which bred curiosity but few sales. The typewriter was overshadowed by a more exciting exhibit, the telephone.

Mark Twain was the most notable early typewriter buyer. He purchased a machine a few months after they went on sale and became the first author in history to turn in a typewritten book manuscript—"Life on the Mississippi"—to a publisher.

The classic story of the typewriter's early struggle is that of the Kentucky mountaineer who returned a typewritten letter he had received with this indignant note: "You don't need to print no letters for me. I kin read writin'."

Others mistook typed letters for printed circulars and threw them away unread.

Great barrier to immediate popularity was a lack of trained operators. In 1878 the first business school to teach typing opened, and Remington brought out a model with upper and lower case letters.

But not until 1882 did the turning point come. In that year the firm of Wycoff, Seamans & Benedict made a deal with Remington to become its exclusive selling agent for the entire world. The triumvirate's first stroke of luck was handed to them by the New York Young Women's Christian Association, which pioneered a typing class for its members.

The course was immediately branded "an obvious error in judgment by well-meaning but misguided ladies." The female mind was considered too flighty to master typing and the female body too frail to operate the heavy machine.

The YWCA's first graduating class of eight girls was instantly hired to work in business offices where previously the only female employees had been scrubbing women at night. The revolution had begun.

YWCA's throughout the country turned out "typewriters," as the girls were called, as fast as they could. Wyckoff, Seamans & Benedict saw where the future lay.

They began to open commercial schools in foreign countries. They went into Germany in 1883; by 1890 the typewriter occupied a prominent place in the businesses of Great Britain, France, and Greece. South America, Asia and Africa followed.

Wyckoff, Seamans & Benedict did so well that within five years they owned the Remington typewriter, including the Ilion factory, all patents, franchises and distribution rights. From 1886 on, Remington Type-Writer and E. Remington & Sons

Pre-typewriter offices were masculine sanctuaries. Executives wrote own letters, dictated to male secretaries.

Female typists were laughed at in the early days but Sholes' machine gave economic emancipation to women.

Typewriter sales spread abroad. Shipment arrives by camel in 1913 in Baluchistan (now part of Pakistan).

were separate companies.

The advent of a practical typewriter coincided with an important change taking place in U.S. business life.

The businessman of 1875 wrote his own letters in longhand with pen and ink or summoned a young man to take dictation and transcribe the letter. Top handwriting speed was 30 words a minute. Copies were made by wetting the original letter with a chemically-soaked cloth and pressing the damp page against a copy book. The damp originals, sometimes illegibly smeared, were then mailed.

But during the last two decades of the 19th Century, small family-owned companies slowly gave way to large corporations. As business grew increasingly complicated, the time was ripe for a device to save executives time and labor.

The typewriter also created monumental changes in society and mores, for it was the chief factor in economic emancipation of women.

During the 1860's, business districts were filled entirely with men. They wore their hats indoors and spit into brass cuspidors. The air reeked of cigar smoke; decoration tended to dark oak which didn't show dirt; and roll-top desks were ideal solution in an era which couldn't care less about clean desk tops.

The doors to these smoke-filled sanctums were firmly shut to women. As late as 1870, only 930 women were working in offices in all 37 states.

Many women were anxious for jobs. They could work in factories, schools, stores or on farms. But there was little a girl with education could do except teach school or be a nurse. White collar jobs in business and commerce belonged only to men.

Typing became first feminine foothold in that world. The typical typist of 1888 didn't have to be at work until 8:30. She was allowed a half hour for lunch and was through by 5:30. Although her starting salary was $6 a week, about half what a man would get for the same work, it was still the best break for women in centuries.

Sholes himself had not been unaware of this. "I feel that I have done something for the women who have always had to work so hard, "he said. "This will enable them more easily to earn a living."

The invasion of highbutton shoes into offices provided cartoonists and vaudeville comedians with typewriter jokes for the next 25 years.

An artist of 1875 envisioned the horrors to follow if women were permitted to work in offices. His sketch shows an office overflowing with hoopskirted ladies — and pandemonium.

The Keith Orpheum circuit abounded with gags like:

"I saw you and your wife walking down Main Street last night."

"Oh, that wasn't my wife. That was my typewriter."

Or—

"Wanna see something? Well, all you have to do is hit the key next to Z and you can see the X raise. X-Rays!"

Remington continued to improve its product with the automatic ribbon reverse (1896) and the decimal tabulator (1898). But by the turn of the century it had competition.

Both Underwood and L.S. Smith were making front-striking typewriters, where each line was visible as it was typed. The Royal Typewriter Co. was offering a machine with exceptionally light, fast touch. Corona and Monarch typewriters were also strongly in the picture.

First popular portable was a Royal. Aimed to women, it was painted in a variety of two-tone colors.

In 1933, International Business Machines entered the typewriter field with an electric machine. The industry regarded IBM as slightly mad. There had been other electric typewriters in 1906 and 1910—both financial disasters. Although the depression slowed down acceptance, the IBM machine eventually heralded a new era of typing ease.

The Department of Commerce now estimates retail typewriter sales at $313 million. An additional $15 million in parts are sold abroad.

Christopher Sholes, the modest pioneer who told people he didn't care to become a millionaire, lived long enough to see his "Type-Writer" come into wide use and become the basis for a new industry. He died in 1890 at the age of 71, a victim of tuberculosis.

Mark Twain, one of the first typewriter purchasers and an enthusiast ever after, wrote the following "testimonial" to the Remington Co. in 1875:

Gentlemen: Please do not use my name in any way. Please do not even divulge the fact that I own a machine. I have entirely stopped using the Typewriter, for the reason that I never could write a letter with it to anybody without receiving a request by return mail that I would not only describe the machine but state what progress I had made in the use of it, etc., etc. I don't like to write letters, and so I don't want people to know that I own this curiosity breeding little joker.

Yours truly,
SAML L. CLEMENS.

Ottmar Mergenthaler

HE UNPLUGGED PRINTING'S BOTTLENECK

Mergenthaler's Linotype transformed typesetting

In 1884, a young German-American inventor named Ottmar Mergenthaler unveiled a machine that Thomas A. Edison — himself perhaps the super-inventor of all time—was to call the "Eighth Wonder of the World."

The machine was the Linotype—the world's first fast, dependable, economical instrument for composition of printer's type.

With its introduction, the printing industry—born 400 years earlier when Johann Gutenberg invented movable type—can be said to have come of age.

Today's printing and publishing industry is a multi-billion-dollar giant, with its volume by 1960 of over $14 billion in the U.S. alone. And Mergenthaler Linotype Co. is one of its major suppliers. The company's 1960 sales were $47.2 million; it produces 65-70% of the hot-metal type-composing machinery in use in the U.S., and its share of the overseas market is slightly higher.

Ottmar Mergenthaler was born in 1854, and grew up in the small German town of Ensingen.

When he was 14, he was apprenticed to a nearby watchmaker. His father was a schoolmaster, and would have liked to send him to high school, but two older brothers were there already, and family funds were running low.

The watchmaker was undoubtedly delighted to get him. A few years earlier, he had created a minor sensation in Ensingen by sneaking into the church tower and repairing the town clock, which had seemed to be hopelessly broken down.

And young Ottmar, who had already decided that he wanted to be an engineer, was perfectly happy with the arrangement.

He spent four years working for the watchmaker by day and attending technical school in the evening.

"Above all, watchmaking taught me precision," he wrote years later, after he had invented one of the world's most complex pieces of machinery. "I learned to temper a spring to the finest degree, to combine the constituents of metal alloys in exact proportions. I learned how to cut out the finest teeth, to make pins. I realized that, if a movement was to work, it must be considered as a whole, that each part had to be perfect in itself and also harmonize with every other."

At the end of his apprenticeship, Mergenthaler emigrated to the

Linotype was christened by *New York Tribune* publisher, Whitelaw Reid. "It's a line of type," he exclaimed when Mergenthaler, demonstrating the complexities of the new typesetting machine, handed him a metal slug.

U.S., and went to work for the son of his former master, who owned an engineering workshop in Washington D. C.

The workshop's main business was the building of patent models for inventors — and, when Mergenthaler was 22, an inventor named Charles T. Moore walked in to ask for a model of a machine he had just developed.

ASSIGNMENT CHANGED LIFE

Mergenthaler got the assignment, and it changed the course of his life.

Moore's invention was a kind of typewriter that produced a transfer of a page for printing by lithography.

It gave Mergenthaler his first glimpse of the printing industry, and he was immediately fascinated by printing's great, unsolved problem—the mechanical composition of type.

He spent seven more years in the Washington workshop, the last five as a partner, devoting all the time he could to experiments with composing machines.

In 1883, when he went into business for himself, his first working model was just a year away.

INDUSTRY NEED DESPERATE

Printers and publishers — especially newspaper publishers, who were just beginning to build up mass circulations — had for several decades been literally desperate for the kind of machine Mergenthaler was trying to invent.

Over the four centuries since Gutenberg's invention of movable type, dramatic progress had been made in printing and most of its related crafts. Printing press design and operation and papermaking had been improved; electrotyping, lithography, photoengraving and photogravure had been developed.

But type was still composed by hand, as slowly and laboriously as it had been in Gutenberg's day.

And the typesetting bottleneck was blocking the entire industry's progress toward high speed, low cost mass production.

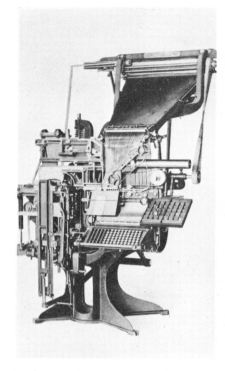

By 1892, when Mergenthaler introduced "star-base" model (above), over 1000 linotypes were in use.

Over 200 19th century inventors had tackled the problem; a number of inventions had been hailed with enthusiasm, won medals and prizes at trade fairs—and promptly broken down in the print shop.

One group of experimenters tried to eliminate type altogether by directly producing an inked transfer for lithographic printing. A second group tried to make use of the principles of stereotyping, with machines that stamped letters one after another onto papier-maché molds for casting in metal. A third simply tried to make machines that could set lead type automatically instead of by hand.

The typesetting machines came closest to success, but they were all too cumbersome, required so many operators that they offered no real economy (the first to be actually installed in a print shop, in 1840, had to be tended by no less than seven men), and, above all, were unable to keep the small pieces of lead type from breaking or sticking.

Ottmar Mergenthaler, during his years of experimentation, tried variations of all three types.

From the papier-maché molds of the stereotype devices, he progressed to metal molds, or matrices, one for each character.

The machine he finally perfected composed these matrices in lines, "justified" their spacing, cast lines of type in molten metal, and redistributed the matrices to repeat the operation. It required only one operator, and set up to 7 lines of type a minute, or more than three times the speed of hand composition. And the sturdy matrices, with sunken impressions of letters, to replace delicate, raised founder's type and to produce solid plates for printing, eliminated breakage.

PROTOTYPE IMPERFECT

Mergenthaler's prototype machine, demonstrated in 1884, did not provide for automatic justification, and its matrices moved on bars rather than independently.

It took him two more years of hard work to correct these deficiencies; but on July 3, 1886, the first Blower Linotype began setting type for the *New York Tribune*.

There was still a danger that the new machine would prove to be uneconomical because of the high cost of the matrices.

When Mergenthaler approached a Baltimore type founder to order 1200 matrices at 6 cents apiece, he was told that the job could not be done for ten times the price.

MADE OWN MATRICES

He solved this problem by designing machinery for high quality, low cost production, and going into the matrix business himself.

He also kept on improving the Linotype.

Before the inventor's death in 1899, three Mergenthaler Linotype plants in Brooklyn, Germany, and England were in full swing, and over 3000 machines were in use.

Today, close to 100,000 Linotypes are setting type—at up to 12 lines a minute—all over the world.

An unsuccessful compositor invented in 1887 by James Paige was called "Mark Twain Machine" because the writer lost fortune promoting it.

The New York Tribune *used first Merganthaler Linotype in 1886. Actual machine with its original operator John T. Miller re-united in 1936.*

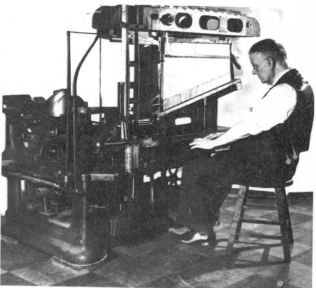

By 1902, sixteen years after New York Tribune *began using machine in U.S., Linotypes had replaced the old hand-typesetting methods at London's Daily Telegraph.*

Mergenthaler Co. exhibits model at an international trade fair in Ceylon where mechanization is catching up.

Today Linotypes are setting type in all corners of the world. Group of Eskimos get demonstration from a compositor working on the Fairbanks, Alaska, News-Miner.

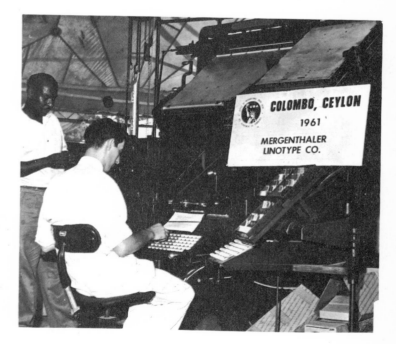

LONG LINES LIFETIME

Theodore N. Vail's faith and flair made long distance telephone practical reality, built up AT&T "empire"

THEODORE N. VAIL

COAST-TO-COAST telephone service became a reality in 1914. *(Below*, wires are strung across Nevada-Utah state line.) Vail had begun securing interstate rights 35 years earlier, when idea of a New York-Chicago call had seemed fantastic.

SAN FRANCISCO-NEW YORK
Nevada-Utah
STATE LINE

THE MAN who did more for the telephone than anyone else but Alexander Graham Bell, who invented it, was Theodore Newton Vail.

Vail was the first general manager (1878-1885) of the original Bell Telephone Co., and twice president of American Telephone & Telegraph Co., which was formed in 1885 as Bell's long distance division and later took the position of parent company which it holds today.

His faith in the future of the telephone was so limitless that he would probably hardly bat an eyelash at the modern AT&T, which has 59.6 million telephones in service. By the early Sixties it was grossing $8.4 billion and leading U.S. industry in assets ($24.6 billion), profits ($1.33 billion) and number of employees (567,000).

He began dreaming of coast-to-coast telephone service in the 1870s, when the telephone appeared to be no more than an ingenious gadget for local communication. He saw that only a national network of affiliated companies under a single top management could provide this kind of service. And he saw—in an age when the typical corporate public relations philosophy was still best expressed by Commodore Vanderbilt's "the public be damned"— that a public utility like the telephone company, near-monopoly though it might be, was peculiarly dependent upon public good will.

Theodore Vail was born in 1845, and grew up in rural New Jersey, the son of an iron manufacturer.

His first few years out of high school were spent as a telegraph operator, first in New York City and then, after the Vail family moved west, in Pinebluff, Wyoming.

In 1869, he joined the U.S. Railway Mail Service as a route agent on an 1100-mile Union Pacific run through the wilderness from Omaha, and began a rise that can only be described as meteoric; seven years later, he was in Washington as General Superintendent of the department.

By 1878, he was getting tired of government service and looking for a job in private business.

The telephone was then barely two years old; Alexander Graham Bell had sent his historic message, "Mr. Wat-

ALEXANDER GRAHAM BELL

son, please come here," to his assistant in the next room of his boarding house on March 10, 1876; he and a few associates had formed the Bell Telephone Co., and were trying to exploit the new gadget's commercial potentialities.

The president of Bell Telephone, Gardiner Hubbard, knew Theodore Vail, and persuaded him to come into the company as general manager.

Vail's Washington friends were staggered.

The First Assistant Postmaster General wrote him, in part:

"I can scarcely believe that a man who holds an honorable and responsible position should throw it up for a damned old Yankee notion (a piece of wire with two Texan steer horns attached to the ends, with an arrangement to make the concern bleat like a calf), called a telephone!"

But Vail was fascinated by the "Yankee notion," and by the administrative challenge of the new business.

Launching a telephone company was very different from manufacturing and marketing an ordinary new consumer product or piece of machinery.

The Bell group had already decided that phones should be rented, rather than sold, to customers, and that service should be provided by central exchanges.

Demand for telephones was mushrooming, but rental fees were not bringing in enough to meet manufacturing costs, and the infant company was facing a law suit against the giant Western Union, which had gone into the telephone business on its own and was violating Bell's patents.

In the summer of 1878, the Western Union telephone was, in fact, far superior to the Bell unit.

Thomas Alva Edison had designed its transmitter, and conversation over a Western Union phone was practically static-free; use of a Bell phone was still, as the inventor's aide, Thomas Watson, had said, "more calculated to develop the American voice and lungs" than to encourage conversation.

Vail spent his first months with the company raising

money, struggling to keep up the morale of discouraged Bell franchise holders who wanted to sell out, and negotiating with Western Union.

By fall, the crisis was past. The company had been reorganized with a capital of $450,000 — a $400,000 increase — and a Boston inventor, Francis Blake, Jr., had come up with an excellent transmitter for the Bell phone.

A year later, Western Union was advised by its attorneys to get out of the telephone business, and the suit was settled out of court.

Vail had not quite put the company on its feet singlehanded; the devotion and personal sacrifice of the other Bell executives had counted for a great deal, and Blake's transmitter was a magnificent piece of luck.

But the new General Manager's energy and optimism, the administrative genius that had carried him to the top of the Railway Mail Service in only seven years, and his vast talents for dealing with people and for fund-raising

INSTITUTIONAL AD CAMPAIGN launched by Vail in 1907 was aimed at removing public distrust of Bell "monopoly." One of the arguments it advanced was that only a national company could afford to maintain service in unprofitable areas.

The Telephone's Burden

EVERY day brings a new use—a new requirement. It is the Telephone's Burden not only to keep pace with business development, but to camp constantly a little across the frontier.

Can you imagine a city, as cities once existed, made up of several "quarters," to each of which was confined a population which spoke a separate language?

You, as the average citizen, would be forced to learn several languages, or to go about the city with an interpreter—a process that would seriously interfere with your business.

If, instead of using different languages, the people of a city used *different telephone systems*, the result would be exactly the same. You would have to keep *each particular brand* of telephone.

It is nobody's *fault* that this is so. The Bell companies are not responsible for the fact that a nation's convenience demands the use of one telephone system, any more than they are that *our language* for a nation is better than a collection of provincial dialects.

The associated Bell companies, with their singleness of purpose and unity of service, *are* responsible, however, for doing their utmost to *provide the system that wholly fits this recognized condition*—that prevents the endless and expensive confusion of many systems.

The Telephone's Burden is to embrace in *one* comprehensive system all that a city, or the whole country, needs in the way of telephone service.

This has made the telephone universal.

To-day's work of carrying sixteen million messages—some of business, some of joy and some of sorrow—is not all of the *day's burden*, either.

Preparing for to-morrow's quota of message-passengers on this great national highway of speech is a labor quite as heavy as to-day's actual work. For in the Bell service to-morrow never comes.

The associated Bell companies' eighty thousand workers are *always* preparing for it—always working to keep pace with the new requirements, forecast by to-day's routine.

People have rapidly developed this *new sense*—the sense of projecting speech. As the sense develops they are learning more about the telephone's possibilities. Twenty million minds are constantly finding new uses for it.

We must immediately adapt the entire Bell system to these new uses.

A realization of this widespread work should clear your mind of doubt, if any exists, that the associated Bell companies are working *with* and *for* the public, striving by the most progressive methods to provide a telephone service that will take your voice anywhere that your thought goes, or your friend goes, or your letter will travel—sometimes even farther than your imagination will carry you—, whether it is half way across the town or half way across the country.

The Bell service is diligently keeping pace with the country's progress, in full knowledge of existing conditions and the necessities of the future.

It goes to the public with such statements as this, in order that all telephone subscribers may understand the position it occupies as a utility, may make their demands on the service intelligently; may readily see that rates must perforce be regulated and continue on an equitable business basis in order to provide the maximum number of subscribers—to make the system universal; that they may fully understand that co-operation of subscriber and telephone company is the *surest guarantee* of good service.

American Telephone & Telegraph Company

And Its Associated Bell Companies

LOCAL AND LONG DISTANCE TELEPHONE

One Policy—One System Universal Service

UNITING OVER 4,000,000 TELEPHONES

Set corporate public relations pattern

had done a great deal to turn the tide. And from then on, these same qualities, coupled with almost prophetic vision and with a rare gift for taking the right step at the right time, were to make him largely responsible for his new company's spectacular success.

Expansion speeded up; it was easy, in a town of any size, to find a young man who wanted to organize and sell stock in a local Bell telephone company.

Vail insisted on the building of exchanges that linked two or more towns, although there was still little demand for such service and most local companies were reluctant to spend the money.

He even began securing inter-state rights.

He was already envisioning a national telephone network in which Bell would be a permanent partner.

Bell stock was soaring; it rose from $50 a share in 1878 to $1000 a share after the Western Union settlement. Vail, who had substantial holdings in the parent company and in the flourishing New York City subsidiary as well, was a millionaire at 35.

When Vail joined the company, in 1878, there were fewer than 10,000 Bell telephones in the U.S. By 1881, there were over 130,000, serviced by 408 exchanges.

In 1884, the first New York-Boston circuit was completed; Vail's dream of a transcontinental network was a few miles closer to reality, and in 1885, the American Telephone & Telegraph Co. was formed for further development of the Bell System's long lines, with Theodore N. Vail as president.

In 1887, with over 50,000 miles of long lines in operation, Vail left the telephone company.

He was in poor health; he wanted more time for his investments; and, very probably, his passion for growth

was bringing him into conflict with the increasingly conservative management of the company.

He had moved during the '80s, with his wife and son, to a magnificent home in Boston, bought a farm in Vermont for summer use, and begun entertaining lavishly and almost continuously at both establishments. His hobbies, with which he expected to keep busy during his retirement, were carriage horses, sailing and stocks.

Ever since he had begun to earn money (or been able to borrow it—thrift was about the only business virtue which Theodore Vail did not possess), he had speculated, always enthusiastically, often brilliantly, sometimes disastrously in ventures ranging from the manufacture of electric storage batteries to a California ostrich farm.

Over the 20 years between 1887 and 1907, his most notable speculative accomplishments were losing practically his whole fortune on a scheme for heating cities by piping hot water underground, and then recouping it in an Argentine electric power development project.

In 1907, AT&T—now the parent company of the Bell System—invited him to come back as president, and he accepted.

During his 20 years of absence, the system had grown prodigiously—and had run into serious trouble.

Insufficient provision had been made for maintenance of existing telephone installations and for purchase of new equipment; many Bell exchanges throughout the country had become badly run down.

And competition had reared its head again—this time, in the form of small, independent, local companies, which, with brand new equipment, shoddy though it often was, were able to offer better service.

The local companies had a psychological advantage,

108

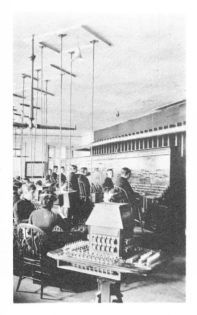

too; anti-big business feeling was running high in the early years of the new century, and the Bell System was a perfect target for attacks as a "monopoly."

However, the public soon found out that competition in the telephone business meant that the average homeowner or storekeeper had to install two or more telephones and keep track of which service his friends or customers patronized.

And, as the new companies began making the same mistake Bell had made and allowing their equipment to run down (many of them had been able to offer low rates by making no provision for maintenance whatsoever), Bell, which had been repairing and refurbishing, began getting business back.

This did not, however, make the giant any more popular.

Back in the presidency, Vail met the challenge of the independents by offering them consolidation practically on their own terms—and many of them were happy to accept.

Then he turned his attention to the public relations problem. He launched an "institutional" advertising campaign—one of the first—with a six-figure budget. He began issuing annual reports of the type common today but practically unheard of then, in which the company's problems and policies were fully and frankly discussed. He encouraged newspaper publicity, and himself wrote a stream of magazine articles on public utilities, in which he did not even hesitate to use the dread word, "monopoly."

He seems to have sincerely believed that the truth—attractively presented whenever possible, of course—could not possibly hurt the Bell System.

In 1908, when Bell's advertising agency, N. W. Ayer, presented an ad with the headline, "One Policy, One System, Universal Service," the company's own advertising director suggested that it might attract the unfavorable attention of trust-busting politicians.

"Is it true?" Vail asked.

The advertising director admitted that it was.

"Very well, then," Vail replied, "let's print it and beat them to it."

Vail's design for public relations, which he was to continue developing until his retirement from the presidency in 1919, has served as a model for the best corporate public relations programs of the present day.

THEODORE VAIL IN HIS 70'S

MAIL ORDER

Richard Warren Sears, founder of the $4 billion Sears,

SEARS *(above)*, clean shaven in his 20s, later cultivated handle-bar mustache to match partner Roebuck's *(below)*. Rosenwald's *(r.)* was more sedate.

THE U.S. mass consumer market of the late 19th Century was less opulent than today's—but it was hungry and fast-growing, and offered dazzling opportunities to imaginative merchandisers.

One of these merchandising pioneers was Richard Warren Sears, founder of Sears, Roebuck & Co., which started this decade with sales of over $4 billion.

Young Sears went into the mail order business in 1886, when large-scale mail order merchandising was a relatively new idea. (His firm's only major competitor, Montgomery Ward, had begun operations in 1873.)

FIRST SEARS STORE was North Redwood, Minn., railroad station where young Sears sold watches. Most small town station agents of 1880s had businesses on the side.

110

MAGICIAN

Roebuck mail order empire, wrote catalogs that talked hard-headed buyers' language

Mail order catalogs were aimed primarily at the nation's largest consumer group, farmers and small town residents, who in 1880 made up 71.8% of the U.S. population.

As Richard Sears, who had grown up in Minnesota farming towns, knew, farmers had little money to spare, and did not want frills.

They did want agricultural equipment, home furnishings and supplies and sturdy work clothes at rockbottom prices. When they splurged a few dollars on a Sunday suit or a watch, they were interested in price first, quality second.

Sears knew, too, that in an age of

stock jokes about country bumpkins and city slickers, the average farmer was afraid of being cheated, or made to look foolish, or both, if he did business with city folks.

It was his knowledge of these facts of rural life, together with a natural talent for and unbounded love of selling, that gave Richard Sears his phenomenal success.

He offered his customers the goods they needed at unbeatable prices, and wrote his catalog copy in such reassuringly folksy terms that fears of city slickers in Chicago vanished when the farmer opened the big book.

Sears, who had left high school

and gone to work as a telegraph operator at 16, was 23 years old and working as a station agent in North Redwood, Minn., in 1886, when one day a shipment of watches arrived from a Chicago jewelery company, addressed to a local jeweler.

The jeweler had not ordered the watches and refused to accept them, so Sears promptly wrote to Chicago and offered to sell them himself.

Then he began telegraphing his fellow station agents up and down the line, letting them know he was in the watch business.

The watches vanished, and Sears ordered more.

He made a $500 profit in six months, moved to Minneapolis, and set up the R. W. Sears Watch Co., in a $10-a-month office furnished with a kitchen table and a few 50¢ chairs.

Business (still conducted largely through station agents) boomed, and in 1887, Sears moved to Chicago, the rail hub of the Middle West.

About then, however, the watches began to come back for repairs, and Sears advertised for a watchmaker.

His ad was answered by a young man his own age, Alvah C. Roebuck, who was hired to repair the watches, and became a partner in Sears' fastgrowing enterprise within a few months.

Roebuck does not seem to have been exceptionally talented, but he had what Sears wanted — boundless admiration for the talents of Richard Warren Sears, and plenty of capacity for hard work. (Sears himself was already working from seven in the morning to 10 or 11 at night.)

The company issued its first catalog in 1887, and began selling to the general public in 1888.

1960 MODEL STORE is part of Tampa, Fla., shopping center. Sears entered the retail field when the automobile made its customers less dependent on mail order catalogs.

Sears decided that a successful mail order merchant had to offer his customers three things: absolute assurance of honesty, a chance to see the goods before being committed to buy, and prices low enough to make up for the fact that mail ordering was still unconventional.

The first catalog, like all its successors, offered a flat money-back-if-not-satisfied guarantee.

The ethical standards of merchandising in the 1880s were not high, and Sears was by no means above bamboozling customers with extravagant adjectives and sky-high claims when he thought he could get away with it.

However, he and other mail order pioneers did a great deal to raise the standards of merchandising.

A catalog had to offer a fixed price and stick to it, unlike a retailer, who could—and often did—charge whatever he thought the customer would pay.

And it had to offer the money-back guarantee to win the business of the suspicious farmers.

So, within a few years, retailers began to realize that they had to adopt the same "customer is always right" policies or lose all their business to the mail order houses.

And manufacturers had to meet the new demand of mail order houses and retailers alike for goods of reliable quality that would not bring a flood of returns.

By 1893, the year in which the Sears, Roebuck & Co. name was adopted, Sears' catalog was offering furniture, dishes, clothing, harnesses and saddles, guns, wagons and buggies, bicycles, shoes, baby carriages, musical instruments and sewing machines as well as watches and jewelry.

Sears wrote every line of catalog copy himself, and supervised its makeup, violating every rule in the advertising man's book.

"White space" was kept to an irreducible minimum, pages were crowded with tiny type and blurred woodcuts.

But Sears, Roebuck customers obviously liked it. The company's 1892 sales volume was $296,368.

The catalog was supplemented by heavy advertising in the so-called "mail order magazines," small monthlies popular with rural readers.

For Richard Sears, there was simply no such thing as too many orders. In fact, he liked to get orders first, then worry about filling them.

His 1895 promotion of men's suits was typical.

He advertised 2000 suits at $4.98 C.O.D., and another 1000 at $8.95, describing them in glowing terms and asserting that "we are the largest handlers of clothing in America."

Orders came flooding in. The clerks in Sears, Roebuck's Chicago offices were swamped; buyers began scouring the market to find the suits, which had existed only in Sears' imagination when the ads were placed, and the shipping department hopelessly jumbled colors, sizes and fabrics.

Such spectacular promotions in-

motion that kept it growing.

Among his promotional schemes were free gift offers, a Customers' Profit Sharing Premium Plan which was, in effect, the forerunner of today's trading stamp plans, and a catalog distribution system under which regular customers got catalogs to pass along to their friends, and received merchandise bonuses for their friends' orders.

Sales passed the $10 million mark in 1900. Sears, Roebuck had gained, and was never to lose, undisputed first place in the mail order field.

Its chief opposition came from country general stores and small town retailers, who were so afraid of mail order competition that they organized public catalog-burnings.

Both Rosenwald and Nusbaum had

	1900 Sales Profits ($ million)		1920 Sales Profits ($ million)		1940 Sales Profits ($ million)		1960 Sales Profits ($ million)	
LEADING MAIL ORDER HOUSES								
Company								
Sears, Roebuck	10.6	0.9	245.4	11.8	704.3	36.1	4036.2	198.7
Montgomery Ward	8.8	0.5	101.7	7.9	474.8	27.0	1222.6	30.7
Spiegel	......	......	n.a.	n.a.	53.5	1.8	268.8	11.8
Aldens*	......	......	7.0	−.3	26.7	.3	114.7	3.4
National Bellas Hess**	n.a.	n.a.	47.7	−1.3	3.4	−.2	48.9	1.3
New Process	......	......	n.a.	n.a.	5.1	.3	22.1	.7

* Known as Chicago Mail Order Co. until 1946.
** Present firm purchased receivership of earlier company of same name in 1932. Original National Bellas Hess was known as National Cloak and Suit Co. until 1927.

creased sales volume to $750,000 in 1895.

They also brought the company to a state of complete administrative chaos, and Alvah Roebuck to physical collapse and early retirement.

The firm's liabilities had risen to more than three times the amount permitted under its charter of incorporation, and Sears began looking for new investors.

He found them in Aaron Nusbaum, who had made a fortune with a soda pop and ice cream concession at the 1893 Chicago Columbian Exposition, and Nusbaum's brother-in-law, Julius Rosenwald, a clothing manufacturer.

Sears retained the presidency of the company, recapitalized at $150,000. Rosenwald became vice president and Nusbaum treasurer.

Julius Rosenwald's talent for administration and finance was as great as Sears' for advertising and sales; from 1895 on, he ran the business while Sears concentrated on the pro-

a preference, incomprehensible to Sears, for knowing how they were going to fill an order before advertising for customers.

Nusbaum was the more conservative of the two, and he and Sears found it impossible to work together. He sold out in 1903.

The clash of personalities between Sears and Rosenwald was less acute; the two men seem to have had the greatest respect for each other.

When Sears retired in 1908, leaving Rosenwald in the presidency, ill health was his most important reason; he died in 1914. His departure ended the most colorful era of Sears, Roebuck history.

Today, over half of Sears' $4 billion sales volume comes from its chain of retail stores, begun in 1925, and more ordering is done by telephone than by mail. But the catalog that Richard Sears made a part of everyday U.S. life is still the cornerstone of all mail order merchandising.

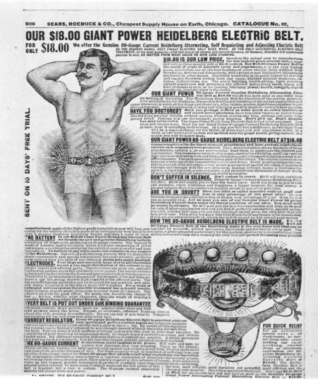

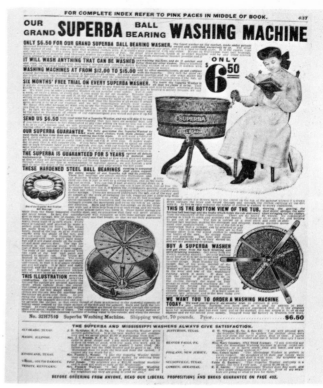

TYPICAL PAGES OF EARLY CATALOGS FEATURED ELECTRIC BELT (SUPPOSED MALE DISEASE CURE-ALL), HAND-CRANKED WASHING MACHINE

CATALOG STYLE grew more conservative after Sears retired. 1913 page shows use of fewer adjectives, more "white space."

1897 CATALOG COVER emphasized company's financial stability, listing bank references and new $150,000 capitalization.

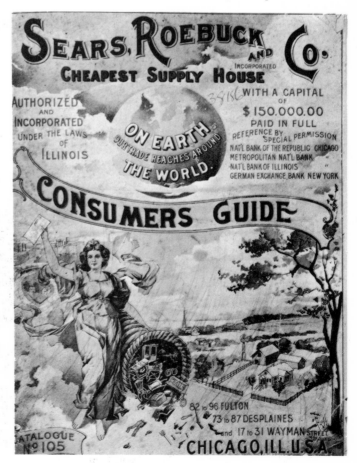

JOHN J. PATTERSON bought factory and rights from James Ritty, saloonkeeper who invented first NCR model in 1879.

MAKING SALES REGISTER

NCR's John Patterson blazed salesmanship's sawdust trail, pioneered "education" of customer

"PEDESTAL PAD," standard in all NCR classes, is used by "The Chief" to demonstrate his personal set of resolutions.

WHENEVER, today, a potential customer listens to a salesman, he is also hearing the ghostly voice of John J. Patterson, who in the 1880s "invented" scientific salesmanship.

His pioneering not only transformed an insolvent little factory into the mammoth National Cash Register Co. (1960 sales, some $450 million), but also established a technique employed virtually every time one person tries to sell something to another.

In 1884, the 41-year-old Patterson, a former coal dealer who never in his life had attempted a direct sale, impulsively paid $6500 for a small Dayton, Ohio, firm which was making—but not selling—a crude type of cash register. (It punched holes in tapes, forcing clerks to report sales, and was the first which recorded cash totals automatically.)

Unfortunately, there was absolutely no market for the machine—stores and offices were still content with traditional methods and equipment. Only a few saloon keepers bought the "thief catcher" to trip up light-fingered bartenders.

Patterson, after adopting the name "National Cash Register," saw that his first job was to create a demand for his register by educating merchants to its use. Both selling and advertising, Patterson decided, must be teaching—teaching people to desire your product. Up till then selling had been order taking. Advertising, for the most part, had been announcement of goods on hand.

He lured 10 full-time sales agents by offering them exclusive territories —a radical idea—and unusually high commissions. By deliberately overpaying, and by refusing to cut the commission rate as a man's sales increased (both startling departures from the business practices of the time), he felt he would push men to sell harder.

A list of 5000 PP's (as he referred to prospective purchasers) was drawn up and bombarded for 18 successive days with NCR circulars. This first known instance of concentrated pressure was so unusual that one merchant returned the 10th mailing with the notation: "Let up. We never done you any harm."

Then Patterson went to work on

SALES TRAINING classes, often taught by Patterson himself, emphasized such points as stay at best hotels, impress potential prospects, don't bore them with dull, long arguments, get them away from their own offices if possible.

his salesmen, who had been receiving a somewhat less than enthusiastic welcome when they visited customers' premises. Resentful clerks and bartenders, who felt the registers were a slur on their integrity, threatened strong arm tactics, staged walkout demonstrations and even sabotaged register mechanisms.

Convinced that salesmen are made, not born, Patterson set about remaking his men within an inch of their lives. He brought out a primer which standardized sales demonstrations by literally spelling out the pitch word-for-word. Basic philosophy of the primer was first to make a friend of a PP and then bring him to a hotel or showroom—away from the distractions of his business—before trying to sell him.

The primer was followed up by a manual which provided answers to every possible objection by a PP.

In the Panic of 1893 he did not retrench, but doubled advertising and intensified sales pressure in a whirlwind tour of front-line trenches—50 towns in 51 days.

Agents really felt the crack of Patterson's whip. Up till then most salesmen had taken the primer with a grain of salt; after this trip they memorized it—or else. During the trip he recognized the need for pool information and pioneered in scheduling regular sales conventions.

It all paid off—NCR really came into its own during the panic. While U.S. business dropped to nothing, NCR had a record year: 15,487 units.

Patterson insisted that 87% of all education was visual, and that the best way to teach was through the eye. This principle was applied in the school, in the primer, and at every conference. Once, at a meeting to discuss production bugs, Patterson had the entire weekly payroll dumped on the platform in a pile of gold and silver coins. His point was that unless every worker "pulled his own weight," there would be no heap to distribute.

One of Patterson's favorite visual aids was diagramming. He also had a system of cartooning or chart talks —for example, pedestal pads on artist's easels became standard equipment in every NCR office. He loved to make little dramas out of sales demonstrations, and would build full sets to simulate a store interior.

Advertising, too, was just another form of teaching to Patterson. He was one of the first men outside of the patent medicine industry to make advertising an integral part of his business. True to form, he had very strong ideas on copy and layout. His rules were: few words and short words; no ad is large enough for two ideas; pictures are more convincing than description (every ad had to have a picture of a register).

Patterson encouraged able men to come to the top, but at the same time his attitude was, "when it gets to the point where a man feels he's indispensable, fire him." Thus, potential threats to Patterson's authority were eliminated.

Industry became dotted with such too-powerful men as Thomas J. Watson of International Business Machines, who went on from NCR to head their own companies.

NCR was organized on Patterson's favorite pattern—the pyramid—with responsibilities carefully delegated so that top management could have time for operational planning. The "Chief" would often pull an executive out of his department for a few days to see how well it ran without him.

Efforts to regulate his men extend-ed beyond their business lives. He ran conventions to teach wives how to help their husbands, suggesting that they avoid late hours, help rehearse sales demonstrations and shop in stores without registers to point out the need to the owner.

Patterson urged his men to cut down on drinking and smoking, take baths more frequently and dress carefully (one agent was fired for "sporting" a white silk scarf and a diamond shirt pin). He even had the head valet at the Waldorf Astoria prepare a booklet on correct dress for every occasion for NCR salesmen.

To give his men a taste of the richer things in life — and thus stimulate them to want more and work harder —he would send executives and their wives to Europe with instructions to spend freely. Clerks would be picked out of departments at random and

WELFARE PROGRAM INCLUDED ON-THE-JOB CALISTHENICS, PROFIT-SHARING FOR EVERY EMPLOYE, INCLUDING ODD-JOB MEN, MESSENGER BOYS

sent to a fine tailor in New York for several suits of clothes.

In taking care of his factory workers—because well-paid people working under optimum conditions will produce more—he embarked on an advanced program of industrial welfare. He started by cleaning the factory and installing showers (men were allowed two baths a week on company time). He ended up with complete, modern, healthy recreational facilities (including lunchtime movies and lectures) and a profit-sharing plan that extended right down to the messenger boys.

The intense drive of his business life, unmixed with any home life whatsoever (his wife had died early and a sister raised his two children), led to chronic indigestion. He found a diet cultist in Europe who prescribed a 37-day starvation cure, from which he never completely recovered.

To regain strength he picked up a trainer in London, brought him back to Dayton and, true to form, soon had all his executives exercising with him. All executives had to be at the factory at 5 a.m. for calesthenics, a rub down, horseback ride and bath. Any executive who refused to join the dawn patrol quickly ceased to be an executive.

Patterson became a real health faddist and for a time would take four or five baths a day. For years he drank a glass of hot, distilled water every half hour.

At 76, Patterson made his son Frederick president, but remained as board chairman to "keep an eye on the store." He died a year later, in 1920.

Today National Cash Register, with an annual volume of $600 million (500 U.S. offices and trading in 120 countries), has expanded into fields even Patterson could not have foreseen. Eighty per cent of last year's sales were derived from such new devices as electronic accounting machines, not even in existence 10 years ago.

But, wherever NCR does business, and whenever NCR makes a sale, the "Chief" is still present. A demonstration easel stands in every office, and his primer and manual still are the basis of every salesman's approach.

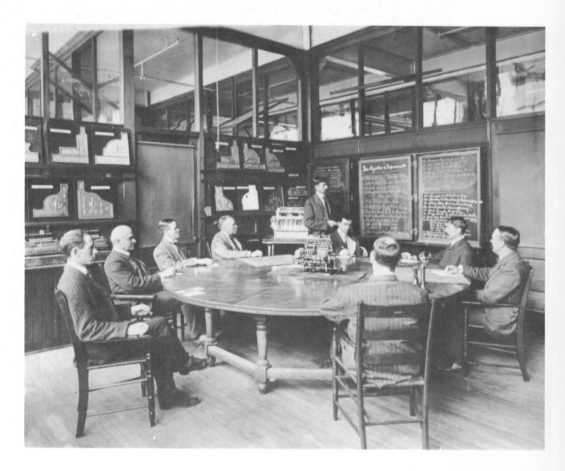

ORGANIZED research and development (*below*, 1904) had top management role. Creativity paid off in big savings.

EMERGENCY department looked like this in 1905. NCR under Patterson was pioneer in improving working standards.

THE EYE, Patterson insisted, was best means of reaching the customer. Advertising art dept. *(above,* 1900) was hub of management planning; all ads included picture of register.

PATERNALISM under Patterson extended to clothes, diet of workers. Company cooking school *(below)* was visited in 1898 by Horace Fletcher (at table), famed dietician of day.

N. C. R. Cooking School

Average weekly Earnings day labor $9.00
family's cost of food $6.00
Scientific Cookery gives better food for $3.00

Oct 28'98

GEORGE EASTMAN

HE CLICKED THE SHUTTER FOR BILLIONS OF SNAPSHOTS

George Eastman invented film, low-priced camera, created $2-billion-a-year industry, turned whole U.S. into nation of camera fans

THE MAN who turned the U.S. into a nation of shutterbugs — and photography into a multi-million-dollar industry — was George Eastman, founder of Eastman Kodak Co.

Back in 1877, when Eastman, then a 23-year-old Rochester, N. Y., bank clerk, took up photography as a hobby, taking a picture called for a back-breaking 70 pounds of equipment, considerable knowledge of photographic chemistry and infinite patience and skill.

Not surprisingly, amateur photographers were a very small, dedicated band—and even professionals were considered slightly crazy by the general public.

Today, photography is probably the No. 1 U.S. hobby. One American in three is a camera fan. Over 2 billion snapshots are shot each year, and total retail sales of cameras, film, and other photographic supplies and equipment are over $2.5 billion.

Eastman Kodak alone had 1960 sales of $945 million — about three quarters from photographic products, the rest from synthetic fibers, plastics and chemicals.

And, while Eastman is the giant of the field simply because it produces every type of photographic goods, it has plenty of competition, both domestic (from such firms as Ansco, Bell & Howell, Polaroid, Du Pont) and foreign, in all its product lines.

George Eastman's contributions to photography were dazzling in their simplicity—he invented film, and he invented a box camera that anyone could use.

Before Eastman came along, the only suitable negative material was glass. Every picture required a separate glass plate, and, since photographic emulsion would not keep, it had to be made on the spot and then applied to the plate, exposed and developed while still wet.

This meant that a photographer setting out for an afternoon's shooting had to take along a camera as big as a soap box, a heavy tripod, a "dark tent" for preparation and developing of his glass plates, a supply of plates in a heavy folder, chemicals, developing tanks and water.

George Eastman, unlike the other photographers of his day, decided that there must be a way to make all this

KODAK SLOGAN made advertising history in late 19th Century, got sales of first box camera off to a fast start.

The Kodak Camera

"You press the button,
- - - - we do the rest."

The only camera that anybody can use without instructions. Send for the Primer free.

The Kodak is for sale by all Photo stock dealers.

A Transparent Film
For Roll Holders.

The announcement is hereby made that the undersigned have perfected a process for making transparent flexible films for use in roll holders and Kodak Cameras.

The new film is as thin, light and flexible as paper and as transparent as glass. It requires *no stripping*, and it is wound on spools for roll holders. It will be known as *Eastman's Transparent Film*. Circulars and samples will be sent to any address on receipt of 4 cents in stamps.

Price $25.00—Loaded for 100 Pictures.

The Eastman Dry Plate and Film Co.
ROCHESTER, N. Y.

PICTURE-SNAPPING became a popular hobby in the 1890s, when Eastman's small cameras, flexible film eliminated wet-plate photography's 70-pound equipment.

misery unnecessary—and set about finding one.

Eastman had left school at 14 and gone to work as a $3-a-week office boy to help support his widowed mother and two sisters. He had studied accounting at home in the evenings, joined the Rochester Savings Bank as a junior clerk at 20, and moved up to a bookkeeper's job and a salary of $800 a year—a fairly substantial one for 1870s.

He was a thrifty, hard-working, intelligent young man who might very well have become a successful banker if he had not almost succumbed to a streak of wanderlust when he was 23. He began planning a vacation trip to— of all places—Santo Domingo, and a friend at the bank urged him to take up photography so that he could bring home pictures of the Central American jungles.

He gave up Santo Domingo for a less adventurous trip to the Great Lakes, but he did become a thoroughly competent wet plate photographer.

By 1878, he was more interested in photography than

CAMERA that revolutionized photography was the 1888 model No. 1 Kodak, basically similar to today's simple models.

in banking, and was avidly reading about the attempts of British photographers to make gelatin emulsions that would remain sensitive when dry so that their plates would not have to be exposed and developed immediately.

Although he had never spent a day in a chemistry class, he began experimenting with a gelatin emulsion of his own in his mother's kitchen.

His hobby became a passion. He worked at the bank all day, mixed emulsions all night, and, as his mother told the story years later, slept through from Saturday night to Monday morning every week.

By 1879, he had invented not only a practical dry-plate emulsion, but also an emulsion coating machine for mass production of the plates.

In 1880, he began running a dry-plate business at night in the loft of a factory building.

And a year later, he went into partnership with Henry A. Strong, a Rochester buggy whip manufacturer who boarded with the Eastman family, and left the bank to devote full time to photography.

Strong, as the older of the two and the more experienced businessman, became president of the new company; Eastman was treasurer and general manager.

By 1883, the Eastman Dry Plate Co. was flourishing, and moved into a four-story building at what is now 343 State St., and still the headquarters of Eastman Kodak.

Eastman then began turning his attention to the development of a light, flexible negative material to replace glass plates, which, even when they could be used dry, were still too bulky, inconvenient and expensive.

By 1885—also the year in which the firm opened its first foreign office, in London—he was advertising that "shortly will be introduced a new sensitive film, which, it is believed, will prove an economical and convenient substitute for glass dry plates, for indoor or outdoor work."

This first film was made of paper, and carried in the camera on a roll holder which substituted for the plate holder.

It was not entirely satisfactory, because the grain of the paper was likely to appear in the print.

FIRST FACTORY of Eastman Dry Plate Co. occupied site where Eastman Kodak's administrative offices stand today.

Eastman pioneered in employe benefits, climaxed career by huge gifts

So Eastman coated the paper with a layer of plain, soluble gelatin, and then a second layer of insoluble, light-sensitive gelatin. After exposure, the gelatin was stripped from the paper, transferred to a sheet of clear gelatin, and varnished with collodion.

This type of film produced satisfactory prints, but Eastman kept on trying to get rid of the paper base. In 1886, he hired a full-time research chemist.

In the meantime, he and Strong were discovering that the professional photography market was far too small for their production potential.

The way to make real money, they decided, was to reach the general public, and the way to do this was to invent a small, light, easy-to-use camera.

In 1888, the first Kodak appeared on the market.

The trade name was invented by Eastman himself; he wanted a short, catchy word that would be easy to spell and pronounce in any language, and he liked the letter "K".

Eastman also coined the famous Kodak advertising slogan, "You press the button—we do the rest."

This was literally true. The No. 1 Kodak Camera sold for $25, loaded with enough film for 100 exposures. When all the pictures had been taken, the owner simply mailed the camera to Rochester with $10 for developing and printing of the old film and reloading with a new roll.

In 1889, the first non-paper-based film—a transparent roll on a base of cellulose nitrate—was marketed, and one of its first buyers was Thomas Edison, who used it to produce the first 35-millimeter motion pictures.

The first folding Kodak camera was introduced in 1890, the first daylight-loading camera and film in 1891.

Use of Kodak dry plates for X-ray began in 1895.

And in 1900, the first Brownie camera—priced at $1 with film that sold for 15¢ a roll—made photography a hobby that practically anyone could afford.

Eastman did not become president of his own company until 1919, when Strong retired. He became chairman of the board in 1925, and served until his death in 1932.

He accumulated a personal fortune of over $100 mil-

121

lion, and gave most of it away during his lifetime—$51 million to the University of Rochester, $20 million to Massachusetts Institute of Technology, and millions more to schools, hospitals, dental clinics and civic associations in Rochester and throughout the world.

His favorite project was probably the launching of the Rochester School of Music and Symphony Orchestra.

He loved music, although his talents as a performer were non-existent; as a young man, he had bought a flute and spent two years trying unsuccessfully to learn to play "Annie Laurie."

He visited Europe every year, and went on a number of African safaris.

Quiet, shy, and straight-laced, George Eastman was nevertheless a popular employer. (Eastman Kodak was among the first major companies to introduce payment for employe suggestions, profit-sharing, a company stock plan and similar fringe benefits.) He was also, for years before his death, the best-known and best-loved citizen of Rochester, N. Y.

And his life's work, the development of photography, still deserves to be called—as it was by the *New York Times* in an obituary editorial—"a stupendous factor in the education of the modern world."

PHOTOGRAPHIC PAPER, film and other photo supplies pour in endless stream from Eastman's giant, highly automated modern Rochester plant, still centered on the original site.

PHILANTHROPIST EASTMAN was camera-shy but posed in 1931 with Rush Rhees, president of Univ. of Rochester, which received $51 million of Eastman fortune.

WHOLESALE VALUE OF PHOTOGRAPHIC PRODUCTS	
Year	$ million
1880	.2
1899	7.8
1909	22.6
1919	88.4
1929	102.8
1939	133.1
1950	432.9
1960	959.0

Source: U.S. Department of Commerce

Thomas Edison, right, was guest of honor at announcement ceremonies of Kodacolor film in 1928 at Eastman House. Although Eastman, left, and Edison had worked together through their companies on the development of the motion picture, this occasion marked their first personal meeting.

122

Lighting contract for Chicago's 1893 World's Fair went to George Westinghouse and his new AC system.

HE ELECTRIFIED INDUSTRY

Westinghouse's AC transformer made
economic distribution of electric power possible

IN DECEMBER, 1880, George Westinghouse of Pittsburgh paid a visit to Menlo Park, N. J.

The purpose of his trip was to see the first public demonstration of Thomas Alva Edison's newly perfected electric light—a dramatic night-time illumination of the entire park.

Like the hundreds of other spectators, Westinghouse went home that night dazzled by the potentialities of electric power. But he had also spotted the weak point in the Edison system—the short range of the direct current produced by its generators—and decided that he could improve upon it.

At 34, Westinghouse was already a noted engineer, inventor, and industrialist.

But in the years ahead, his contributions to the development of electric power—not only as a light source, but also as the workhorse

of industry and transportation— were to win him a place among the greatest technological pioneers of his amazing era.

Westinghouse was born in 1846, the son of a well-to-do machine shop owner in upstate New York.

He began working part-time in the shop while he was still in his early teens, rigging up ingenious devices to speed his chores and spending most of his time building model engines.

Then, after two years of active service in the Civil War and a semester at Union College—all that was needed to persuade his culturally ambitious father that he had no bent for the liberal arts—he went into the family business full time.

Before he was 21, however, he had patented his first major invention and launched his own manufacturing firm.

The invention was a railroad "car

replacer"—a mechanism that hoisted derailed cars (frequently seen in those pioneer days of railroading) back onto the track in a fraction of the time it had taken train crews to do the job manually.

The fast-growing business of railroading was as challenging as a young engineer of the 1860's and 70's could find. It gave Westinghouse his start, and he never lost his enthusiasm for it. (By a pleasant coincidence, he even met his wife—with whom he was to spend over 40 unusually happy years—on a train trip.)

Shortly after he perfected his car replacer, he began working on the device that the railroads needed most urgently — an efficient, quick-acting brake.

The trains of the 60s were brought to a halt by a cumbersome arrangement of handwheels on each platform, linked to chains that ran

123

George Westinghouse spotted weak point in Edison's system, put together transformer used in today's AC.

Early (1886-89) Westinghouse power plants grew rapidly. Many small belt-driven alternators were used.

beneath the cars and tightened brakes as the wheels were turned.

A crew of skilled brakemen needed half a mile's leeway to bring a train to a smooth stop, and disastrous collisions were common.

Lack of the right brake was holding back the railroad's expansion more than any other single factor —bigger, faster trains could have been built and put into operation, but they almost literally could not have been stopped.

For more than a year, Westinghouse experimented with various steam-powered braking devices, but they were all too cumbersome.

Then he came across a magazine article that described the revolutionary compressed-air drilling equipment being used in the construction of the Mont Cenis tunnel through the Alps.

There, he saw, was the answer— compressed air could be used equally well to power a compact braking system.

Within a few months, he had applied for patents on his air brake and was trying to peddle it to the railroads. But railroad men from Commodore Vanderbilt on down simply laughed at the idea that air could be used to stop a train.

In the meantime, Westinghouse's car replacer business was running into trouble. Sales were falling off, and the young inventor's partners (both older men and business veterans) were trying to edge him out of the company and keep the pat-

ents for the device.

Westinghouse managed to win the patent fight, however, and left the family home in Schenectady to head for Pittsburgh, the fast-growing center of the iron and steel industry. There, he hoped, he would find a larger company interested in taking over the car replacer.

He not only succeeded in this venture, making a profitable arrangement with the firm of Anderson & Cook, but also, within a few months, found a local railroad that was willing to give the air brake a try.

In April, 1869, the air brake got its first run—from Pittsburgh to Steubenville and back on the Steubenville Division of the Panhandle Railroad.

And a few minutes out of Pittsburgh, it showed what it could do.

The train was chugging along at 30 miles an hour when its horrified engineer saw a horsedrawn wagon no more than two blocks ahead of him on the tracks. No team of brakemen could have stopped the train in time to avert disaster.

But the air brake did—just four feet from the horses, which had gone out of control in their fright and were plunging sideways toward the locomotive.

The rest of the run, during which all scheduled stops were made smoothly, was anticlimactic — the brake had already sold itself to Panhandle, and to every other railroad in the business.

Three months later, the Westinghouse Air Brake Co. was chartered, with a capitalization of $500,000. Westinghouse, at 23, was on his way.

For most of the next two decades, he devoted himself primarily to the railroad equipment business, developing scores of automatic safety and control devices that made vital contributions to the program of rail transportation.

His second company, Union Switch & Signal, was founded in the year of 1881.

In the mid-80s, almost as a sideline, he turned his attention to natural gas.

His interest was aroused when he discovered a natural gas well on his own property. Within a matter of months, he had developed and patented a "system for conveying and utilizing gas under pressure" that overcame hitherto insurmountable obstacles to the efficient use of the hard-to-handle fuel. Then he organized a public utility company to serve all of Pittsburgh, and went back to business.

As the 80s moved on, Westinghouse was increasingly involved with electrical as well as mechanical engineering. He experimented with — and finally rejected — electricity as a supplementary power source for a bigger and better airbrake for long freight trains that he perfected in 1886.

And, from the day of his visit to Menlo Park in 1880, he was con-

124

New atomic-powered generating station in Mass. West-inghouse Electric designed and developed the reactor.

Westinghouse tapped gas on grounds of own home, later developed effective methods of drilling. conveying.

cerned with the problem of electrical distribution.

Like Edison himself, and unlike most of the other inventors of the day, Westinghouse had seen the value of staff work in science and engineering, and had hired a brilliant team of research workers. It included men like Nicola Tesla, Guido Pantaleoni, and Oliver Shallenberger, whose formal education and scientific understanding were greater than his own.

And this team joined him in the task of finding a substitute for the Edison direct current system.

The trouble with DC was that it could only be generated at low voltages, and that distribution of electricity was thus limited to a very short range—only a mile at the time of the demonstration.

Westinghouse wanted to develop a system that would permit generation at very high voltages, and delivery of power to points near and far at whatever voltage was needed—in other words, to "alternate" current from high to low pressure.

The difficulty—so great that it seemed insurmountable to Edison and to most of the other electrical engineers of the day—was control of those very high voltages.

The first breakthrough came when Westinghouse heard about the development in England of a device called a "transformer" to reduce voltages in electrical circuits.

He promptly dispatched Pantaleoni to England to obtain the U.S.

patent rights for the transformer and bring it home.

When it arrived, he pronounced it theoretically sound but faulty in mechanical design—and began literally taking it to pieces and putting it together again.

Soon he had a working model of the transformer used in all alternating current systems today.

He patented it in 1886—six years after Menlo Park—and, in the same year, established the Westinghouse Electric Company.

Westinghouse Electric's revenues were to soar to $4 million by 1890, making Westinghouse, at the peak of his career, the head of a giant corporation as well as of half a dozen smaller ones. (By 1960 Westinghouse Electric Corp. sales totaled $1.2 billion and Westinghouse Air Brake's $170 million.)

The transformer was the last of the many developments that made possible the distribution of electricity by alternating current.

By the fall of 1886, the first AC system—supplying power to Lawrence, Mass., from a Westinghouse experimental laboratory at Great Barrington, Mass., four miles away —was ready to go into operation.

It was a complete success, and demonstrated not only that AC could carry power farther than DC, but also that it was much cheaper.

However, Edison and his coworkers refused to admit that AC was safe, and a substantial proportion of the public agreed with them.

The battle between Westinghouse and Edison interests was to rage for 10 years—until Westinghouse Electric and Edison General Electric pooled their patents in 1896.

Each side bombarded the public with newspaper and billboard advertising; Edison himself wrote an article for the influential *North American Review* on the dangers of AC, and Westinghouse offered a rebuttal in the next issue.

Newspaper editorials took sides in the controversy.

Charges of bribery, fraud, and criminal libel flew back and forth.

Of course, there were occasional fatal accidents when AC wires were strung too low; and these were greeted with newspaper headlines like: "THE WIRE'S FATAL GRASP;" "ONE MARTYR MORE;" "AGAIN A CORPSE IN THE WIRES."

AC got perhaps it worst advertisement when New York State announced that in the future, criminals would be electrocuted (by alternating current) rather than hung.

Nevertheless, AC gained ground.

The turning point came in 1892, when the city of Niagara Falls called for bids on a complete power system—and Westinghouse won out over Edison G.E.

The following year, Westinghouse brought off one of the most spectacular coups of his career— one that proved that he (again, like Edison) had a sense of public rela-

Downtown Pittsburgh reflects peaceful benefits of world's first full-scale atomic-electric generating station for civilian needs only (Shippingport, Pennsylvania).

tions that was far ahead of his time.

The sponsors of the Chicago World's Fair had announced that the Fair would be illuminated by no less than 250,000 electric lights.

Westinghouse Electric and Edison General Electric were the only two firms in the country able to bid for the gigantic contract — and Westinghouse underbid its rival by more than $1 million.

The Fair, Westinghouse believed, would provide such a magnificent showcase for the powers of electricity—and the products of the firm that won the contract—that he was willing to lose hundreds of thousands of dollars to get the job.

But Edison refused to admit defeat, and promptly went to court to challenge Westinghouse's right to use the Sawyer-Mann electric light bulb, on the ground that this bulb—the patent for which Westinghouse had recently acquired—was so similar to the Edison bulb as to be a patent infringement.

The court decided in favor of Edison.

Westinghouse met the challenge by the simple expedient of designing a new bulb that worked on a different principle. It was by no means as good as the Edison bulb, but perfectly adequate for a few months' service at the Fair.

Then came the crash production program. New machinery was built and installed in a new factory, and in a bare five months, the 250,000 light bulbs were produced.

The bright lights of the Fair's "Magic City" drew "ooh's" and "ah's" from thousands of visitors, and rave notices in the nation's press. And the giant Westinghouse installation that supplied the power, open to the public, proved to be one of the most popular attractions.

Moreover, Westinghouse did better than break even on the deal, and prompt cash payment from the grateful Fair management helped tide the company over the Panic of 1893.

By the turn of the century, with the Westinghouse-Edison patent war a thing of the past, alternating current was accepted as—in the words of the great British scientist, Lord Kelvin—"the only practical and economical solution for the problem of electrical distribution."

George Westinghouse, in the meantime, had turned his attention to the problems of electric power for industry.

A British engineer, Charles Parsons, had invented a turbine engine in 1884. And Westinghouse, once again recognizing a good thing when he saw it, bought the U.S. patent rights for the equipment and began the job of perfecting it.

The result was the Westinghouse-Parsons turbine generator, the most powerful engine ever built. (He provided his own showcase for the new advance by immediately scrapping all the power-producing devices in his factories and replacing them with Westinghouse - Parsons generators).

Also in the 90s, he went to work on the world's first electrically powered urban transit system; the motor that made possible large-scale development of electric trolley lines was perfected in 1902.

Then, in the early 1900s, he rounded out his career by developing the first electric locomotive for the railroads.

Two years before his death in 1914, he won a particularly satisfying honor. To his already impressive collection of awards, decorations, and honorary degrees, he added the Edison Medal—an annual award granted by the American Institute of Electrical Engineers in commemoration of the career of the great inventor of the incandescent bulb.

"It is perphaps somewhat ironic," the award read, "that he whom we are to honor tonight has disagreed violently over a long period of years with the man in whose honor this medal was founded. But those of us who know Thomas Edison as a generous and just man know that he regards his defeat in one battle as a great victory in the march toward progress."

Today's engineers would put it another way — George Westinghouse did as much as any man of his generation to advance the "state of the art" in electricity.

Frederick W. Taylor

MANAGEMENT MAN

**Frederick W. Taylor showed industry that
"there's a best way to do everything"**

Today's industrial management men owe much of the challenge, creativity, and complexity of their jobs to Frederick Winslow Taylor, 19th Century consulting engineer.

It was Taylor who persuaded the skeptical businessmen of his day that management is, in many ways, an exact science—and that the front office is a vital link in production.

A happy combination of personal assets made Taylor the greatest of the turn-of-the-century management pioneers.

He was a brilliant engineer — so good that he would undoubtedly have gone to the top in design engineering if he hadn't been more interested in making machines operate efficiently than in building them. He had a natural affinity for scientific methods of investigation, and the imagination to apply them to the practical problems of industry — problems that he understood because he had worked on the factory floor himself. He knew how to

handle people — hardboiled factory hands and hidebound board chairmen alike — and win them to his credo that "there is a best way to do *everything*." And he had what can only be described as a passion for industrial productivity.

The father of "scientific management" was born, in 1856, into a well-to-do, cultured Philadelphia family.

He spent much of his childhood traveling in Europe with his parents and older brother and sister. (As an adult, he s p o k e almost flawless French, and German at least good enough to enable him to swear back fluently at the German-born workers in the Philadelphia steel mill where he began his career.)

Then, when he was 16, he was sent to Exeter to prepare for Harvard and a career in the law. Two years later, he passed his Harvard entrance examinations with honors — but he had worked so hard that he was suffering from acute eye strain, and was in no shape to

begin poring over the fine print in Blackstone.

Years later, when he was about to send one of his sons off to Milton Academy, he wrote to a friend: "I should have preferred Exeter, but there is no restriction whatever at Exeter on the hours in which the boys can study, and I thought it would be better for Robert to be where he was obliged to have lights out at 10 o'clock."

Back home in Philadelphia at 18, with college postponed indefinitely, Taylor decided that the life of a young gentlemen of leisure was not for him — and apprenticed himself to a small machining and pattern-making shop. (None of his biographers mention any parental opposition to this move, but it's hard to believe that his family was not, at the very least, somewhat startled.)

Four years later, he moved on to the Midvale Steel Co. Times were hard, and the only job open for the young machinist was one as a yard

"Never examine anyone but a first-class man"

laborer — but he soon moved up to lathe operator and then to "gang boss," or assistant foreman. (In six years, he was to become the company's chief engineer.)

In 1878, as Taylor soon found out, factories were jungles.

Mechanization of industry was making giant strides; factories were getting bigger; workers' tasks more specialized — and duller; personal supervision harder to maintain; and management techniques were lagging far behind.

The economic slumps of the '70s had brought heavy unemployment, and to most workers, the equation was simple: lower output per man equals more jobs to go around.

Morale and productivity were low, and labor-management relations were simple and brutal: the foreman was expected to drive his men to produce more; the men, it was assumed, would produce as little as they could and still hold their jobs.

Frederick Taylor spent his first two years as a gang boss driving his crew of lathe operators as hard as he could. He was successful enough to be marked by management as a young man to watch. But he was so cordially disliked by some of the workers that there were rumblings in the plant about the possibility of his getting a bullet through his head on his lonely walk home. "I was a young man in years," he said later in his career, "but I give you

my word that I was a great deal older than I am now, what with the worry, meanness, and contemptibleness of the whole damn thing. I made up my mind either to get out or to find some remedy for this unbearable condition."

The "remedy" that occurred to him in the early 1880s was as simple as it was revolutionary — instead of assuming that a man's daily output had to be either as much as could be forced from him or as little as he could get away with, establish scientifically what it could reasonably be expected to be.

His immediate superior, William Sellers (one of the great engineers of the 19th century) was immediately interested in the idea of the experiment that proved to be industry's first time-motion study, and gave the young foreman permission to go ahead.

Taylor took one machine and one skilled worker out of production ("Never examine anyone but a first-class man," he was to tell his lecture audiences later on), got waste steel from the factory yard, and began investigating, one by one, all the possible variables in the job of metal cutting: speed, shafting, and belting of the machine; shape and temper of the tools; the feeding of tool into metal; composition, preparation, and availability of materials; the methods and motions of the worker.

When the best way to handle each

of these facets of the job had been found, and the ideal production rate, based on maximum efficiency, had been calculated, the new techniques were put to practice in the Midvale Steel shop.

The result was an increase in output amounting — for some men — to several hundred per cent. Taylor had proved for the first time that "there is a best way to do everything."

The Taylor System of scientific management as it was to evolve over the years had four parts: study of the job to find the best way to do it; setting of production standards based on the results of the study; detailed planning of plan operation for greatest efficiency; and finally, maintenance of the established standards.

Running a factory along these lines called for hitherto unheard-of quantities of paperwork; in 1911, Taylor had to reassure an audience of Dartmouth business administration students that his system was not just "the printing and ruling of a lot of pieces of blank paper and spreading them by the ton about the country."

It also involved a new emphasis on personnel work — training men in proper techniques and placing them in positions where they were at least theoretically capable of doing "first class" jobs.

In short, it demanded a higher degree of organization than U.S. industry had ever known, and created more complex responsibilities for management.

Stubborn Management

Taylor said at Dartmouth that "in the work of changing from the old to the new system, nine-tenths of our troubles are concerned with those on the management side . . . they are infinitely more stubborn, infinitely harder to make change their ways, than the workmen." In actual fact, the Taylor System was to meet bitter opposition from both management and labor for many years.

Until 1895, however, it was virtually unknown outside the Midvale Steel Co.

In that year, Taylor presented a paper called "A Piece Rate System" to the American Society of Mechanical Engineers, which he had joined ten years earlier after taking night

Booming steel mills of late 19th century (below, a Carnegie plant) gave Taylor the perfect proving ground for "scientific management."

school degree in mechanical engineering.

The ASME was not just a technical society; it was actually the nation's first management forum, and the center of the U. S. "management movement" that was just getting underway in the '80s.

Serious study of the problems of management in big business can be said to have begun with Henry R. Towne's presentation of a paper entitled "The Engineer as Economist" to the ASME in 1886.

Discussions at ASME meetings during Taylor's first years there centered almost entirely around systems of incentive pay to raise productivity, and Taylor's idea that a day's work could be scientifically measured to set production standards was met with considerable skepticism.

For that reason, he presented the 1895 paper — his first report on time-motion studies — as part of a discussion of a new kind of wage scale; even so, it sparked the controversy over "scientific management" that was to rage for most of the rest of his life.

By then, he had left Midvale Steel.

From 1890 to 1893, he served as general manager of the Manufacturing Investment Co., where he began to apply "scientific management" techniques to accounting and office work.

In 1893, he became an independent consulting engineer, and spent the next eight years introducing the Taylor System to a succession of clients, the most important of whom was Bethlehem Steel.

His assignment at Bethlehem was virtually a top-to-bottom overhaul of the company's production facilities; the work he did on coal and ore shoveling is typical both of his method and its results.

He found that each man on the shoveling crew used his own shovel, and used it for materials ranging from rice coal at 3½ pounds a shovel load to wet ore at 32 pounds.

So, selecting two "first-class shovelers" and paying them double wages for the investigation period, he set about finding out what an optimum shovel load would be.

He found that the men shoveled fastest and with least fatigue with exactly 21 pounds on the shovel.

The next step was to stock up on shovels of different sizes, one for each type of material, so that all

the workers would always have a 21-pound load to handle.

When each man came to work in the morning, he found a colored slip in his box. The color told him (many of the workers were illiterate) which size of shovel to take from the tool room for the day.

A yellow slip meant that the man hadn't met his shoveling quota for three of four days in a row. When this happened, a supervisor spoke to him, and watched his shovel. "In nine cases out of ten," Taylor recalled, "the man had simply forgotten something about the art of shoveling" — which, of course, had also been studied.

"A Game of Chess"

Obviously, all this cost money — for the study itself, the new shovels, the tool room, the office where each day's work was planned in what Taylor called "a game of chess with 500 men," and the executives to staff it. Wages went up, too, since the workers were paid a premium for meeting their quota.

However, the cost of handling a ton of material dropped from between seven and eight cents a ton to between three and four cents, with a net saving for Bethlehem in the first year of $70,000-$80,000.

This ideal combination of higher wages and lower labor costs was exactly w h a t Taylor believed his system should always achieve.

He also believed that "scientific management" would put an end to labor-management friction by setting up objective standards for labor's output and rewarding individual performance in such a way as to make high production equally desirable for both sides. He even thought it would make labor unions unnecessary.

The unions, however, disagreed.

Organized labor's quarrel with the Taylor System sprang largely from the "differential rate" wage scale that generally went with it.

This was, in Taylor's words, a "modification of straight piece work that consists in paying a higher price per piece, or per unit, or per job, if the work is done in the shortest possible time and without imperfections than if the work is done in a longer time or with imperfections."

Usually, or at least in theory, the basic rate in a Taylor System shop was set high enough so that the man who produced as much as time-motion studies had indicated,

would be paid substantially more — 30 to 100 per cent more, Taylor claimed — than he had before the system was initiated. A man who fell short of his quota might earn no more than he had before, or even less.

It could be assumed that no one would produce much *more* than the studies had proved he could.

This wage scale did remove the greatest drawback of the straight piece work system — the vicious circle in which high production might skyrocket payroll costs until management decided to cut the piece rate, thus making the workers work perhaps twice as hard for the same pay and removing their incentive to raise their production any further.

But the unions felt that it still fell far short of giving labor a fair share of the profits created by increased productivity, and continued their battle for a "day rate."

They also maintained that time-motion studies and production quotas simply put too much pressure on the worker.

Writer, Lecturer

Taylor retired from his private consulting practice in 1901, and spent the remaining 14 years of his life writing and lecturing.

He also took on several unpaid assignments — notably, one for the U.S. Army that precipitated a wave of strikes among civilian employes at the arsenals he was trying to reorganize along Taylor System lines.

The strikes led to a Congressional committee hearing in 1911 on "The Taylor System and other systems of shop management" at which Taylor testified, defending his methods, for weeks on end.

The committee report was non-committal, saying simply that it could find no evidence that the Taylor System was unfair to labor.

But the hearings had tremendous publicity value; and so did the publication of two of Taylor's major papers in the popular and respected *American Magazine*.

And evidence that "scientific management" methods did work — even if they were not a panacea for all the ills of business and industry — had, after all, been slowly accumulating for over 15 years.

From 1912 until his death in 1915, Taylor found himself sometimes reminding his lecture audiences that there were, after all, things efficiency experts *couldn't* do.

CHAMPION OF U.S. LABOR

Gompers dedicated his life to elevation of the masses, improvement of factory conditions. He made the voice of U.S. labor heard around the world

In the 1850s a commonplace sound echoed through the narrow streets of London's East Side slums:

"God, I've no work to do. Lord, strike me dead — my wife, my children want bread . . ."

The pitiful wailing of the unemployed had a profound effect on young Samuel Gompers.

"That cry, ringing through the streets day after day, never failed to draw me to the window . . . to watch these men struggling against despair," he wrote 60 years later in his autobiography.

It became the most important influence to shape his life.

More than any one of the powerful merchant princes in U.S. business history, Samuel Gompers was responsible for the emergence of modern industrial America. By his insistence on "more, more" for labor, he forced mechanization and spurred our industrial revolution.

During his lifetime Gompers towered over all other labor leaders; his legacy remains the bedrock on which present-day unionism rests. For more than 40 years he served as president of the American Federation of Labor, from its feeble birth in 1886 until his death in 1924.

As time went on he was regarded by most of the nation as labor's elder statesman and, although the AFL only included one-tenth of the total employed, he took it upon himself to speak for all labor. Few questioned his right to do so.

Despised both by reactionary industrial czars and radical left-wing elements (for entirely different reasons), he was revered by millions who looked to him as their champion.

Born in 1850 into a poor family of Dutch Jews who had migrated to London, Gompers had a brief four-year education and, at 10, was apprenticed to a shoemaker. However, he complained the noise of the shoemaking establishment hurt his ears and he switched over to cigar-making, his father's trade.

Persistent poverty soon prompted the Gompers family to make a second move, this time to the United States. The Cigarmakers Society of England had established an emigration fund. Instead of paying unemployment benefits, it helped pay members' passage to America.

The Gompers family arrived in New York in 1863 after seven weeks at sea. Their new four-room home on Houston Street looked more spacious than the one-room flat in London, but the neighborhood was similar. Gompers recalled that opposite their house was a slaughterhouse, behind it a brewery.

For the first year and a half he and his father made cigars at home. But always of a gregarious nature, he soon found many friends, attended night school at Cooper Union, and joined local social clubs. Eventually he almost forgot he was not a native-born American. (He fathered the AFL's anti-immigration policy.)

At 14 Gompers joined the Cigar-

AFL President Samuel Gompers (sixth from right) often met with prominent leaders of the business community, steel scion Charles M. Schwab (fifth from right) and Presidential aspirant Herbert Hoover (2nd from left).

National guardsmen were called in to quell rioting of striking American Railway Union members during the famous 1894 Pullman Strike in Chicago.

Steelworkers battled federal troops during bloody 1892 Homestead riots.

makers' Local No. 15. He went to work in a factory and immediately began to participate in union activities. So evident were his qualities of leadership that when fellow employees, some of them 40 years his senior, wanted to present grievances to the boss, he was selected as their spokesman. His level-headed arguments often won the desired terms.

On his seventeenth birthday he married a girl who worked in the same shop and 20 months later their first child was born. Five more followed and, because his income for many years was small and irregular, the family often suffered privations.

Gompers became more and more involved with union activities, especially when the depression of the 1870's caused severe unemployment among the cigarmakers.

Gompers and Adolph Strasser, another active labor man, obtained control of the weak Cigarmakers International Union and tried to strengthen it. Their reforms, startling for those times, included uniform initiation fees and dues, centralized control over strikes, and the levy of $2 per member for a strike fund.

Finally in 1878, when the cigarmakers' distress had grown extreme, the union risked its first walkout. "It was a wonderful fight," said Gompers, despite the fact the union was forced to capitulate after five months.

"Although we did not win, we learned the fundamentals . . . which would assure success later."

The strikers went back to work, but Gompers was blacklisted for many months.

Gompers' spirit of combat was to be of great use, for the country was entering a dynamic and turbulent era when modern industrial America began to emerge from its infancy.

From colonial days until the Civil War, few workers had any consciousness of class. Those few unions which did organize found themselves stymied by the old common law of conspiracy.

But the ending of slavery assured industrial capitalism a dominant role in the U.S. economic system. Overnight the economy mushroomed. By 1894, the U.S. had jumped to first place in world production of industrial goods.

Rapid growth was accompanied by heavy concentration of capital and the birth of giant corporations. Monopolies sprang up in many branches of industry. Survival often depended on cutthroat competition.

With the introduction of machinery, most workers were no longer individual, dignified craftsmen, but generally adjuncts to the machine.

"There are too many millionaires and too many paupers," editorialized the *Hartford Courant*. America was indeed a land of contrasts.

Furious speculation and overbuilding came to a brief halt with the depression of 1873. It lasted seven years. Wages were slashed and labor unions crushed. The new industrialists used the same ruthless tactics on workers as they did on competitors.

"I can hire one-half of the working class to kill the other half," boasted railroad magnate Jay Gould.

Warfare was declared and from the 1870s on, guns, spies, and troops played a prominent role in U.S. labor relations. Many industrial battles were settled in this way.

During these chaotic times the first important national labor organization began to make itself known. Activities of the Noble Order of the Knights of Labor were cloaked in darkest secrecy with rituals similar to the Masons and Odd Fellows. But in 1878 when the depression had produced a new consciousness in American workers, it came out into the open, rallying all labor to its slogan: "An injury to one is the concern of all."

Labor solidarity was its main objective and no group of workers was excluded — skilled and unskilled, white and Negro, male and female. The Knights even admitted employers.

Its goals were lofty; elevation of humanity, education, political action. Workers were urged to found producers' co-operatives or work in harmony with employers.

"I shudder at the thought of a

131

American unionism owes its life to crusading efforts of Gompers

strike," said one of its leaders. It was this non-militant attitude, so out of keeping with the rebellious times, which brought its demise.

In the meantime a rival, the American Federation of Labor, had risen, with Samuel Gompers as its president and co-founder. Its aims and methods were a far cry from the Knights.

"A struggle is going on . . . between the oppressors and the oppressed of all countries," the preamble to its constitution declared, "A struggle between capital and labor . . ."

While the AFL recognized the struggle, it did not intend to change the system. It merely wanted a bigger share of the pie.

"Pure and simple unionism" was their philosophy. Concentrate on immediate objectives; never mind about grandiose ultimate goals.

In structure the AFL was founded on voluntarism or "a rope of sand," as Lenin called it. Each local had complete independence.

A serious flaw in their organization was a snobbish emphasis on skilled workers, labor's aristocracy. It had little interest in the non-skilled, even though mass produc-

tion would eventually put the majority of labor into that category.

When Gompers took on the job of its presidency (no one else wanted it), the youthful organization became his personal baby. At an annual salary of $1,000, he settled in an 8 x 10 office with tomato crates for files and enthusiastically set out to build the Federation. He worked tirelessly, doing every conceivable job including that of errand boy.

He wrote in March 1887: "My official duties are taking up my entire time and energy . . . I have not had the pleasure of partaking of afternoon or evening meals (Sunday included) with my family for months."

Evidently there were other reasons for his absence from home. A member of the AFL Executive Council wrote to a friend in 1892: "I am rather inclined to think Sam is a model husband as the haunts that used to know him now mourn his absence; his favorite pool room has closed up its doors."

Physically a startling person, he had a huge torso, short legs, and a pipe-organ voice. He used all his incongruous parts to gain and hold attention; his contemporaries de-

scribed him as "a born actor."

He combined this personal dynamism with shrewdness. His old battles in the cigarmakers union had taught him the value of a strong treasury. Accordingly, the AFL charged high dues and initiation fees. Strike funds, unemployment insurance, sickness, old age and disability benefits — all were available to members. (Gompers later opposed Federal unemployment insurance, workmen's compensation and social security on the grounds that unions should provide for their own.)

In politics he advocated non-partisanship, refusing to identify the AFL with either major party. "Reward our friends and punish our enemies" was his policy.

In fighting for better conditions he tried to make the AFL respectable in the eyes of the general public. Even though he once studied German to read Karl Marx in the original, he hated being labeled a radical.

His later violent animosity toward socialism and communism was partly because these ideologies bore a foreign connotation. He insisted the U.S. labor movement should be purely American and work out its own philosophy and techniques.

His idea of unionism reflected typical American practicality. He set up an efficient, business-like union, not unlike the workings of business itself.

The Federation grew slowly during its early years, from less than 150,000 members in 1886 to 278,000 in 1898. But powerful industrialists administered many devastating defeats to it.

Corporate Staying Power

Two bitter strikes proved to Gompers that his strongest unions could not yet withstand the attack of a giant corporation.

For nearly five months in 1892 the Carnegie Steel Co. and the Amalgamated Assn. of Iron and Steel Workers, one of the most powerful unions in the country, waged war at Homestead, Penna. The steel company imported 300 armed Pinkerton detectives and 8,000 National Guardsmen to crush the union. A triumphant Carnegie re-established the 12-hour day and cut wages

Immigrants formed backbone of early U.S. labor movement. N. Y. strikers demand 8-hour working day, rally to slogan "In Unity is our Strength."

132

to subsistence level. Forty years elapsed before the industry effectively organized again.

In 1894, the American Railway Union, led by Eugene Debs, struck the Pullman Palace Car Co. in Illinois. Despite a call for Federal troops, trains stood still all over the country. Finally the strike was broken by a court order against the union for interfering with the operation of mail trains.

(Although the injunction was not a new legal instrument, this was its first important use against labor. Afterward, it became a popular weapon.)

The ARU sent an urgent telegram to Gompers, asking him to come to Chicago to support a city-wide strike. Gompers came but refused to give his blessing. He said the railway strike was already lost and further agitation might endanger the long-run interests of labor.

For this stand he was severely criticized by both radicals and some sections of labor.

Labor's Magna Carta

Despite his individualism, his disdain of money (he died a poor man) and his selfless devotion to labor, Gompers was pompous and self-righteous.

Consistently throughout his long tenure as AFL leader, he defied the membership when it favored radical programs. For all of his progressive speeches, he became exceedingly conservative as the years passed.

He often was not able to rise above flattery and adulation. In 1914 his lobbying finally resulted in a bill which would exempt unions from being sued for restraint of trade. To him, the Clayton Act was labor's Magna Carta.

But so pleased was he with the friendly spirit of Congress and so emotionally insistent on the exact wording of his favorite theory — ". . . the labor of a human being is not a commodity or an article of commerce" — that he compromised on a crucial clause.

It originally stated "nothing contained in the anti-trust laws . . . shall apply to labor . . .", but the final wording was considerably weaker. His oversight enabled the courts to interpret the Act very liberally. Not until 1935 did the Wagner Labor Relations Act change the situation.

The period of World War I was

Management and labor rub elbows during Union Square labor rally in N.Y. Outdoor meeting (above) afforded workers opportunity to air grievances. Even the ladies had their say in early labor disputes. Below, group of striking telephone operators line up for picket duty in Boston, 1916.

one of great activity and gratification for Gompers. Rising above labor partisanship, he renounced his previous pacifism and became a national leader and patriot.

The favorable Wilson administration helped labor get a fairer hearing in industrial disputes and AFL membership doubled. After the war Gompers was disappointed not to be included in the peace delegation, but he was sent to Europe as head of a labor goodwill mission.

There he felt doubly betrayed when the post-war era brought a retrogression in industry-labor relations. With war-time restrictions lifted, prices soared. Labor, asking for higher wages to meet increased living costs, found itself threatened with the open shop and lockouts.

Its power and prestige went into a temporary decline as Gompers reached the end of his life. As a result of a half century of intense exertion and free living, his health began to deteriorate. He contracted Bright's disease and became almost blind.

In December, 1924, he traveled to Mexico City for a meeting of the Pan-American Federation of Labor but became ill. He wished to die on American soil and was moved across the border to San Antonio.

For more than 50 years he had struggled to further organized labor.

"The trade union is the great fact of my life," he said. His monument is today's approximately 18 million union members.

HE
BEAT
THE HEAT

Willis Carrier, inventor of mechanical air conditioning, designed world's first temperature-humidity control system for a Brooklyn printing plant in 1902, founded Carrier Corp. in 1914. Today, air conditioning is a $4-billion-dollar industry and has brought cool comfort to millions of homes

NEW YORK was even hotter and damper than usual in the summers of 1900 and 1901, and as the summer of 1902 drew near, a Brooklyn printing firm decided that it had to stop just talking about the weather.

The paper the plant used was one size on dry days, another on humid ones. Colors overlapped, color runs rarely matched from day to day, and flow, and drying rate of ink were irregular.

So the company, Sackett-Wilhelms, called in the Buffalo Forge Co., manufacturers of blowers, heaters and exhausts, to design a temperature-humidity control system.

Buffalo Forge turned the problem over to its most promising young employe, engineer Willis Carrier.

In August, 1902, the world's first industrial air conditioning went into operation at Sackett-Wilhelms—and today's $4 billion air conditioning industry was born.

Willis Carrier came from an upstate New York farm family. He was 25 in 1902, and a year out of Cornell, where he had taken a degree in electrical engineering.

He took the Buffalo Forge job after graduation with some misgivings, since the company had nothing to do with electricity. But a campus recruiter (they were around, even then) had made him a good offer, and he liked the idea of living with relatives in Buffalo.

Carrier spent his first months at Buffalo Forge designing drying systems for coffee and lumber and a forced draft system for boilers.

He soon decided that the branch of engineering he had stumbled into was woefully lacking in basic data. So he started working overtime on development of formulas and compilation of tables — and, within six months, had prepared a formula for selecting draft fans for maximum boiler efficiency, minimum fan horsepower.

The Buffalo Forge management was sufficiently impressed to establish a research department and put Carrier in charge of it.

He next came up with data on heater coils which—once he had persuaded the older engineers to use his tables—saved the company $40,000 in the next heating season.

So it was hardly surprising that when the temperature-humidity control order arrived from Sackett-Wilhelms, Willis Carrier got the job.

Mechanical temperature control was already a reality in 1902—although decidedly a luxury item.

The first commercial ice-making machine had been invented by a Florida doctor, John Gorrie, in 1851, and in the 1880s, mechanical refrigeration began to spread throughout the U.S. Madison Square Theatre and Carnegie Hall were ice-cooled; so was the New York Stock Exchange, after its members asked, "if they can cool dead hogs in Chicago, why not live bulls and bears in New York?"

But, although air could be cooled, circulated and moistened fairly successfully, its humidity could not be reduced — and, especially for indus-

134

trial use, humidity control was just as important as cooling.

Years later, Carrier described his first humidity-control experiment:

"We rigged up a roller towel arrangement with loosely woven burlap which we kept flooded with a saturated solution of calcium chloride brine. We drew air through the burlap with a fan. Readings of dry-bulb and wet-bulb temperatures told us the amount of moisture removed from the air by the brine.

"Everything about the test was operated manually except the fan—a man dipped brine from a barrel and poured it over the cloth, and a man turned the rollers."

This test was abandoned in a week. The calcium chloride did reduce moisture, but it left the air so salty that it would have rusted machinery.

The next experiment involved circulation of cold air through heater coils, balancing the temperature of the coil surface and the rate of air flow to produce the dew point temperature at which the air had the right humidity for printing.

This method worked. On July 12, 1902, Carrier turned in finished drawings to Sackett-Wilhelms.

But it was not until several months later, in the fall of 1902, that Carrier hit upon the principle of "dew point control," the basis of modern air conditioning engineering.

He was waiting for a train on a foggy night in Pittsburgh, and suddenly realized that he was pacing back and forth in the ideal medium for moisture control.

If he could create "fog" by saturating air with water, and then control its temperature at saturation, he could produce exactly the desired amount of moisture in air.

Since he was still supposed to be working on heaters, blowers and exhausts for Buffalo Forge, it was spring of the next year before he was able to start working on his new idea.

His "Apparatus for Treating Air" was finished in 1904 and patented on January 2, 1906.

As orders started coming in, Carrier—now head of the company's Engineering Department at 29—began to take an interest in the marketing of his moisture-providing brainchild.

He compiled a sales catalog, including technical data which, when published in 1911 as "Rational Psychrometric Formulae," would establish air conditioning as a full-fledged branch of engineering.

The catalog also listed potential markets for cooling apparatus—theatres, churches, restaurants, ships, soap, leather, glue and textile factories, tobacco warehouses.

Home air conditioning was still only a day dream, and for the next 20 years, cooling installations were to be sold primarily for improvement of products and processes — the textile industry was the first large-scale customer—rather than for the comfort of people.

In 1908, the air conditioning in Buffalo Forge's business was grow-

SALES AND PROFITS OF LEADING AIR CONDITIONING EQUIPMENT MANUFACTURERS 1928-60

(in $ millions)

Company	1960 Sales	1960 Profits	1948 Sales	1948 Profits	1938 Sales	1938 Profits	1928 Sales	1928 Profits
Carrier	256.8	5.0	54.5	5.2	10.6	—.7	2.4	.1
Worthington	194.4	7.7	92	8.4	17.7	.7	15.3	.7
Trane	102.5	6.7	22.6	1.8	3.6	.2	......	....
Fedders	68.8	4.5	20.1	1.7	3.9	.1	n.a.	.3
York	merged with Borg-Warner Corp.		56.5	5.6	14.2	—.1	n.a.	.9

NOTE:

Four of the billion dollar corporations, General Motors, Chrysler, General Electric and Westinghouse, are also leaders in the air conditioning field. Separate figures for their air conditioning sales are not available.

OPENING of New York's first air conditioned movie theatre, the Rivoli, on Memorial Day, 1925, was a highly publicized event. It was also a nerve-wracking one for Carrier, who had spent all night in the theatre setting up the new equipment.

ing so fast that the company decided to form a subsidiary, Carrier Air Conditioning Co. of America.

Carrier was the new company's vice-president, and Irvine Lyle its sales manager.

Lyle was another of Buffalo Forge's most promising young men. As New York district sales manager, he had brought in the Sackett-Wilhelms order six years before, and he and Willis Carrier were close friends.

Carrier Air Conditioning flourished for six years, winning new customers in industry after industry.

In 1914, however, with the threat of war making business conditions uncertain, Buffalo Forge decided to cut back — and the new subsidiary was the first to go.

Carrier and Lyle were promised that their jobs with the parent company were safe, but they were still heartsick over the decision.

Together with five of the subsidiary's other key men, they decided to go into business on their own.

The seven pooled their savings—and their borrowing power—to form Carrier Engineering Corp. with a total capital of $32,600.

Salaries in the new company were at what one of the founders later described as "subsistence level," and its two-room headquarters in Buffalo was sparsely furnished with second-hand furniture.

But 40 contracts came in during the first year, and Carrier Engineering was soon in the black.

Renamed Carrier Corp. after a 1930 merger with Brunswick Kroeschell and York Heating & Ventilating, it still holds an important place in the industry Carrier pioneered.

The industry as a whole has now

MONSTER refrigeration machines used in early air conditioning systems were complex and cumbersome. Carrier's development, in early 1920s, of simpler refrigeration equipment for manufacture by Carrier Corp. was vital growth.

RAILROAD AIR CONDITIONING was introduced by Baltimore & Ohio on its crack New York-Washington trains in 1930. Cool comfort of pullman cars and diners aroused businessmen's interest in air conditioning for their plants, offices, homes.

placed air conditioning units in 5.5 million U.S. homes. Factory air conditioning is commonplace, and summer comfort is offered by 90% of the nation's theatres, 50% of hospitals, 27% of Class A office buildings, 35% of motels, 20% of stores, and 3% of churches.

Willis Carrier's dream of the air-conditioning of whole cities from a single central plant may be just around the corner.

SACKETT-WILHELMS air conditioning equipment, Carrier's first installation (in artist's conception, *above*, with young Carrier at center) was designed to provide temperature of 70 degrees in winter, 80 in summer, constant humidity of 55%. To maintain these conditions, it had to remove 400 pounds of water an hour from the air.

FIRST AIR COOLED HOME was Minneapolis mansion of Charles G. Gates. Equipment, specially designed by Carrier, was 20 feet long, six feet wide, seven feet high. Small home units, introduced in the late 1920s, were not common till 1940s.

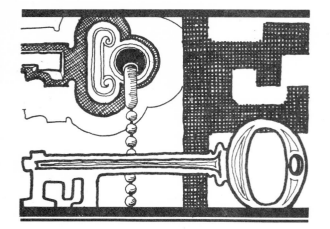

THE CUSTOMER IS ALWAYS RIGHT

BACK in the early 1900s, there were two kinds of hotels.

There were the luxury ones—big city palaces like New York's brand new Waldorf Astoria, and their smaller-scale counterparts in smaller cities and towns—where guests were surrounded by red plush, gilt trim and potted palms and smothered with attention.

And there were all the rest—where rooms were usually uncomfortable and chilly, service inept, and bathrooms one-to-a-floor or even fewer, and where a lone traveler was lucky if he didn't have to share a double room (and bed) with a complete stranger.

Then, in 1907, a successful restaurant owner named Ellsworth Milton Statler built a new hotel in Buffalo, N.Y.

Twenty years later, Statler Hotels in a half a dozen cities had become the home-away-from-home of millions of middle-class Americans.

Statler standards of solid comfort and unpretentious service had revolutionized hotel-keeping—and Statler efficiency had made it big business.

Today 14,000 U.S. hotels take in over $2.7 billion a year. The gross 1960 income of the industry's largest company, Hilton Hotels Corp., which absorbed the Statler chain in 1954, was $230 million.

E. M. Statler (he disliked his first and middle name, and rarely used them) was born in Somerset County, Pa., the son of an impecunious German Reform minister.

The Statler family moved west to Bridgeport, Ohio, in 1869, and three years later, when Ellsworth was only nine years old, he went to work as a furnace-tender in the local glassworks.

The work was hot and grueling, and the pay fifty cents for a 12-hour day.

The McClure Hotel, across the river in Wheeling, W. Va., must have seemed like Paradise in comparison when Ellsworth moved there at 13 to take a job as bellboy for $6 a month plus room, board and tips.

Two years later, he had advanced to the job of head bellboy.

It was about then that a phrenologist from Boston came to town.

Young Ellsworth stopped in for a reading of his

E. M. STATLER believed in fussless comfort, bath in every room. He pioneered hotel standardization and today's $2.7 billion-a-year hotel industry

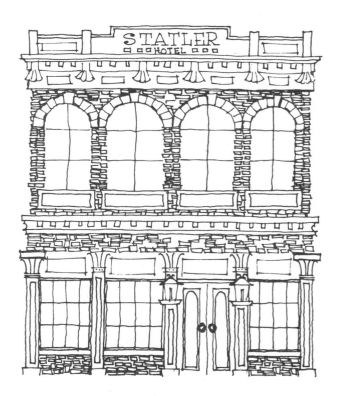

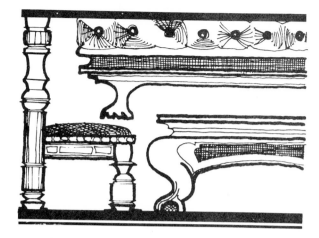 

character from the bumps on his skull, and received a report that amused (or annoyed) him so much that he kept it for the rest of his life.

He was told that he often felt "unworthy, inferior, insignificant," that although he was really "smarter than you consider yourself," he would "pass along through life without being especially noted for anything," and that he ought to try farming or mechanics as a career.

Before he was out of his teens, Statler was well on his way toward proving the phrenologist had been spectacularly wrong.

He moved up at the McClure to become night clerk, then day clerk, and, when he was about 18, he leased the hotel's billiard room.

His younger brother, Osceola, was a superb billiard player, and Statler promptly installed the boy behind the McClure's green baize tables.

Soon fashionable Wheeling was flocking to the hotel to watch Osceola Statler, still in short pants, take on billiard champions from out of town.

Statler's next venture was a bowling alley, in an abandoned vaudeville house next door to the McClure.

Then came his first restaurant, the Pie House.

The tables at the Pie House were set with eggshell china and the best silverplate. Its menus featured minced ham and chicken sandwiches (Statler's own invention) and pies home-baked by the proprietor's mother and sisters. Its coffee was strong and hot, and it was soon the most popular eating place in Wheeling.

By the time Statler was old enough to vote, he was making $10,000 a year.

In 1894, he moved to Buffalo and opened a larger restaurant—the only near-disastrous venture of his business career.

The good citizens of Buffalo, he soon discovered, were simply not in the habit of dining out, and were especially suspicious of a restaurant run by a stranger.

Within a few months, he was deep in debt and facing the loss of his Wheeling properties as well as of the Buffalo one.

However, the Grand Army of the Republic was coming to Buffalo for its annual "encampment," and Statler decided to see to it that the Civil War

veterans ate at Statler's.

In a city-wide newspaper and billboard advertising campaign, he offered an almost unbelievable meal for twenty-five cents: oyster bisque, olives, radishes, fried smelts with tartar sauce, potatoes, lamb with green peas, duck with apple sauce, salads, ice cream and cake, coffee, tea, or milk, and as many helpings of everything as the diner could put away.

By the end of the first day of the GAR encampment, his cashier was literally knee-deep in quarters.

It was more surprising that Statler managed to make a profit on his twenty-five-cent banquet; but he did. He was out of debt by the time the GAR left town.

And he had begun to lure local customers, too.

Within a year or two, the restaurant was a Buffalo institution.

By 1901, when Buffalo's Pan American Exposition was about to open, Statler had $60,000 in the bank, his credit was good, and he was ready for his next big move.

He had wanted a hotel of his own ever since his bellboy days at the McClure, and the Exposition gave him a perfect opportunity for a trial run at hotel-keeping.

In less than six months, spending 18 hours a day at the site, he supervised the building of a huge, cheap temporary hotel that covered nine acres and offered accommodations for 5000 people.

The summer of 1901 was cold and wet, and the Exposition was a fiasco. (It ended in national tragedy when President William McKinley was assassinated on the steps of its Hall of Music.)

But Statler's hotel broke even.

Three years later, Statler built a second huge, temporary hotel for the St. Louis World's Fair. This time the fair was a spectacular success, and the hotel made a profit of $300,000.

And after another two years, the first permanent Statler Hotel opened in Buffalo.

It was followed, during its founder's lifetime, by Statlers in Cleveland (1912), Detroit (1915), St. Louis (1918), New York (1919), and Boston (1927). (Three more hotels—in Pittsburgh, Washington, D.C., and Los Angeles—were added to the chain

private ∗ bathrooms

before its sale to Hilton.)

Right from the beginning, Statler offered the average American traveler more comfort and convenience than he had ever hoped to find in a moderate-priced hotel.

Even the first Buffalo Statler had a bath in every room—a luxury that was not offered by many of the "luxury" hotels of the day.

Statler simply decided that private baths would make competitive sense. His hotel, he was sure, would always be the first in town to be sold out.

Moreover, he built the baths so economically—back-to-back, and in vertical shafts that carried heating as well as plumbing pipes—that plumbing costs for the Buffalo Statler were only 30% higher than they would have been with one or two public bathrooms on each floor. (The "Statler Plumbing Shaft" is standard in most of today's multiple dwellings)

Statler Hotels were also the first to offer telephones—and later radios—in every room. They were the first to supply such small conveniences as circulating ice water, full length mirrors, and closets instead of clothes pegs.

Guests found well-stocked writing desks and even small sewing kits in their rooms, and got free morning newspapers.

Statler service offered fewer Continental flourishes than did service in the luxury hotels—Statler himself was deeply convinced that the average hotel guest wants to be made as comfortable as possible and then let alone. But its motto, from 1907 on, was "the customer is always right."

As the Statler chain grew, its operation was simplified, streamlined and standardized. Identical silver, china, and linens were bought in quantity and used in all the hotels. A basic decorating scheme was adopted so that furniture was interchangeable. And a guest who liked the apple pie at the Boston Statler could be sure he'd like it in St. Louis, too.

No cost-cutting detail was too small to escape Statler's attention.

He noticed, for instance, that it took a maid unnecessary seconds to make a bed with a sheet that had a wider hem at the top than at the bottom, because she had to make sure the sheet was turned the right way around, so introduced sheets with identical hems at both ends.

And he gave the same attention to details that might make Statler guests a little more comfortable.

It was his own idea to place the keyholes in all his hotel rooms above the doorknob instead of below, so that customers who had had a few too many in the bar could unlock their doors with a minimum of fumbling.

E. M. Statler built and operated hotels the way his contemporary, Henry Ford, built automobiles.

And by the time of his death in 1928, the Statler Hotel was a national institution almost in a class with the Model T.

THREE DECADE'S HOTEL GROWTH

(Year-round operation, 25 or more rooms)

	1929	1935	1939	1948	1954	1958	1960 (Est.)
TOTAL INCOME -$ BILLION-	.9	.6	.8	1.9	2.1	2.2	2.4
NO. OF HOTELS -1000S-	11.9	11.4	14.1	14.5	11.4	10.4	NA
NO. OF ROOMS -MILLIONS-	.1	.9	1.1	1.2	1.1	1.	NA

OPERATION INDICES -1929=100-	1930	1935	1940	1945	1950	1955	1960
TOTAL SALES	90	71	85	163	192	224	240
ROOM SALES	91	64	76	133	167	200	220
RESTAURANT SALES	88	80	96	200	225	251	277
ROOM RATES	97	72	81	101	142	185	225
OCCUPANCY	65	60	64	91	81	72	65

Sources: Totals from Commerce Department; index figures from Horwath & Horwath, leading hotel accountants.

Summary: Hotel industry, after reaching its depression low in 1935, is now operating at well over two-and-one-half times the 1929 sales level. The comparatively low occupancy percentage can be attributed to the proliferation of motels.

Life is service. The one who progresses is the one who gives his fellow men a little more. a little better, service. —E. M. Statler.

At 18, E. M. Statler was a hotel clerk at $50 a month; at 21 he was making $10,-000 a year in his restaurant business.

140

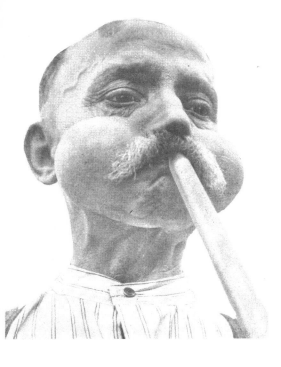

GLASS GIANT

Untutored Mike Owens replaced blowpipe with machine, founded $2-billion-a-year glass industry

A T THE TURN of the century, glass was made much as it had been for over 2000 years.

The last major advance in glass production had been the invention of the blowpipe around 300 B.C.

Then, in 1903, a West Virginian glass blower named Michael J. Owens perfected a machine that produced glass containers mechanically.

A few years later, a second Owens machine made possible automatic production of plate glass.

These two inventions catapulted the ancient craft of glassmaking into the ranks of modern industry.

Horatio Alger Career

And they launched Mike Owens on one of the least publicized but most spectacular Horatio Alger careers in the annals of U.S. business.

Today, the annual sales volume of over 200 U.S. glassmaking firms is more than $2 billion, and "Owens" is probably the most famous name in glass.

The direct descendants of Mike Owens' companies, Owens-Illinois Glass Co. and Libbey-Owens-Ford Glass Co., are second and third in the industry (Pittsburgh Plate Glass is first). And the leading producer of glass fiber for insulating materials and fabric is Owens-Corning-Fiberglas Corp., largely owned by Owens-

Painting, made in 1910 to symbolize revolution in glass production, shows Owens standing in front of early model automatic bottle machine, inspecting a clear glass bottle which the machine has just produced.

 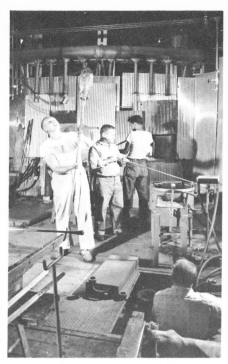 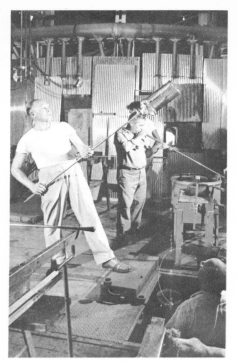

Some 750 highly skilled craftsmen still employ age-old "hand blowing" for special products. Photos show

(l. to r.) worker blowing air pocket in molten glass, "spinning" container into shape, then lowering it

into mold. Bulk of such work today is to meet specifications for specialized laboratory equipment.

Illinois and the industry's fourth largest firm, Corning Glass Works.

Mike Owens was born in Mason County, W. Va., in 1859, and went to work as a furnace stoker in a Wheeling, W. Va., glass plant when he was only 10.

The master blowers in the Wheeling plant dipped "gathers" of molten glass from the furnace by hand, formed it by blowing it through pipes, and gave the finished glass containers their final shape with hand tools.

Hand glassblowing was—as it still is today, although it plays a much smaller role in the industry—a highly skilled and highly paid craft.

But the unskilled work of the glass plants was done by children like Mike Owens, who earned 30¢ for a 12 to 14 hour day.

Owens' mechanization of the industry, 30 years later, was to help put an end to its use of child labor.

His first invention, hit upon when he was still in his early teens, eliminated the job of the "mold boy," who squatted on the floor beside the master blower, opening and closing his mold. Young Owens sank the mold into the floor, and provided a foot treadle so that the blower could open and close it himself.

Owens was a master blower at the age of 15.

And by the time he was 20, he had become a leader in the American Flint Glass Workers' Union.

He first came into contact with his future employer, sponsor and partner, Edward Drummond Libbey, when he was sent to Cambridge, Mass., to organize a strike at Libbey's New England Glass Co.

He was so successful that the New England Glass Co., a family business founded in 1818, turned "runaway shop" and moved to Toledo, Ohio, where it was renamed Libbey Glass.

Union Leader

However, the budding young labor organizer seems to have made a quick decision that he was really more interested in the production end of the glass business.

Six months later, he turned up in Toledo, asked Libbey for a job, and —surprisingly enough—got one.

He rose quickly to become Libbey's plant manager, and soon began thinking about a machine to replace the glass blower in bottle production.

Mike Owens was perhaps unique among inventors in that he could not really invent.

Totally lacking in technical training, he could not even read a blueprint. And he would probably have had a hard time operating one of his own machines.

But he knew glass, and had an

almost instinctive understanding of the principles upon which a glass blowing machine would operate.

When he had decided how his machine would work, he told his parish priest about it. His description was so clear that the priest warned him against telling anyone else — "from what you've told me, I could go out and have this thing built."

However, Mike Owens had gone as far as he could go—somebody else would have to build the machine.

With Libbey's backing, he took his idea to a talented engineer and designer named Emil Bock.

"Put It in Iron"

"Put it in iron," he said when Bock handed him his first baffling set of blueprints.

And "put it in iron" Bock did.

The first crude machine, christened the "bicycle pump," sucked up molten glass, placed the gob inside a steel mold, and puffed a mechanical breath of air into the mold to produce a glass bottle.

The first few bottles were so misshapen that they could never have gone on the market, but they proved that the machine worked.

Slowly over the next few years, it was perfected, enlarged, and put into motion.

Six, then eight, and finally 15 "bicycle pumps" were mounted on a rotating steel framework that circled like a merry-go-round in front of a pot of molten glass. As each unit passed over the pot, it dipped, scooped up a measured quantity of glass, and went on. When it returned, seconds later, it had blown and discharged a standard-sized bottle.

The machine that went into production in 1903 weighed 100,000 lbs., contained 10,000 parts, and could turn out 400,000 bottles every 24 hours. (Top production for a master hand blower with four assistants was 216 bottles in a 14-hour day.)

Libbey and Owens then went into partnership to form the Owens Bottle Machine Co.

At 44, the erstwhile labor organizer was a management man, and—as companies throughout the industry began leasing the revolutionary new machines—an extremely wealthy one.

Plate Glass Machine

Owens next turned his attention to mechanization of flat or plate glass production, still an expensive, small-scale operation in which workmen blew huge glass bubbles and flattened them by hand.

He developed a machine that drew glass automatically from the furnace in sheet form, and established a second company, still in partnership with Libbey — the Libbey-Owens Sheet Glass Co.

In 1917, the first Libbey-Owens plant opened in Charleston, W. Va. —a plant in which no human labor was needed from the time the raw materials entered it until the continuous sheet of glass came from the oven ready for cutting.

Mike Owens died in 1923, and Edward Libbey two years later.

In 1930, Libbey-Owens Sheet Glass Co. merged with Edward Ford Plate Glass Co. to become today's Libbey-Owens-Ford.

In 1929, Owens Bottle Co. acquired the Illinois Glass Co. and became Owens-Illinois. And six years later, Owens-Illinois absorbed the original Libbey Glass Co., where plant manager Mike Owens had gotten his start and the glassmaking revolution had begun.

Owens never retired, died in harness at directors' meeting in 1923.

Latest model of automatic glass container machine is expected to increase production rate to 1200 per minute.

THEY TAUGHT THE WORLD TO FLY

Wright brothers made first powered flights, founded today's huge industry

Orville (l.) and Wilbur (r.) in 1909 at Ft. Myer, Va., where first military plane was tested for Signal Corps.

BACK IN DECEMBER, 1903, taxpayers who felt like complaining about governmental extravagance could point to the $100,000 Federal grant made to the Smithsonian Institution for—of all things—development of a heavier-than-air powered flying machine.

The machine, built by one of the nation's leading scientists, Dr. Samuel Pierpont Langley, had been tested twice. And, as most sensible citizens had felt sure it would, it had plunged ingloriously into the Potomac on both occasions.

Few people even noticed the short, garbled accounts that appeared in a handful of newspapers a week later, describing a successful flight made at Kitty Hawk, N. C., by two scientific unknowns named Orville and Wilbur Wright.

Today, of course, the Wright brothers are ranked with Edison and Bell among the handful of inventors who made the most dramatic and decisive contributions to 20th Century technology.

It is less well remembered that they were also pioneer aircraft *manufacturers*, founders of today's $6.5 billion U.S. aircraft industry.

Wilbur and Orville Wright (born in 1867 and 1871 respectively) were two of the five children of Milton Wright, a bishop of the United Brethren church.

They were the only members of their family who did not go to college.

Instead, they went into business together in Dayton, Ohio as soon as they left high school, and, by the mid-1890s, were moderately successful bicycle manufacturers.

Then, toward the turn of the century, a casual interest in aeronautics that they had shared ever since their teens began turning into a full-fledged hobby.

It was hardly surprising, in a world that had seen the making of so many technological miracles over a few decades, that there were scientists, inventors, and amateurs like the Wright brothers who believed that

New era of history confronts panoplied old during Wilbur Wright's triumphal 1908 tour.

man would one day fly.

In fact, a great deal of progress in aerodynamic theory had already been made.

Men had been taking to the air for short flights in lighter-than-air balloons for over a century, and in heavier-than-air, unpowered gliders for several decades.

Toy models of powered heavier-than-air craft had been flown.

But all attempts to get a man-carrying "flying machine" off the ground had failed.

Part of the trouble was that nobody knew enough about flying to build a craft that would fly, and to handle it in the air.

The glider enthusiasts were just beginning to put the theories of flight to practical test for seconds at a time; most of the would-be aircraft builders who preceded the Wrights had never been off the ground.

The inventor of the airplane would have to be his own test pilot. He would need not only the scientific understanding and mechanical talent required for any great invention, but also a high degree of physical courage and skill.

And he would have to be lucky. Even unpowered gliding, the indispensable preliminary to powered flight, was an extremely dangerous sport.

In 1899, Wilbur wrote to the Smithsonian Institution, explaining that he wanted to begin experiments in flight "to which I expect to devote what time I can spare from my regular business," and asked for a reading list.

After a year of intensive study, the brothers began building their first glider, and by the spring of 1900 were corresponding with the U.S. Weather Bureau about the best location for flying it.

They also wrote to Octave Chanute, a retired civil engineer who was one of the nation's leading students of aeronautics.

Both Chanute and the Weather Bureau recommend-

AT FIRST, FEAT WAS IGNORED

ed the Carolina coast as having the desired winds.

So, in September, 1900, the brothers set off for their first "vacation" in Kitty Hawk.

They returned in 1901, and again in 1902.

By the end of their third season, with the advice and encouragement of Chanute, they had consolidated, revised and in certain respects completely revolutionized the existing body of aerodynamic theory.

Their 1902 glider was larger and more airworthy than any ever built. It contained all the control elements necessary for stable flight. It was, in fact, an airplane without motors or propeller.

These the brothers built over the winter, and in the fall of 1903 they went back to Kitty Hawk for the fourth time.

"I see that Langley has had his fling and failed," Wilbur wrote to Chanute in October, after the Smithsonian Institution flying machine had lurched into the Potomac for the first time. "It seems to be our turn to throw now, and I wonder what our luck will be?"

On December 15th, after two more months of gliding practice, they flew the powered plane.

The longest of the four flights they made that morning (before the wind overturned the little plane on the ground and damaged it beyond repair) lasted only 57 seconds.

But, in Orville's words, it was the "first in history in which a machine carrying a man raised itself by its own power into the air in full flight, sailed forward without reduction of speed, and landed at a point as high as that from which it started."

Triumphantly, Wilbur and Orville telegraphed their brother Lorin, back in Dayton, to give the news to the Associated Press.

However, public cynicism about flying machines was at its height after the recent fiasco on the Potomac, and the Dayton AP man turned down the scoop of a lifetime with the comment that if the flight had lasted 57 *minutes,* Lorin might have a story.

Inaccurate Accounts

A few accounts of the flight, most of them wildly inaccurate, did leak into the press over the next few weeks. But the first full report (written by Chanute for *Popular Science Monthly*) did not appear until March, 1904.

By then, Wilbur and Orville had decided to stop pretending to be bicycle manufacturers who flew for a hobby, and became aircraft manufacturers.

They finished their second plane, larger and heavier than the first, in May, and began flying in a 68-acre cow pasture.

In September, they reported joyfully to Chanute that they were able to "circumnavigate the field." Before the year's end, they were making five-mile flights.

Then, in November, they began trying to negotiate the aircraft industry's first government contract.

It took them three years.

Their first letter to the War Department got a form reply, obviously designed for "flying machine" cranks, completely ignoring the fact that the Wrights had

Spain's King Alfonso sits in plane, chats animatedly with Wilbur, after demonstration during 1908 tour.

Brothers flank President Taft after he presented them Aero Club of America Medal at White House, 1909.

asked for no development funds, but had actually offered to build a practical aircraft for military reconnaissance and communications. It added up to "no."

Extremely disappointed and desperate for customers (their savings from the bicycle business were fast running out), the Wrights began negotiating with the French and British governments.

But a year later, when they were making 25-mile flights and drawing hordes of curiosity-seekers and reporters to the cow pasture, they were still waiting for business.

It was not until early 1907 that President Theodore Roosevelt (who had helped launch the Langley project when he was Assistant Secretary of the Navy in 1896) read about the Wright plane and passed the word along to the War Department to do something about it.

The red tape began to unwind.

In the summer of 1907, an Aeronautical Division of the Signal Corps was formed, and shortly thereafter advertised for bids on a two-passenger aircraft

146

with a useful load of 350 pounds, a 125-mile range and a 40-mph cruising speed.

The public, the press and even most of the nation's aeronautical experts — everybody, in fact, but the Wright brothers — decided that the government had finally taken leave of its senses.

The Wrights, however, had practically written the Signal Corps' specifications (bids were merely a legal formality) and knew that they could build the plane.

The brothers' year of triumph was 1908.

Wilbur, flying in France (where negotiations with the French and British were coming to a successful conclusion) became a popular hero almost overnight. So did Orville, flying under War Department auspices in the U.S.

Birth of Industry

In 1909, the Wright Company became big business.

The brothers, who had earlier refused several offers of substantial financial backing, accepted an offer from an impressive group of multimillionaires (including Cornelius Vanderbilt and Howard Gould).

In exchange for all rights to their U.S. patents, they received $100,000 in cash, 40% of the stock of the new corporation, and a 10% royalty on every plane it sold. Wilbur became company president.

Two years later, Wilbur died, and Orville retired shortly thereafter.

Even before Wilbur's death, the aircraft industry had started to grow, and a bitter patent war between the Wright Co. and its first major competitor, Glenn Curtiss, had begun.

The court battles dragged on until 1917, when they were ended by the formation of an aircraft industry patent pool for wartime production.

In 1914, Curtiss, who was fighting for his business life, took to the air in the 1903 Langley flying machine (so drastically remodeled that Langley would never have recognized it) in an attempt to prove that the Wrights had not invented the first airplane at all.

Orville Wright was so angered by the Smithsonian Institution's support of Curtiss' claims for the Langley machine that he sent his and Wilbur's original Kitty Hawk plane to a British museum.

The Smithsonian did not publish an official retraction until 1934, and the Kitty Hawk plane did not come home until 1948, the year of Orville's death.

By then, the aircraft industry had long since come of age, under the leadership of men like Glenn L. Martin, Donald Douglas and William E. Boeing.

But it was the Wrights who, as a plaque in the Smithsonian Institution states today, "as inventors, builders and flyers . . . developed the airplane, taught man to fly and opened the era of aviation."

First Wright plane made four free, controlled, powered flights, first in history, at Kitty Hawk Dec. 15, 1903.

Wilbur (r.) piloted first Army test plane at speed of 42.5 mph July 30, 1909.

HOW MAGAZINES WENT NATIONAL

Cyrus H.K. Curtis led the turn-of-the-century publishing revolution that created the mass circulation magazine; S.S. McClure dramatized its power as a national opinion-maker

I N 1883, A 33-YEAR-OLD publisher named Cyrus H. K. Curtis launched an unpretentious little women's magazine called *The Ladies' Journal*, edited by his wife.

Ten years later, 36-year-old Samuel Sidney McClure, owner of a small newspaper feature syndicate, brought out the first issue of a general-interest monthly called *McClure's Magazine*.

By the turn of the century, *The Ladies' Home Journal* (the extra word crept into the magazine's title early in its life) had almost a million readers; *McClure's* had 360,000.

And a dozen other magazines— *Munsey's, Delineator, Cosmopolitan, Pearson's,* to name a few—had reached circulation heights (300,-000 to 700,000) that would have dizzied any publisher back in the

1870s and 80s, when probably only *Harper's* boasted more than 100,000 readers.

Magazine publishing was coming into its own—as a big business and a major social and economic force.

Cyrus Curtis was the leader of this publishing revolution.

His *Journal* was the first magazine to win and hold the loyalty of a truly national audience.

He pioneered modern techniques of magazine circulation-building, promotion, distribution, and market research.

He was the first magazine publisher to grasp the potentialities of advertising as a money-maker.

He laid down the principles upon which the relationship between advertiser, advertising agency, and magazine are still based.

And, because he wanted his readers to trust the advertising pages in Curtis publications as they did the editorial pages — he fought for high standards of advertising ethics.

S. S. McClure's career as a publisher was short, and his influence on the industry far less pervasive than Curtis'.

But, between 1902 and 1906, he made magazine reading more exciting for more people than it had ever been before—and demonstrated the power of the national magazine as a molder of public opinion.

The influence of *McClure's* during the years when it was running exposes of business and politics was so great that William Allen White (writing in Curtis' *Saturday Evening Post*) called McClure one of the 10 most important men in the

Curtis, a now successful publisher of a successful women's magazine, takes over the Saturday Evening Post in 1899.

Ladies' Home Journal began as Mrs. Curtis' women's page in small weekly. Shown is art room of early Curtis offices.

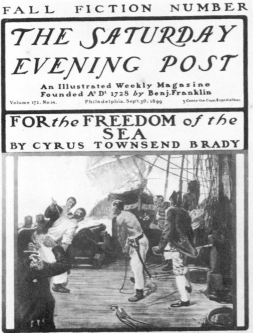

FALL FICTION NUMBER

THE SATURDAY EVENING POST

An Illustrated Weekly Magazine
Founded A⁰ D¹ 1728 *by* Benj. Franklin
Volume 172. No.14.   Philadelphia. Sep't 30. 1899   5 Cents the Copy, $2.50 the Year.

FOR *the* FREEDOM *of the* SEA
BY CYRUS TOWNSEND BRADY

The Curtis Publishing Company Philadelphia

United States.

Although magazine publishing did not become a major industry in the U.S. until the days of Curtis and McClure, it has a long, honorable history that begins in 1740 with the publication of Benjamin Franklin's *General Magazine and Historical Chronicle for all the British Plantations in America.*

(Even earlier, in 1729, Franklin had founded the *Pennsylvania Gazette,* which was to be renamed *The Saturday Evening Post* 100 years later and which became a Curtis publication in 1899. But during its first century of life, the *Gazette* was more newspaper than magazine.)

By the end of the 18th century, 98 small magazines—most of them written by and for the intellectual elite of the 13 colonies—had appeared, and many of them had already disappeared.

All through the 19th century, magazines multiplied (there were 700 by 1865), their audience broadened and their influence grew.

Only Local Circulation

Outside the big cities, books were scarce and expensive, libraries few and far between, public education rudimentary and public entertainments practically non-existent; magazines were a major source of fun for thousands of Americans.

They attracted the finest talents of their day—Thoreau, Poe, Emerson, Hawthorne, Richard Harding Davis, James Russell Lowell were all "magazinists."

High Level Reading

Many of them *(Harper's, Atlantic, North American Review)* were solidly highbrow, and even those that catered more to popular taste (like the rechristened *Saturday Evening Post*) offered pretty substantial fare along with serialized fiction and light features.

Special-interest publications began to spring up. The first women's magazine, *Godey's Ladies' Book,* was founded in 1830, the first farm magazine, *Country Gentleman* (later to become the third Curtis publication), in 1853.

A sampling of new magazine titles from the late 1860s includes: *Carriage Monthly; National Baptist; Christian Witness: Good Health; Temperance Advocate; Art Journal; Ball Players' Chronicle; Sporting Times; Velocipedist, Communist.*

All the magazines of the first three quarters of the century, however, had small circulations.

And while a few of the more distinguished were known throughout the country, circulation was generally local or regional.

Advertising was a minor source of revenue. Before the 1860s, in fact, many reputable publications simply refused to accept it—and with some reason, since most of the advertising that did find its way into magazine pages was for dubious patent medicines.

After the Civil War, however, things began changing fast.

The new railroads that spanned the continent made national distribution feasible for the first time; the Postal Act of March, 1879, gave second class mailing privileges to magazine publishers—an important economic incentive for circulation-building.

The nation's economy was growing by leaps and bounds — total value of U.S. manufactures rose from $2 billion in 1860 to $5 billion in 1880 and $9 billion in 1890.

New Advertising Media

And manufacturers who aspired to reach a national market began planning advertising campaigns and looking for advertising media.

Americans were as hungry for reading matter as ever—and more of them belonged to the educated middle class with money to spend. New magazines began springing up faster than ever; there were 1200 in

LEFT *Women employees' rest, off-duty room had well stocked library.*

Cyrus Curtis spent a great deal of energy promoting his magazines as a medium for mass advertising, and one year spent $310,000 in his own national advertising campaign.

1870, 3300 in 1885. Many of today's leaders (*McCall's, Good Housekeeping, Popular Science, Cosmopolitan, National Geographic,* and *Vogue*) were founded between 1870 and 1885.

Mass Magazine

The stage was set for the entry of the national magazine — and then came Cyrus Curtis.

Curtis was born in Portland, Me., in 1850; his father was in the home furnishings business.

He began his career in the magazine business at the age of 13, when he bought an ancient handpress for $2.50 and started turning out a two-cent weekly called *Young America* that sold briskly to Portland's teenagers.

In 1879, after a few years as a drygoods salesman in Portland and an advertising solicitor in Boston, he settled in Philadelphia and founded a small weekly called *The Tribune and Farmer.*

The Tribune and Farmer soon acquired a women's page, edited by Louisa Knapp Curtis, who was to keep her job in her husband's organization until 1889.

The page was so successful that Curtis decided to make it a separate magazine, issued monthly as a supplement to *The Tribune and Farmer.* The first issue of the Ladies' Journal appeared in 1883, containing articles on gardening, fashion, child care, cooking, and needlework, plus an illustrated serial.

Journal's circulation hit 25,000 at the end of its first year, 100,000 in 1885 and 700,000 in 1889.

In that year, it came of age.

Curtis arranged a $200,000 line of credit with N. W. Ayer & Son (one of the leaders in the new business of advertising) and launched a massive ad campaign for his magazine; before the year was over, he was to spend a total of $310,000. He doubled the *Journal's* subscription price—from 50c to $1 a year—and hired a professional editor, a brilliant 25-year-old named Edward Bok.

The price rise cost the magazine about 250,000 low-income readers; Curtis immediately set about rebuilding his circulation by announcing a subscription contest with $500 as first prize to the reader who brought in the most new subscribers.

Wide Editorial Interest

Bok began broadening the magazine's editorial content with culture ("Forgotten Graves of Famous Men," "Gladstone's Love of Reading and Bismarck's Literary Taste"); exotic people and places ("How Zulu Women Sew"); and human interest ("Unknown Wives of Well-Known Men").

He introduced a column for girls, in which "Ruth Ashmore" (he wrote it himself until he found a suitable woman contributor) told her young readers to "learn to say no" and advised them on dress, manners, and romantic problems.

But the *Journal* remained primarily a service magazine for housewives, and the quality of its service was high. By the mid-90s, Curtis and Bok had hired a doctor to run the magazine's health column, and experts in their fields to head its other service departments — child care, household management, cooking, beauty.

Model Home Plans

In 1895, the *Journal* began running plans for simple, practical, well-designed model homes that led one eminent American architect, Stanford White, to say a few years later, "I firmly believe that Edward Bok has more completely influenced American architecture for the better than any man of his generation."

"Get the right editor and you'll have the right magazine," Curtis once said. "Then it's only a selling proposition."

All through the '90s he worked at "selling" the *Journal* to readers and national advertisers.

By the end of the decade, the *Journal's* circulation was breaking even its own records, Curtis Publishing Co. was solidly in the black, and its owner was ready to perform his second publishing miracle—the transformation of the *Saturday Evening Post.*

Cyrus H. K. Curtis

Edward Bok

Samuel Sidney McClure

150

The Ladies' Home Journal

Christmas 1903

THE CURTIS PUBLISHING COMPANY, PHILADELPHIA

By 1903 The Ladies' Home Journal *had a million readers, the first magazine to win a national following.*

The Journal *set a format for women's magazines to come, with columns on beauty, deportment, health problems.*

By the turn of the century, the Journal *had become the fashion style-setter for women all over the country.*

Part 2

HOW MAGAZINES WENT NATIONAL

McClure and the "Muckrakers"...
Curtis and the Saturday Evening Post...
National magazines and national advertisers...

In 1893, ten years after the founding of the first great mass circulation magazine, Cyrus Curtis' *Ladies Home Journal,* Samuel Sydney McClure launched his *McClure's Magazine.*

At 35, McClure was a veteran of publishing—just as Curtis had been when he founded the *Journal* at 33.

He was born in Ireland, emigrated to the U.S. as a boy of nine, and began working his way through

Knox College at 17.

Soon after he left college, in 1882, he took his first magazine job—as editor of *The Wheelman,* a publication for bicycling enthusiasts.

Then, a few years later, he went into business for himself, founding the first newspaper syndicate.

McClure saw—probably because he had been a poor boy himself—that newspaper publishers could make money by catering to a large

audience that was hungry for fiction and unable to afford books and magazines.

The first offerings of his feature service to the small weekly newspapers it served were "reruns" of old short stories and serials from popular magazines.

As the syndicate grew, it began buying novels from major writers of the day—Kipling, Hardy, Stevenson, William Dean Howells,

George H. Lorimer wove the Saturday Evening Post *into the broad fabric of middle-class American life.*

Ida Tarbell and Lincoln Steffens were two of the writers who made McClure's *such a powerful reform*

force that editor S. S. McClure was called "one of the 10 most important men in America" in the early 1900 s.

Frank Stockton—and serializing them across the country.

It was a substantial success.

And by the early '90s, McClure was able to begin preparations for a magazine of his own—a mass circulation monthly for the vast new audience created and made accessible by the sweeping economic and technological changes of the 1870s and '80s.

It would sell for only 15¢ a copy, 10¢ less than the newsstand price of most of the better magazines. (Virtually the only major magazine to sell for less than a quarter before 1893 was, of course, Curtis' *Ladies Home Journal*, the first to reach the new mass audience; *Journal* subscriptions cost $1 a year.)

McClure hoped to have the general interest, popular-priced field to himself for a year or so at least—but he was quickly disappointed.

Price War

The appearance of his 15¢ magazine launched a price war—*Cosmopolitan*, seven years old and making its bid for mass circulation under the new ownership of John Brisben Walker, promptly went down to 12½¢ and Frank A. Munsey entered his *Munsey's Magazine* in the race by cutting its price from a quarter to a dime.

McClure's had rough sledding for its first few years—its days of glory were still ahead.

But by the mid-'90s, it was obvious that the popular-priced monthly had come to stay.

Cyrus Curtis, meanwhile, with the *Journal* solidly in the black, was beginning to look around for a second magazine.

$1000 Bargain

In 1897, he found a bargain—the *Saturday Evening Post*.

The *Post*, founded by Benjamin Franklin in 1729, had flourished until the mid 19th century and gone downhill steadily ever since.

In 1897, it was a shoddy 16-page weekly offering little but bad fiction; circulation was down to 2000.

Curtis bought it for $1000.

During its first year of life as a Curtis publication, it remained virtually unchanged; an assistant editor of the *Journal* put it out in his spare time.

Then Curtis hired a young reporter named George Horace Lorimer as editor, and went into action.

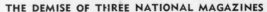

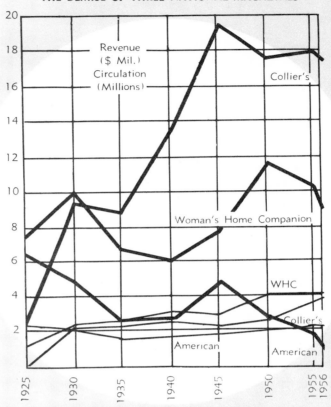

Source: Magazine Publisher's Association

The first recognizable modern issue of the *Post* appeared on September 30, 1899.

It had a color cover and a two-color ad (from Quaker Oats), ran 32 pages with 32 columns of paid advertising in all. Its contents included a story by Bret Harte, the first article in a series called "Men of Action," and an editorial by Lorimer that announced:

"There is nothing worthy or permanent in life that is not clean, and in its plans and purposes the new *Saturday Evening Post* preaches and practices the gospel of cleanliness. It appeals to the great mass of intelligent people who make homes and love them, who choose good lives and live them, who seek friends and cherish them, who select the best recreations and enjoy them."

Once again, as with Edward Bok for the *Journal*, Curtis had found the perfect editor. Lorimer, who was to stay with the *Post* until 1937, had laid down the guidelines that were to make it as brilliantly successful as a middle-class family magazine as was the *Journal* in the women's field.

And once again, Curtis launched a massive campaign to build circulation and bring in major advertisers. He cut the magazine's single copy price to a nickel, and poured almost a million dollars into promotional advertising in its first two years.

In 1899, he and Lorimer were probably the only two people in the publishing — or advertising — business who believed that the *Post* had a future; less than 10 years later, they had proved themselves right.

153

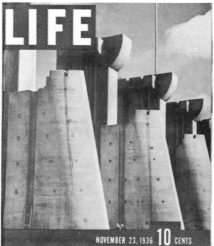

National magazines got bigger than ever in the 20th century under leadership of publishers like Henry Luce (Life,

Advertising begins to play a leading role in mass magazine publishing

The magazine's circulation began to rise as soon as Lorimer took over the editorship; it reached 250,000 in one year (1900), 700,000 in 1904, and over a million in 1908.

Its advertising revenues lagged behind for the first two years, but when they began to climb, they climbed fast — from $159,000 in 1900 to $1 million in 1905, $3 million in 1909.

It was during these same years that *McClure's* enjoyed its meteoric rise to fame as the voice of the "Muckrakers."

Magazines had often served as agents of social protest and reform before; the leading periodicals of the 19th century had campaigned against slavery in the '50s and '60s, political corruption and business monopoly in the '70s and '80s. And, of course, Bok of the *Journal* had begun crusading on public issues of interest to women almost as soon as he took over.

But *McClure's* was the first general interest publication to show how powerful a magazine's voice could be in the new era of national distribution.

McClure had, from the time he launched his magazine, intended to offer his small town readers news and commentary as well as fiction.

Then, in the late '90s, he met Ida Tarbell, who was already a well-known biographer, in Paris.

He hired her as a *McClure's* staff writer, and assigned her to write a history of Standard Oil.

He was rather expecting a generally favorable piece, emphasizing the great trust's efficiency in production and distribution.

What he got—a carefully written and strictly factual expose of the company's use of bribery, fraud, and violence to attain power—must have staggered him when it reached his desk.

But he printed it.

And almost overnight, *McClure's* became the leader in the battle against corruption in business and government that had begun in the '70s and was reaching its climax in the first decade of the new century.

Miss Tarbell was soon joined on the *McClure's* staff by Lincoln Steffens, probably the most famous "muckraker" of them all.

His two great exposes of political corruption, "The Shame of the Cities" and "The Struggle for Self-Government," ran in the magazine.

Then came the third of the trio, Ray Stannard Baker, who concentrated on railroad management, labor-management relations, union racketeers.

From 1902 to 1906, these three—and others, like Josiah Flynt, with "The World of Graft" and "The Powers that Prey"—kept *McClure's* readers, and much of the nation, in a ferment.

The magazine was so widely respected as a leader of the national reform movement that its writers were invited to the White House to discuss their findings with the President, Theodore Roosevelt.

Then, as suddenly as *McClure's* had risen, it fell.

Editors' Squabble

In 1906, Tarbell, Steffens, Baker, and the managing editor, John Phillips, quarreled with McClure and left the staff. (The subject of the dispute was an odd one—McClure had decided to implement his views on reform by founding a model community and a string of impeccably run commercial enterprises, and was becoming more interested in planning his Utopia than in running his magazine.)

The writers and Phillips all moved over to the staff of the *American*, and a few years later, *McClure's* was sold.

It survived until 1933, but was never again outstanding.

McClure himself abandoned his business plans, and lived in scholarly retirement until his death in 1947.

154

THE READER'S DIGEST

THIRTY-ONE ARTICLES EACH MONTH FROM LEADING MAGAZINES—EACH ARTICLE OF ENDURING VALUE AND INTEREST, IN CONDENSED AND COMPACT FORM

FEBRUARY 1922

1936), Mr. and Mrs. DeWitt Wallace (Reader's Digest, *1922), Gardner Cowles* (Look, *1937).*

In its four short years of ascendancy, however, *McClure's* had proved that the new national magazines could be what their relatively small-scale 19th century predecessors had never been — opinion-makers more powerful than the daily newspapers.

McClure also proved that controversial editorial content did not necessarily scare away advertising.

McClure's advertising lineage soared during its four years as a reform leader; advertisers, whether they liked the "muckrakers" or not, could hardly afford to ignore the magazine's circulation. And many of them seemed to feel that an ad in *McClure's* was a guarantee of their own integrity.

By 1911—the year in which Cyrus Curtis, undistracted by visions of Utopia, bought the 58-year-old *Country Gentleman* as his third magazine, it was clear that national magazines and national advertising were made for each other.

And Curtis, who had been the first to see—and capitalize on—the potentialities of this fact, was also playing a key role in development of the relationships between advertiser, agency, and medium.

Modern Publishing Concept

His basic contributions were two —the enforcement of modern principles of ethics in advertising, and the development of the agency commission system.

He laid down the principle that Curtis publications would not accept dubious advertising in the early 1890s, when the *Journal* still needed all the ads it could get, astonishing the industry by refusing to have anything to do with patent medicines, which were then the largest single source of advertising revenue.

He began studying the problems of advertising agency recognition. In 1898, when agencies were still relatively new, most magazine advertising came directly from manufacturers, and rate-cutting was a common practice.

In 1901, the first Curtis contract went into effect, providing that the publisher would accept no advertising from any source at less than his published rates; that the agency, in its turn, would charge its clients the full Curtis rate; and that the agency would get a 10% commission plus a 5% discount for cash.

The support offered by the contract system, which was quickly adopted by other major publishers, greatly strengthened the agencies and stimulated the development of advertising as a major industry in its own right.

By the time of Curtis' death in 1933, national magazines were in their heyday. *Time* and *Fortune* had been launched by young Henry R. Luce (*Life* in **1936**), the *Reader's Digest* by DeWitt Wallace, and *Look* (1937) by Gardner Cowles.

Total per-issue magazine circulation had reached 174 million; and general and farm magazines carried more than $9 million worth of advertising per issue.

Cyrus Curtis, the father of this giant industry, might easily have thought of a slogan—"Never underestimate the power of the national magazine."

		1960		1950		1940		1930		1920	
		Circulation (mils.)	Revenue ($ mil.)	Circ.	Rev.	Circ.	Rev.	Circ.	Rev.	Circ.	Rev.
Founded	Magazine										
1922	READERS DIGEST	12.6	34.7	*	*						
1936	LIFE	6.8	138.8	5.3	80.4	2.9	18.9				
1870	MCCALLS	6.6	31.6	3.9	9.9	3.2	5.9	2.5	8.3	1.3	2.5
1883	LADIES HOME JOURNAL	6.6	28.3	4.5	22.5	3.7	6.8	2.6	15.6	1.9	11.1
1728	SATURDAY EVENING POST	6.4	105.0	4.0	63.2	3.3	27.3	2.9	47.6	2.1	36.2
1937	LOOK	6.3	59.1	3.1	17.8	1.9	1.3				
1922	BETTER HOMES & GARDENS	5.0	25.6	3.6	19.6	2.3	3.9	1.4	2.7		
1885	GOOD HOUSE KEEPING	4.9	22.7	3.1	15.4	2.4	7.6	1.9	11.9	N.A.	N.A.

TOP EIGHT MAGAZINES

Source: Magazine Publisher's Association

155

BIGHEARTED BANKERS

Arthur J. Morris and A. P. Giannini sparked revolution in banking by rolling out welcome mat for small depositors and borrowers

IN 1904, a 34-year-old San Francisco businessman named Amadeo Peter Giannini opened a small bank that he called the Bank of Italy.

And just six years later, in Norfolk, Virginia, a 28-year-old lawyer named Arthur J. Morris launched his Fidelity Savings and Trust Co.

Over the next few years, the careers of these two young men were to revolutionize banking and finance, and open up new room for growth not only for the banks, but for the entire U.S. economy. (As for their own ventures, Giannini's was to become the world's largest bank, the Bank of America, which today has resources of more than $13 billion; Morris's was to grow into a multi-billion dollar network of "Morris Plan" banks.)

What they did was simple enough —they made banking services, and low-cost instalment credit in particular, available to the average wage earner and small businessman for the first time. But this, in the staid, marble-and-mahogany world of early 20th century banking, was a startlingly radical idea.

Two Americans with backgrounds more different than A. P. Giannini and Arthur J. Morris can scarcely be imagined. Giannini was the son of Italian immigrants; Morris came from old Virginia stock. Giannini entered banking via the wholesale produce markets of colorful, fast-growing turn-of-the-century San Francisco; Morris from the tradition-steeped University of Virginia (where he was first in his law school class).

But they shared a deep concern for the financial problems and needs of the average man, "the little fellow," as Giannini called him, and had great faith in his financial responsibility. They were both bold, imaginative businessmen who knew how to recognize a big idea when they had one. And both were men of exuberant energy; they loved their work and thrived on it.

Arthur J. Morris still does. At 80, he is the active board chairman of Financial General Corporation, the giant holding company that has succeeded the "Morris Plan" banking organization. He gets back to his Park Avenue office from lunch faster than his secretaries, spends six hours a day in the saddle when he visits his South Carolina shooting plantation, and is launching a long-term program for the introduction of "Morris Plan" banking in Europe. "The good Lord's taken care of me because I've taken care of 160

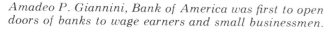

Arthur J. Morris of Financial General Corp. has devoted his life to what he calls "democratization of credit."

Amadeo P. Giannini, Bank of America was first to open doors of banks to wage earners and small businessmen.

million other people," he says.

Morris knew A. P. Giannini well, and declares flatly that he considered him to be "the greatest living banker." One suspects that Giannini, who died in 1949, would have returned the compliment.

Giannini's story begins first. He was born in 1870, in San Jose, Calif., 50 miles from San Francisco. His father was a young Italian who had arrived from Genoa two years earlier and taken over the operation of a small hotel.

When Amadeo was seven, his father was killed in a quarrel with a workman. His mother, who had been not quite 16 when her first son was born, soon married a young man named Lorenzo Scatena who had worked his way from Italy before the mast and in 1877 was hauling produce to market for the farmers of the Santa Clara Valley.

In 1882, the family moved to San Francisco. Scatena entered the wholesale produce market and quickly worked his way up in it to become one of the business leaders of San Francisco's Italian colony in North Beach.

Young Amadeo was fascinated by his stepfather's business, and joined L. Scatena & Co. as soon as he finished grammar school and a short commercial course. At 21, he was a full partner.

Ten years later, married and the head of a growing family of his own, he sold his half-interest in the firm and "retired." He was worth several hundred thousand dollars, largely invested in North Beach real estate, and he may have been thinking about going into politics.

But in 1902, his father-in-law, another wealthy North Beach Italian-American, died, and young Giannini took over the management of his estate. Among the responsibilities this entailed was a directorship of the Columbus Savings and Loan Association, a prosperous and conservative North Beach bank.

Giannini hadn't attended directors' meetings for more than a few months when he decided that the Columbus was failing to give real service to the Italian community— and missing its own best chances for growth.

The Columbus, like every other bank in San Francisco—and in the United States, for that matter—had never given credit to an applicant who did not have substantial collateral, and was not even interested

Among Giannini's many contributions to modern banking was development of branch system; above, first Bank of Italy branch at San Jose, California.

in small savings and commercial accounts. Banks, its directors believed, were for the well-to-do.

Giannini thought banks should be for everybody; and, when he failed to make any headway with his ideas at Columbus, there was only one thing to do.

One day early in the spring of 1904, he burst into the office of James J. Fagan, an old friend and a vice president of downtown San Francisco's big American National Bank. "Giacomo," he said, "I'm going to start a bank. Tell me how to do it."

On October 17, 1904, Giannini's Bank of Italy opened its doors. It was capitalized at $300,000, in $100 shares which had sold like hotcakes. Its board of directors was solidly Italian-American, with the single exception of the Irishman, Fagan, and consisted largely of younger, up-and-coming members of the North Beach community, although the older generation was represented by none other than Lorenzo Scatena. It had three salaried employees, one of whom, assistant cashier Armando Pedrini, had been hired away from Columbus Savings and Loan.

Giannini had insisted on Pedrini, and had guaranteed to pay his $150-a-month salary himself if it was too much for the payroll—not only because he was a promising executive, but because he was hand-

some and charming; "The women are crazy about him," Giannini told his economy-minded co-directors. And Giannini's new kind of bank was going to be a place where people enjoyed doing business.

The Bank of Italy took in $8780 from 28 depositors on its opening day, and passed the $100,000 mark in December, 1904.

At the end of 1905, its first full year, its deposits were over $700,-000, its assets over $1 million, and it had $239,318 out in loans.

Most of the bank's first customers were the small tradesmen, workers, and housewives of North Beach—people who had kept their money in mattresses before Giannini went after their business.

And go after it he did, in a complete departure from traditional, conservative banking practice. He canvassed the neighborhood, talking up the advantages of interest-bearing savings accounts. And when new customers (many of whom could not write English) came timidly to the bank, the staff patiently initiated them into the mysteries of passbooks and deposit slips.

Giannini himself scorned a private office; his desk was out in the open on the bank's main floor, where he amused a brood of children while their mother made a deposit, or presented a proud new father with a five-dollar gold piece for the baby, reminding him that

157

Credit for wage earners

just one dollar would open a savings account.

Right from the start, the Bank of Italy made many small loans—business loans, home mortgages, and even personal loans with no collateral, for amounts as low as $25.

In spite of its rapid growth, the bank was still relatively small as it began its second year. It was not yet a member of the San Francisco clearing house; its checks were cleared through James Fagan's American National Bank. Giannini also used the larger bank's vaults for safekeeping of his cash reserves; every night, sacks of currency traveled downtown to American National by horse and buggy. Fagan's affectionate name for the Bank of Italy was the "baby bank;" to most of the city's leading financiers, it was just "that little Dago bank up in North Beach."

Then, on April 18, 1906, San Francisco was devastated and its business life paralyzed by earthquake and fire. The Bank of Italy came through the crisis with flying colors. Giannini and his staff fled the city as the fires spread, with the bank's cash and other valuables hidden in produce carts from L. Scatena & Co. Five days later, they were back in business, in makeshift quarters down on the waterfront, and Giannini, with unquenchable confidence in the city's ability to rebuild itself, was making loans right and left. The "baby bank" was mak-

ing the financial community sit up and take notice; most of the larger banks did not manage to resume normal operations for a month.

Eighteen months later, the bank weathered a second crisis, the financial panic of 1907. Thanks to Giannini's keen sensing of the economic climate, loans were curtailed, gold reserves increased and deposits built up in time. During the first days of the panic, gold bars were piled high behind the tellers' window — such a reassuring sight for nervous customers that the bank's deposits actually increased during the panic period. Once again, the Bank of Italy had shown the way; it was even able to lend gold reserves to the big Crocker National Bank.

Faster every year, the bank grew. It opened its first San Francisco branch office in 1907, its first out-of-town office in 1909, in Giannini's old home town, San Jose. In 1913, with assets close to $16 million, it invaded Los Angeles, shattering tradition once again by actually *advertising* for customers.

The story of its 60 years of development into today's giant Bank of America is full and fascinating. But the foundations upon which Giannini built his banking empire were laid in those first few years in San Francisco.

Today, Giannini's kind of banking, with active solicitation of new business, full facilities and friendly personal attention for everyone, conscientious and imaginative service to customers and to the community, is the kind most Americans expect. In the early 1900s, the Bank of Italy was decades ahead of its time.

However, although he encouraged the applications of small borrowers

1913 newspaper ad announced Bank of Italy's new low-cost loan services "catering to the small depositor."

for business and personal needs, Giannini was not primarily concerned with instalment credit—certainly not with its development on a nation-wide scale.

The father of "pay-as-you-go" budgeting, with all it has meant to the average American family and to the national economy, was back East in Norfolk, Virginia.

In the year of the San Francisco fire, young Arthur Morris was five years out of law school and already a partner in a thriving firm.

He had studied law because his mother's family had produced lawyers for more generations than anybody could remember; but his father was a merchant and banker, and his interest in banks was at least as great as his interest in Blackstone, and his law firm did a great deal of bank work.

It was for this reason that, in the spring of 1906, a $2500-a-year railroad clerk came to the Morris law office. His wife was ill, and he had

Bank of Italy met its first great challenge when fires and earthquakes ravaged San Francisco in April, 1906.

Burned out of its first home, the bank managed to start emergency operations ahead of its bigger competitors.

Wholesaler Giannini married banker's daughter Clorinda Cuneo in 1893. In 1936, their son Mario succeeded A.P. as president of Bank of America.

been to every bank in Norfolk trying to borrow the $500 he needed for her hospital care. Every one had turned him down.

When Arthur Morris heard the story, he was surprised and indignant; it seemed to him that the man was as good a credit risk as plenty of wealthy citizens with the collateral the banks required.

A week later, he sent the clerk to a bank where the loan had been arranged; he didn't tell him that he, Arthur Morris, had guaranteed it.

Over the next six months, he arranged 40 loans totaling $32,000 in the same way, and did not lose a penny.

Shortly thereafter, he hired a team of researchers for a nationwide survey of the credit situation; 80% of the people surveyed had no access to bank credit, and had to borrow from "loan sharks" at interest rates of 10% a month and up.

The local bankers he talked to saw nothing wrong with this situation, doing business with small borrowers would be disastrously uneconomical, they said, and moreover, easy access to bank credit would undermine working people's thrift. They could always borrow from family and friends in a time of need, couldn't they?

But Morris just didn't see it that way. He felt, on the contrary, that a man who could borrow from a bank at a fair interest rate, on the "collateral" of his character and earning power, and repay the loan in sensible instalments, was more likely to develop economic initiative and independence than one who couldn't.

And in 1910, with $20,000 capital (half his own, half raised from skeptical friends), he opened his "little old hybrid bank," the Fidelity Savings and Trust, for the primary purpose of providing personal instalment credit for wage earners.

"Everybody in Norfolk criticized me and ridiculed me," he recalls today, "with the exception of one person, and that was my mother."

But the balance sheet of Fidelity Savings and Trust was soon to prove that he knew just what he was doing.

In its first two years of operation, the bank loaned $159,000 (over $60,000 for automobile loans — a considerable boost for the infant automobile industry and its credit loss was only a fraction of one per cent.

At the end of 1911, Morris went to Atlanta on legal business, and met a local insurance man named W. Woods White who had been campaigning for years to curb the excesses of the loan sharks. Wood was immediately enthusiastic about Morris' new kind of bank, helped raise $50,000 to start one in Atlanta, and persuaded the *Atlanta Constitution* to give the new undertaking extensive coverage.

When Morris got back to Norfolk, mail began pouring in from people all over the country who had read or heard about the *Constitution's* stories on "Morris Plan" banking, and who wanted to find out how such banks could be organized in their cities.

And in 1912, the Fidelity Corp. of America was organized with $500,000 paid-in capital—much easier to

raise than the original $20,000 had been — to establish "Morris Plan" banks as far West as Denver.

Two years later, Morris telephoned Fergus Reid, a prominent Norfolk businessman with Wall Street connections, and said, "Mr. Reid, this is too big for Norfolk."

He himself was just beginning to realize how big it was—how instalment credit was not only offering a useful service to deserving people, but was also, by increasing mass consumption, providing a steady stimulus for economic growth.

On the day after Labor Day, 1914, the two men left for New York to raise the $25 million that Morris had decided he needed to build a nationwide network of banks.

The trip was a triumph; just about everybody who was anybody on Wall Street, from J. P. Morgan on down, chipped in, and "Morris Plan" banking was big business.

Three years later, in 1917, Morris organized the first credit life insurance company, and the Morris Plan structure was complete.

Morris estimates that his banks have lent $133 billion over the past 53 years, with a credit loss of no more than one quarter of one per cent. (Today, of course, all the banks founded as "Morris Plan" institutions have become full-service commercial banks, while virtually all banks of non-Morris Plan origin also offer instalment credit.)

And he does not believe that instalment buying, even at its present high rate ($50 billion outstanding in mid 1960s) is likely to run away with itself — not, he says, in the hands of "experienced lenders."

Horsepower carried Bank of Italy assets to safety in Francisco fire.

159

CONQUEST OF THE BEARD

**King Gillette's invention of the safety
razor changed the face of the times
by ending male bondage to whiskers**

ONE EARLY MORNING in 1895, a 40 year-old traveling salesman with a well-lathered face glared into his shaving mirror and muttered words that men have said for centuries when confronted with a dull razor.

The frustrated shaver was King Camp Gillette, successful peddler of bottle caps and a man who had dreams of inventing something—he didn't know what.

As he stood staring at his straight razor, the picture of what is known today as the safety razor came to him, crystal clear in every detail.

His vision was destined literally to change the face of men in the 20th century and to create a new U.S. industry which now has annual sales close to $500 million (including accessories).

The safety razor gave men an easy, quick, economical shave for the first time in history. It vastly altered the fashions of the times by fostering the rapid demise of the beard.

King Gillette was a self-made man. Born in Fond du Lac, Wisconsin, in 1855 and educated in Chicago, he was forced to shift for himself after the Chicago Fire of 1871 wiped out his father's business.

From the age of 21 on, he prospered as a traveling salesman in the U.S. and England.

Although untrained mechanically and possessing no particular technical ability, Gillette, the salesman, yearned to invent something. Once he systematically went through the alphabet, listing every conceivable item which man might need.

In 1891, Gillette took a new job with the Baltimore Seal Company,

King Camp Gillette's mustachioed face has appeared on 100 billion blade packages over last 60 years.

a manufacturer of bottle stoppers. He became good friends with William Painter, inventor of the stopper and originator of the cork-lined tin cap known as the Crown Cork. (Baltimore Seal later became Crown Cork & Seal Company.)

On a visit to Painter's home in Baltimore, the talk drifted to inventions, a fascinating topic to both men. One of Painter's remarks had a profound effect on Gillette.

"King," he said, "you are always

thinking of inventing something. Why don't you try to think of something like the Crown Cork? When once used, it is thrown away and the customer keeps coming back for more."

After this advice, Gillette became obsessed with inventing a device which could be used and thrown away.

It occupied his thoughts for four years until the summer of 1895.

"I was living in Brookline (Mass.) at the time," Gillette reminisced in a 1918 article. "On one particular morning I started to shave and found my razor dull. It was not only dull but it was beyond the point of successful stropping and it needed honing, for which it must be taken to a barber or cutler.

"As I stood there with the razor in my hand, my eyes resting on it as lightly as a bird settling on its nest—the Gillette razor was born.

"I saw it all in a moment, and in that same moment many unvoiced questions were asked and answered more with the rapidity of a dream than by slow process of reasoning."

The cumbersome straight razors of the 1890s consisted of a sharp edge backed by a bulky support. Gillette saw that the backing was a waste when the same result could be had by putting a fine edge on a small piece of steel.

Why not sharpen two opposite edges of a thin, uniform steel strip, and hold the blade in place with a clamp and a handle?

"I stood there in a trance of joy," Gillette later recalled. "Fool that I was, I knew little about razors and practically nothing about steel."

Before invention of the safety razor, daily shaves were a luxury only the wealthy could afford. An 1861 engraving shows Virginia gentleman relaxing with his newspaper while waiting patiently for his turn in the chair.

So great was his delight that he immediately wrote to his wife who **was** visiting in Ohio:

"I have got it. Our fortune is made!"

His enthusiasm was somewhat premature. Eleven years of work and experimentation were to pass before he would collect a single dollar in dividends on the invention.

At a Boston hardware store he purchased pieces of brass, steel ribbon used for clock springs, a small hand-vise, and files. With these raw materials and no mechanical training Gillette produced the first model of the safety razor with disposable blades.

He made endless sketches (some used later in patent suits) and then came, in Gillette's own words, "the hour of trial." Eight years of trial, in fact, before the safety razor was introduced on the market in October, 1903.

Gillette believed that razor blades could be made cheaply since steel ribbon sold for 16 cents a pound. He calculated a pound would yield 500 blades.

"I did not know then that the steel to be used must be a particular quality and it would cost many times what I supposed per pound."

He was to spend over $250,000 in laboratory tests before this question of steel was solved.

To his surprise, he found that no one was interested in his razor. Investors were cold and technicians didn't think the idea worth bothering with.

Even his friends regarded the razor as a joke and often greeted

Charles Evans Hughes, U.S. Supreme Court Justice, sported popular 1900 beard-mustache combo.

him with: "Well, Gillette, how's the razor?"

For nearly six years he experimented with blades, searching out machine shops in Boston, New York and Newark for advice on how to harden and temper thin steel. Everywhere he was told to stop wasting his money and drop the radical idea.

"But I didn't know enough to quit," he said later. "If I had been technically trained, I would have quit."

During this period of discouragement all he had to show was the crude model he had fashioned himself in 1895.

The first significant development came in 1900 when William E. Nickerson, a graduate of the Massachusetts Institute of Technology,

entered the picture. While the idea of the safety razor belongs solely to Gillette, its development into a practical instrument was the work of Nickerson.

In a loft over a fish store located next to a wharf where Boston's garbage was dumped, Nickerson refined the original razor and developed a process for hardening and sharpening sheet steel.

In 1901, Gillette finally persuaded some friends to raise $5000 to help him form a company and start manufacturing the razor.

The first razors appeared on the market in 1903. Sales for that year came to 51 razors and 168 blades.

But the following year razor sales leaped to 91,000 and blades to 123,000. By 1908, annual blade sales had passed the 13 million mark and, by 1917, one million razors and 120 million blades were being sold yearly.

The conquest of the beard seemed well underway.

But thousands of years before Gillette provided an easy method to "Look Sharp," the removal of hair from men's faces had been a concern of kings, generals and poets.

Early Egyptian razors were made of flint and copper and sharpened with sandstone. The invention of bronze made possible a sharper razor which retained its cutting power longer. About 2500 B.C., iron and steel furnished even more efficient materials for razors.

Romans wore long beards until 200 B.C. when Scipio Africanus, conqueror of Hannibal, became the first daily shaver. The unshaven face soon became the mark of peasants and slaves.

Luxuriant whiskers have swelled masculine egos since dawn of time

The first time a young Roman noble shaved was the occasion for a feast day. His shorn beard was dedicated to the gods. Nero preserved his beard in a gold box set with pearls.

About this time the first barber shops came into existence.

Beards became popular again in Rome around 120 A.D. when the Emperor Hadrian grew one to hide ugly scars on his face. For the next 200 years beards were in style until the time of Constantine the Great in 300 A.D. His shaving made a smooth face fashionable once more.

Barbers flourished in the Middle Ages. They not only shaved customers and cut hair, but also practiced the painful art of bloodletting which was a popular remedy for all ailments.

Shakespeare made numerous references to shaving in his plays. In "Love's Labor Lost" there are mentions of "the razor's edge invisible" and "I could not endure a husband with a beard on his face."

Shaving in the U.S. has had a long and varied history. American Indians pulled out their beards, using clam shells as tweezers. George Washington owned a fine set of straight razors and was kept clean shaven by a servant.

In Civil War days whiskers were back in style, a fashion which continued through the 1890s. By that time the Egyptian bronze razor had changed only slightly to the straight edged concave razor. Only the rich could afford a daily shave by a barber or valet. Others possessed one or two hook-type straight razors and shaved once or twice a week.

During World War I, razors began to sell in quantities never dreamed of by its inventor.

When the U.S. entered the war, Gillette's output went almost exclusively to the Armed Forces. Men who had never heard of the safety razor were issued a Gillette. As a result, self-shaving became widespread and servicemen carried the habit over into peacetime.

In 1921, Gillette weathered his first storm of competition. The company's basic patents were due to expire, leaving the field open for anyone to make the razor and blade. Other manufacturers prepared to flood the market with imitations.

Six months before the expiration date, Gillette brought out a new model to sell for $1. (Until that time razors had sold for $5 or higher.) The company made record profits that year.

Biggest Little Thing

In 1930, Gillette merged with a competitor, the Auto-Strop Company, and continued to expand through the years prior to World War II. During this time the one-piece razor was developed. A new manufacturing process produced the Gillette Blue Blade. A thin blade followed and shaving creams were later added to the product line.

There are few U.S. companies whose advertising is better known to the public than Gillette's. In 1939, the company decided to take a gamble and invest a substantial share of its annual advertising budget in radio sponsorship of the World Series.

The Yankees took the Series in only four games and Gillette sold 2.5 million razors. Since then, sports events have formed the backdrop for the company's advertising. Gillette Safety Razor Company

is also among the oldest television advertisers. It sponsored boxing events on TV back in 1944.

Major product improvements mark the company's recent history. In 1947, the company brought out a blade dispenser which did away with paper-wrapped blades and permitted insertion of the blade directly into the razor.

The first adjustable razor was introduced in 1957 and was followed by the Super Blue Blade in 1960.

In the 60 years since King Gillette sold his first razors, the company has turned out over a billion razors and 40 billion blades. It now has factories in Argentina, Australia, Brazil, Canada, England, France, Germany, Switzerland and Mexico.

In 1948, the company embarked upon a diversification program. It acquired The Toni Company, manufacturers of home permanent wave kits. In 1955, it bought up the Paper-Mate Company, producer of ball point pens. The company entered the hospital supply field in 1962 with the purchase of Sterilon Corporation.

Recently Gillette Safety Razor set a new sales record of $276 million. About 72% came from the Safety Razor Division.

The company's trademark, the face of King Gillette with wavy black hair and a full mustache, has been reproduced on blade packages over 100 billion times.

Just before Gillette died in 1932 at the age of 77, he was heard to remark:

"Of all the little things that have been invented, the razor is one of the biggest little things ever issued from the U.S. Patent Office."

Royalty promoted bearded elegance in late 1800s. King Leopold of Belgium (left) and Austria's Emperor Franz Joseph (center) were models of European fashion. U.S. journalist Jos. Pulitzer (right) wore shaggy Vandyke.

IMAGE MAKER FOR PR

Ivy Lee persuaded U.S. industry that good public relations is good business, raised PR man's status in eyes of public

IVY LEE, the almost legendary public relations man, did some of his most successful image-making for the public relations business itself.

It was during his lifetime — and, to a great extent, in the light of his career—that the "publicity man" was metamorphosed from a rather shady purveyor of dubious news releases into a valued counselor to heads of corporations and even, on occasion, heads of state.

Ivy Lee's formula for good publicity relations was a blend of ethics, imagination, and plain horse sense.

He made PR respectable by applying to his own practice the principles of constructive action and fair play with the press and the public that he advocated to his corporate clients. And, during his 30 years in the business, he laid down guidelines that have become articles of faith for today's second generation of PR men.

Ivy Ledbetter Lee was born in Cedartown, Ga., in 1877, the son of a Methodist Episcopal minister from whom he apparently inherited his persuasive gifts.

The Rev. Dr. James Wideman Lee was an extremely popular preacher and author; one of the books he edited, *The Earthly Footprints of Christ and His Apostles,* sold more than a million copies.

Dr. Lee also had a lively interest in big business — rare in the disillusioned South of Reconstruction days, where industrialization was generally regarded as a kind of Yankee blight. And this, too, he passed on to his son.

Young Ivy graduated from Princeton in 1898, and soon arrived in New York with "a raincoat, a diploma, and five dollars."

Presumably, there were ample financial reserves back in Cedartown; but Ivy Lee was neither the first well-heeled college graduate nor the last to enjoy seeing himself as a Horatio Alger hero.

And he lost no time in making good — with a cub reporter's job on the New York *Journal.*

From the *Journal,* he moved on to the *Times* and then the *World,* developing into a seasoned financial reporter.

Then, in 1903, he took his first public relations job — managing a New York City mayoral campaign for the Citizens' Union. A year later, he went to work for the Democratic National Committee.

Public relations at the turn of the century was just emerging as a fast-growing field in which an ambitious young man with newspaper training could make a lot of money.

Nobody, though, as yet dignified it with the term "public relations." It was "press agentry," and press agents were generally looked down upon, particularly by newspaper editors, as a loudmouthed breed whose job was to get the client's name in the paper whether it belonged there or not — or, if the client was in trouble, to keep him out of the news when he ought to be in. (This contempt crept into the copy of a Denver *Republican* reporter in 1909: "New press agents are being born every minute. You can hear 40 of them howling in every city block.")

As for turn-of-the-century big business, it was still largely indifferent or hostile to the idea of public relations.

Many major firms had already decided that it paid to advertise their product, and more were following suit every year, in full color in all the major publications of the day.

But the notion that it might also pay to publicize the company itself — and to take public opinion into account when framing corporate policy — seemed like nonsense to tycoons who were still inclined to agree with Commodore Vanderbilt's "The public be damned!"

Big business' hand was forced by the crusading journalists called "muckrakers," and by the trust-busting activities of the Teddy Roosevelt administration.

When company after company was being accused of graft, corruption, and callous indifference to the welfare of its employees and the general public, when public opinion was hastening the passage of regulatory legislation, changes clearly had to be made.

In 1902, U.S. Steel began issuing an annual report that gave full details about company operations.

In 1903, American Telephone & Telegraph (later a pioneer in the field of institutional advertising) started to give its employees special training in "meeting and dealing with the public."

In 1906, Standard Oil hired a press agent, J. I. C. Clarke, at the then phenomenal salary of $20,000 a year.

And also in 1906, a group of Pennsylvania coal miners hired 29-year-old Ivy Lee. So, a few months later, did the Pennsylvania Railroad.

With these two accounts to launch a business of his own, Lee issued a declaration of principles:"

"Our plan is, frankly and openly, on behalf of business concerns and public institutions, to supply the press and public of the United States with prompt and accurate information concerning subjects which it is of value and interest to the public to know about."

One of Lee's great assets as a public relations counselor was undoubtedly his fascination with the workings of industry and his liking and admiration for the men who hired him.

He was entirely convinced that if the big corporations met the press and the public half way, they would get fair treatment.

He put this theory into practice soon after he went to work for the Pennsylvania Railroad, when there was a disastrous crash on a Pennsylvania line. The railroads had always taken the attitude that the

Lee's successes sparked PR's postwar development

less said about accidents, the better; reporters had sometimes had to exercise considerable ingenuity to get even the bare facts on rail disasters. Lee shocked his employers by actually providing free transportation to the scene of the crash, and going along with the reporters to answer their questions.

The obvious corollary to Lee's faith in frankness with the press was his conviction that a company was bound to get the publicity it deserved — that no public relations counsel could make a firm appear honest, progressive, and public-spirited if it was not. Therefore, it followed, it was the public relations counselor's job to advise his clients on how to behave.

"When I started out in this work," Lee told an interviewer in the '20s, "there were two courses open to me. I could tell my clients what they wanted me to tell them. That, of course, would please them. But it would never get me very far. The other course was to tell them what I thought irrespective of their opinions. If my judgement was

Lee mobilized public support for American Red Cross, World War I.

right, they would come to respect it. If I were wrong, I would soon find out. In either case, I'd eventually find my level."

Today, these arguments are as familiar to public relations men and management men alike as two plus two equals four. In the years before World War I, they were startling, to say the least.

But Ivy Lee put them across.

In 1910, he gave himself a leave of absence from public relations and sailed for Europe, where he spent the next two years opening offices for a New York brokerage firm and lecturing at the London School of Economics.

Soon after his return to New York, Ivy Lee met John D. Rockefeller, Jr., and a long and mutually profitable friendship began.

The time was April, 1914. The militia had fired on strikers at the Colorado Fuel & Iron works in Ludlow, Colo., which was largely owned by the Rockefellers; and the Rockefeller family, whose press relations had never been good, was in very hot water.

Lee advised the younger Rockefeller to go out to Colorado, and "Junior" went. He spent two weeks there, wearing denims and listening to the workers' stories — and came back determined to break down the barriers that he felt his family's millions had created between it and the rest of the nation. (Later, he was to describe the Colorado strike as "one of the most important things that ever happened" to the Rockefellers.)

In June 1914, Ivy Lee was retained by "Junior" at $1000 a month. And he soon had crotchety old John D, Sr., who had been bitterly opposed to him, passing out dimes to children.

With the Rockefeller account, Lee's reputation as a "physician to corporate bodies" (an epithet coined by a *Herald Tribune* writer) was made and his future assured.

His business expanded steadily over the next 20 years. He worked hard at it; he was an omnivorous reader and included newspapers from all over the U.S. in his daily diet of print. And he made a thorough study of his clients' business interests. (Joseph M. Ripley,

editor of the publishing trade paper *American Press*, wrote in 1926 that "he probably knows more about the inner workings of more big corporations than anyone else in America.")

Lee never revealed his full client list, maintaining — rather contradictorily, in view of his commitment to frankness with the press—that the relationship between a public relations firm and its clients was sometimes a confidential one.

But he was known to have such diversified accounts as American Tobacco, Armour, Chrysler, Portland Cement, Thompson-Starrett; Harvard and Princeton Universities; the Guggenheims, the Red Cross, the Episcopal diocese of New York, the Waldorf Astoria, the New York Interborough subway, and the Republic of Poland.

Not everybody, of course, saw him as a "physician to corporate bodies." To people who were suspicious of big business and disturbed by the growing power of public relations, he was a "corporate dog robber," "little brother of the rich," "Minnesinger to millionaires," and, inevitably, "Poison Ivy."

He called himself a "publicity man" at first, later an "advisor in public relations," and described his work — in particular, his relations with newspaper editors—as "apply-

IVY LEDBETTER LEE

ing common sense to the obvious."

He applied "common sense to the obvious" throughout the 1926 *American Press* interview that gives one of the best summations of his PR philosophy:

"If I were an editor, I should welcome every particle of information which any publicity man could give me, and then I should go to work to develop the story in my own way..."

"If the publicity man is a barrier against newspaper men getting to the source of information, he has no right to be there. That does not mean that a newspaper man has a right to ask every man in a responsible position to give him a personal interview on any question he may wish to ask. But it does mean that he is entitled to a first-hand answer to every legitimate question . . .''

"Any idea that there is any inherent virtue or vice in 'free publicity' is, to me, perfectly absurd. And these men who object to 'free publicity' are just as logical as it would be for them to object because a store puts so many attractive things on its shelves. They don't have to buy these things, and they don't have to use this publicity."

He also emphasized that he insisted on dealing with the men at the top in his client firms: "I get my facts from the man who has them,

and when I'm sure of these facts, and only then, I present my plan to the man who is to pass on it."

Lee liked to boast that he had only once asked an editor to withhold a story—when the Associated Press got a tip on a $5 million donation to a Harvard fund, and he was afraid that premature announcement of this windfall would reduce other donations.

And, he maintained, he had only once spoiled a reporter's scoop — when a Hearst man was about to break the story of Abby Rockefeller's engagement. Feeling, he said, "that the story of a girl's engagement is one that should be given out by her and just as she wants it," he gave the reporter his come-uppance by releasing the announcement to all the papers.

Lee was convinced that advertising and public relations techniques could be used to further international understanding as well as to improve relations between businesses and the public. (He was, incidentally, a strong supporter of paid advertising as part of an overall public relations campaign.)

He once suggested that the USSR might take ads in U.S. newspapers to tell its side of the story on the subject of its World War I debts.

Here again, of course, he was ahead of his time—although govern-

ments today are more likely to use advertising space to boost their export products and tourist attractions than to air controversial issues.

Lee visited the Soviet Union twice, and was an outspoken advocate of U.S. recognition of the new regime there. He denied, though, that he ever had an account from the Kremlin.

He did have one controversial foreign client—a German die trust that paid him $25,000 a year in the early '30s for advice "as to what I considered to be American reactions to what has taken place in Germany, and as to what, if anything, could be done about it."

Since what had taken place in Germany was the rise to power of Adolf Hitler, his acceptance of the account raised an ethical question that is still current in the public relations business — should a PR consultant take on any work, and if so, of what kind, for a client he regards as anti-social?

Ivy Lee himself may never have worked out the answer; he died in 1934.

Just a year earlier, he had reorganized his firm as Ivy Lee & T. J. Ross, taking into senior partnership a younger man named Thomas Joseph Ross, who had been with him since 1919. Among the other partners were Joseph Ripley, who had left the *American Press* to join Lee in 1930, and Lee's two sons, James and Ivy, Jr.

(Today, "Tommy" Ross is the head of the firm, now called T. J. Ross & Associates and still a leader in the field; Ripley is still a member. James Lee left in 1962 to run a resort hotel in Vermont, and Ivy, Jr., has his own public relations firm in San Francisco.)

Ivy Lee had stiff competition in the last years of his career—notably, from two young men named Carl Byoir and Edward L. Bernays.

But he was still high man on the totem pole. *Time* Magazine paid him a backhanded compliment when it mentioned the printed cards that announced the formation of Ivy Lee & T. J. Ross: "The cards did not state what business Messrs. Lee & Ross were in, but it is unlikely that anyone had to ask."

Elderly and intensely publicity-shy John D. Rockefeller, Sr. mellowed under Lee's tutelage; in 1930, Boy Scouts made him honorary Tenderfoot.

CEREAL STORY

W. K. Kellogg sired packaged cold cereal flakes, revolutionized nation's breakfast habits, and started the trend toward "convenience" foods

THE FIRST "convenience foods," forerunners of today's billion-dollar industry, were the packaged cold cereals that revolutionized U.S. breakfast habits half a century ago.

And the man behind the revolution was Will Keith Kellogg, co-inventor — and promoter extraordinary — of the cereal flake.

Today, W. K. Kellogg's most famous brain child, Kellogg Corn Flakes, is still the nation's largest selling cold cereal. The company he founded, The Kellogg Co., processes more than 700 million pounds of cereal a year (Corn Flakes and half a dozen other brands), and by 1960 sales passed the $258 million mark.

Kellogg was born in 1860, 14th in a family of 16. His father was a Battle Creek, Mich., broom manu-facturer, and young W. K. left school at 14 to become a traveling salesman for the family business.

After three years on the road in southern Michigan and a year in Dallas as manager of a family friend's broom factory, he went to work for his older brother, Dr. John Harvey Kellogg, who was superintendent of the Battle Creek Sanitorium.

Dr. Kellogg was a brilliant physician with a powerful personality and limitless capacity for hard work; under his guidance, the Sanitorium was well on its way to becoming an internationally famous institution.

It offered its patients "every device and facility known to modern therapeutics for the cure of disease," including water therapy (over 200 kinds of baths, douches and fomentations), light treatment, diathermy, vibration and mechanical massage.

The doctor also prescribed plenty of fresh air and sunshine — a revolutionary idea in the 1880s and '90s. (His views on the treatment of tuberculosis, amply vindicated in the 20th century, were branded as "heresy" by the Boston Medical Association.)

Sanitorium menus were carefully planned, with calories counted and nutrients measured (here, too, Dr. Kellogg was ahead of his time). They were also strictly vegetarian, and sugar, alcohol and tobacco were forbidden. (Patients on the road to recovery sometimes escaped to a nearby steak house for a meat meal, a glass of whiskey and a cigar.)

By the 1890s, the Sanitorium was treating 500 patients a year, and Will Kellogg, working a 15-hour day like his brother, was, in effect, its executive director.

Its salaries, however, were low. The future inventor of Corn Flakes was making only $87 a month, and his financial prospects looked so bleak that for a time, he considered quitting his job and going West for a fresh start — but finally decided to stay with his brother.

Dr. Kellogg was constantly on the lookout for new foods to meet the dietary needs of his patients and to make his vegetarian meals tastier.

He had been experimenting with cereals ever since the 1870s, and in 1894, when he was trying to produce flaked wheat, he enlisted his brother's aid.

The two Kelloggs began boiling batches of wheat at night in the Sanitorium kitchen and running the cooked grain through rollers. The resulting dough was sticky, gummy and unappetizing.

Then, one day, a batch of wheat was cooked, set aside, and forgotten.

When the brothers came back to it, 48 hours later, it was undeniably moldy, but they decided to run it through the rollers anyway — and, to their amazement, it came off in flakes!

They tried toasting the cereal in the oven, and discovered that it emerged crisp and (making allowances for the moldiness) tasty.

The Kelloggs had stumbled upon the principle of "tempering" cooked cereal to equalize the moisture throughout the batch, the secret of successful flaking.

They overcame the serious disadvantage of mold by storing the boiled grain in tin-lined bins.

The wheat flakes made a hit with Sanitorium patients, and were soon being produced in modest quantities, as were other Sanitorium health foods, for shipment to health-conscious out-of-town customers.

By the late '90s, Will Kellogg was devoting most of his time to his mail order food business, and in 1890, he persuaded the Sanitorium's board of directors to set it up as a separate company, Sanitas Food Co., with its own factory.

At about the same time, he began trying to boil and flake corn. It proved harder to work with than wheat, but Sanitas put a thick and not very tasty corn flake on the market early in the 1900s.

Battle Creek, in the meantime, was turning into a cereal boom town. Between 1902 and 1904, no less than 42 cereal companies sprang up. But most were extremely small operations, selling on a mail order basis and promoting their products primarily as health foods.

W. K. Kellogg, however, had decided that there was no reason why everybody shouldn't eat dry cereal—not for its health-giving virtues, but just because it tasted good.

The idea was a revolutionary one, at a time when the typical American breakfast still consisted of such items as steak, fried potatoes, hot corn meal mush or oatmeal, bread with molasses—and perhaps a piece of pie.

Bankers, taking a dim view of the Battle Creek cereal boom as many of the small companies began to fold, were doubtful that most housewives would ever accept a factory-cooked cereal, and one that was to be served cold, at that.

W. K. Kellogg gambled future on conviction cereal flakes would win public acceptance on own merits, not merely as health food.

But Kellogg found a backer, a former Sanitorium patient named Charles D. Bolin, who was able to raise $35,000 to launch the Battle Creek Toasted Corn Flakes Co.

(The corn flakes had improved since their invention. Kellogg had found that corn grits produced a thinner, crisper flake than whole corn; and, in the face of his brother's

stern disapproval, he had sweetened them with sugar. They had become one of Sanitas' most popular products, and Kellogg decided that they were the best bet for the mass market he was aiming for.)

Dr. Kellogg retained stock in the company until 1911, but he took no part in its operation.

Will Kellogg, at 46, was on his own.

He began advertising Corn Flakes in April, 1906, only two months after the new company was incorporated, with $2092 worth of space in six midwestern newspapers, and went on to launch a national advertising campaign in all media.

Production of Corn Flakes rose from 105 cases a day at the end of 1905 to 1000 cases daily by midsummer, and orders were coming in faster than they could be filled.

The company's first *Ladies' Home Journal* ad, in July, 1906, began:

"This advertisement violates all the rules of good advertising.

"Four thousand dollars has been paid for this space to call the attention of the six million readers of the *Ladies' Home Journal* to a new breakfast food which, at the time this notice is written, less than 10 per cent of the readers of the *Journal* can purchase."

It went on to extol the product and explain that the company was working night and day to produce enough Corn Flakes to satisfy everyone.

A year later, when 4000 cases of Corn Flakes a day were rolling out of Battle Creek and the company was still 300 carloads behind on its orders, the plant burned to the ground.

The fire was a disaster, not only financially (the young company had reinvested its profits, as fast as they came in, in new equipment and a bigger work force), but also competitively.

Six rival producers of corn cereal had gone into business over the past year, and they were sure to gain ground while the Kellogg plant was closed.

On the day after the fire, a Chicago architect arrived in Battle Creek to begin planning the new factory.

But when Kellogg visited the De-

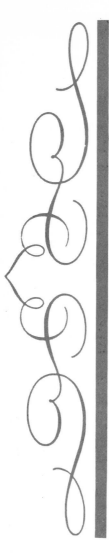

Kellogg began advertising corn flakes in April 1907, two months after new company was incorporated. Campaigns pioneered in talking to consumer.

troit manufacturer who supplied his rollers—the only one in the U.S. with facilities for making this equipment —he was told that a competitor had just placed an order for all the rollers the firm could produce over the next several months—planning, presumably, to put them in storage while Kellogg's Corn Flakes vanished from grocers' shelves.

Back in Battle Creek, and wandering unhappily through the ruins of the old factory, Kellogg discovered that his original rollers, though damaged, were in repairable condition. **He telephoned the equipment manufacturer and persuaded him to take on the repair job.**

The old rollers traveled to Detroit marked with acid, to avoid a factory mix-up with the competing cereal firm's new ones, and returned to Battle Creek in a freight car manned by a Kellogg employe.

And within five months, the new plant was in operation.

"Now we can turn out 4200 cases a day, and that's all the business I ever want," Kellogg told his son, who had recently entered the firm.

It was not, however, all the Corn Flakes the public wanted.

A generous advertising budget ($1 million a year by 1915), lively advertising campaigns, and massive distribution of free samples kept sales rising. So did heavy spending on new equipment, packaging and product research, and introduction of new brands of cereal.

By 1920, production had reached 24,000 cases a day.

W. K. Kellogg served as president of his company until 1929, and as board chairman until 1946. He died in 1951 at the age of 91.

Shortly before World War I, he asked the company treasurer to go over his personal finances, and was astonished to learn that he had already accumulated $1 million. (Before he died, his contributions to charity, largely through the W. K. Kellogg foundation, were to exceed $45 million.)

"Well, I never expected to be worth that much," he remarked mildly.

W. K. Kellogg, whose top salary before he was 45 had been $1044 a year, was probably telling the truth.

Young, successful Henry Ford poses proudly in office, had already bought out early partners.

HE MADE THE FORDS ROLL BY

Ford made first car in 1896,
in 1908 concentrated on low-cost Model T,
sold 15 million by 1927

HENRY FORD'S Model T, first marketed in 1908, was the original "compact" car.

The development of the "T", which almost overnight turned the automobile from a toy for the rich into an adjunct of everyday U.S. life, makes Ford the key figure of an industry whose early days are crowded with illustrious names.

Henry Ford was born on a Michigan farm in 1863.

The only side of farm life that attracted him was the opportunity it afforded for tinkering with machinery, and when he was 16 he left home to become an apprentice machinist in Detroit.

For the next few years, as apprentice and journeyman, he worked on steam and gasoline engines; in 1888, he joined Edison Illuminating Co. as a mechanical engineer.

Four years later, in 1892, Charles Duryea invented the first U.S. automobile. And Henry Ford, like every other young mechanic in Detroit, was electrified by the event.

The first gasoline-powered motor car had been demonstrated in Paris by Gottlieb Daimler, inventor of the high speed internal combustion engine, only six years earlier, and the first practical automobiles were already being manufactured by the French firm of Panhard & Levassor, whose engineers had added to Daimler's vehicle such basic features of automobile design as clutch, gear-box, and transmission.

The U.S. industry, which was to surpass the French in production in 1903 —coincidentally, the year in which Ford Motor Co. was founded—got off to a slow start in the '90s.

The horse and buggy hung on because, as Charles Duryea ruefully remarked, "oats were too cheap."

The first U.S. automobiles, made almost entirely by hand, were not only too expensive for most potential customers, but also so undependable that "automobileers" were the laughing stock of their horsedrawn friends and neighbors.

And the noisy, dirty "horseless carriages", which ran—when they did run—at such breathtaking speeds, were considered by many citizens to be a menace to life and limb.

When Thomas Edison declared in 1895 that the "horse is doomed," few Americans agreed with him.

Among those who did, however, was a fast-growing group of manufacturers in Detroit, which was the natural capital of the new industry because it was

Bearded naturalist John Burroughs, inventor Thomas Alva Edison, share ride in sturdy Model T piloted by Henry Ford himself.

MODEL T CONCEPT REBORN IN MODERN COMPACT

already the center of the carriage, bicycle, and marine engine industries, and had plenty of machine shops, metal working establishments, and skilled labor.

Ransom Olds turned his Olds Motor Works to automobile production in 1899; Henry M. Leland, a manufacturer of bicycle parts and marine engines, formed the Cadillac Motor Co. in 1900.

But the first Detroit-made automobile had made its jerking, sputtering maiden run in 1896, and its builder had been Henry Ford.

Ford began working on a car of his own as soon as he read the reports of Duryea's triumph.

Still working full time for Detroit Edison, he turned out three experimental models between 1896 and 1899.

Then, in partnership with Tom Cooper, a retired bicycle racing champion, and C. H. Wills, an engineer, and with the backing of a group of Detroit financiers, he founded the Detroit Automobile Co.

This first business venture was a financial fiasco; so was the Ford Automobile Co., formed with the same partners under the auspices of another group of financiers in 1901.

The trouble was that Ford and his associates were trying to sell a high-priced racing car, even further out of the average buyer's reach than the Oldsmobile and Cadillac, which were by then enjoying considerable success in a limited market.

However, Ford was making a reputation for himself, both as a brilliant engineer and as a daring racing driver. (He raced his own cars in competition until 1904.)

In the summer of 1902, he produced his last and most famous racer, the "999," which was so fast that neither Ford, Cooper nor Wills wanted to risk bringing their business careers to an untimely end by taking it into competition.

Driven by Barney Oldfield, one of the first great professional auto racers, the "999" won a spectacular triumph in a major meet, and attracted the attention of a prosperous coal dealer, Alex Y. Malcomson.

Ford and Malcomson became co-founders of the Ford Motor Co. in the fall of 1902, and their first car, practical and relatively inexpensive, priced at $850, went on the market in 1903.

"The most reliable machine in the world," its advertisement in *Motor World* Magazine ran. "A two-cylinder car of ample power for the steepest hills and muddiest roads. The same genius which conceived the world's record maker — the "999" — has made possible the production of a thoroughly practical car at a moderate price."

Ford Motor Co. sold 1700 of these cars in 15 months, and earned small fortunes for its backers.

Malcomson, intoxicated by this quick success, promptly invested in another automobile company, failed, and in 1906 had to sell out his Ford holdings to avoid bankruptcy.

Ford and the company's business manager, James Couzens, who was to be number two man in the organization until 1915, bought him out for $175,000.

Public suspicion of "horseless carriages" was melting away in the early years of the new century, and Ford Motor Co., like its competitors, continued to prosper.

All the cars on the U.S. market, however, were still luxury items.

Ford Motor Co. introduced five models between 1903 and 1908; the cheapest—the original $850 model—was competitive with the least expensive of the "merry Oldsmobiles," and the others ran as high as $2000.

But Henry Ford had begun to dream of a really cheap "farmer's car."

And quite suddenly, early in 1908, he decided that henceforth his company was going to produce one single low-priced model, and that all Ford cars would be as standardized as "pins or matches."

The result, of course, was the Model T, a light, tough, accessoryless black box on wheels.

The "T" bore some resemblance to earlier Fords, and to Oldsmobile, Cadillac, and French Renault models.

But the design features that, together with its overall simplicity and economy, made it unique, were the work of Ford and the men around him.

These included an ignition system with a built-in magneto; a system of "splash" lubrication; a new and superior type of rear axle; three-point suspension and "planetary" transmission.

Even in its first year, when it was priced at a moderate but not rock-bottom $850 (in the years ahead, its price was to drop to $575), the car was a spectacular success.

For one thing, it was far easier to drive than other cars on the market—an important feature in a day when most prospective buyers still had to learn to drive.

And it could travel the roughest country roads, climb stony hills and slog through mud—even more impor-

tant when the vast majority of roads throughout the U.S. were still relics of the horse-and-buggy era.

The Ford assembly line was born of necessity as Model T sales soared.

It was obviously impossible to turn out thousands of cars a year in a factory where mechanics wasted time moving from job to job or waiting for stockboys to bring them parts.

First came the grouping of machines, with parts and tool bins, in the order in which they would actually be used, rather than in separate departments for each type.

Then came the installation of inclined slide, leading from one bench to the next, to eliminate the need for carrying or passing of parts from man to man.

Equally important was the increasing specialization of each worker's task; a skilled mechanic who formerly would have put an entire part together now merely performed a single operation on the part-in-the-making and passed it along.

By 1913, "line production" was in use on all the feeder lines that led to the final assembly floor.

There, men still moved from chassis to chassis, and, with parts arriving from the feeder lines faster and faster, chaos reigned.

In 1914 came the final step—a moving belt powerful enough to carry cars along the final assembly line was developed.

In the summer of 1913, it still took 12 hours and 28 minutes to put a Model T together; eight months later, the time had been cut to 98 minutes.

And on February 7, 1920, Ford attained his "life's desire"—a car-a-minute production rate.

The Model T was discontinued in 1927. It died because the car buyers of the prosperous '20s were beginning to demand elegant styling and solid comfort, and, as yearly model changes became fashionable, a new institution —the used car lot—sprang up to meet the needs of low-income customers.

A trend in automobile manufacture and marketing that did not begin to reverse itself until the late 1950s had begun.

However, the "T" had made automotive history. It had sold 15 million units for a $7 billion gross, and could take most of the credit for launching the U.S. public's love affair with the internal combustion engine.

Famous "999" was so fast Ford, himself a racing driver, relinquished controls to champion Barney Oldfield (at wheel).

Assembly line, which eventually turned out car a minute, brought Ford international fame as genius of mass production.

HE LAUNCHED THE OUTBOARD MOTOR

Today's multi-billion-dollar recreational boating industry was born in 1909, when Ole Evinrude developed the first practical outboard motor

SOME 5.5 MILLION OUTBOARD-POWERED PLEASURE CRAFT THIS SUMMER ARE PLYING U.S. WATERS, COASTAL, GREAT LAKES AND INLAND

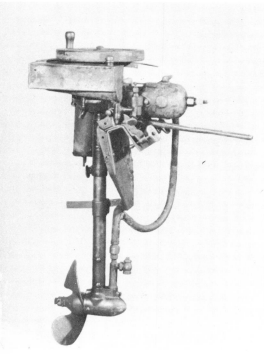

THE FIRST EVINRUDE OUTBOARD MOTOR

OLE EVINRUDE was prolific inventor, wife Bess a shrewd promoter and business-woman. Together they made a unique team, created a billion-dollar industry.

MILLIONS of U.S. families, taking to the nation's lakes and bays in their own small boats this summer, owe a vote of thanks to a Norwegian-American farm boy whose Viking blood ran away with him—Ole Evinrude, inventor of the first practical outboard motor.

When the first Evinrude outboard went on the market in 1909, the J. P. Morgan dictum on pleasure boat ownership ("if you have to ask what it costs, you can't afford one") began to pass into history.

Today, there are 8.0 million craft in the recreational boating fleet, many of them bought on the instalment plan—and at least 5.5 million are powered by outboard motors.

The growth of the recreational boating industry during the past decade alone has been staggering.

In 1949, when the pleasure fleet numbered only 2.5 million, boat owners spent $780 million on their hobby. By the early Sixties, they were spending $2 billion a year and the figure is climbing higher yearly.

By mid 60s according to Outboard Boating Club, more than 12 million pleasure boats were afloat, and the annual boating bill averaged at least $3.5 billion.

Ole Evinrude was not the first inventor to see profitable possibilities in a device that would take the work out of propelling a small boat.

In 1873, a Frenchman developed a gigantic, ponderous contraption that moved a barge on the Seine before the astonished gaze of Napoleon III. But it was too slow to be practical.

Twenty years later, at the Chicago Fair, William Steinway, of the piano family, exhibited a crude outboard of pipes and gears topped by a heavy internal combustion engine. Clamped to a skiff, it made the craft sputter, back-fire and churn across Lake Michigan. But it created such clouds of oily smoke that it would hardly have been suitable for pleasure boating.

In 1905, Cameron B. Walker of Detroit invented an outboard motor that came close to workability, but its configuration was impractical.

And then came Ole Evinrude.

His contribution, essentially, was to simplify the outboard's basic shape—his motor. a single-cylinder "one-lunger," was perched directly upon the single, straight driveshaft which, extending downward vertically into the water, turned the propeller. It was actually *outside* the boat itself, securely clamped to the rear transom.

The man who was finally to turn the outboard motor from an idea into the foundation of a billion-dollar industry was born on a Wisconsin farm in the late 1870s, the son of Norwegian immigrant parents.

His formal education ended with the third grade.

Ole's father had his heart set on turning the boy into a farmer, but Ole decided while he was still in his early teens that he liked machinery better than cows and corn, and water better than dry land.

When he was 14 he began building a sailboat. His father found it half finished in back of the barn, a family story goes, and axed it into kindling wood.

Ole promptly began another one—well out of sight of the farmhouse, this time. And when Andrew Evinrude found the second boat—a seaworthy 16-footer—he decided that trying to keep his son down on the farm was hopeless.

So, at 16, Ole left home and went to work as a machinist in the nearby town of Madison, Wisc.

He moved on to Pittsburgh, then Chicago, and finally Milwaukee, where he went into business for himself as a pattern-maker.

He built his first engine—a gasoline model for "horseless carriages"—in the basement of his boarding house, and went into partnership with a friend to manufacture it.

The firm of Clemick and Evinrude was soon a going concern, and hired a bookkeeper, a tiny, energetic Irish girl named Bess Cary.

In 1907, Ole and Bess were married, and one of the most remarkable husband-and-wife teams in the history of U.S. business was soon on its way to success.

Two years later, after their only son, Ralph, had been born, Ole began working on an outboard motor.

He and his two brothers-in-law launched it, attached to a rented rowboat, in April, 1909, and, to their delight, it put-putted cheerfully along at five miles an hour.

DECADE OF OUTBOARD GROWTH (Sales—$ millions)		
	Outboard Marine Co.	Total Industry
1950	$26.2	$37
1951	28.2	40
1952	33.4	47
1953	49.3	70
1954	63.2	90
1955	73.2	105
1956	106.3	152
1957	124.8	178
1958	130.8	189
1959	139.3	200
1960	171.4	225

Ole built a second motor, lent it to a friend, and the next day got an order from the friend for 10 more—with cash on the line.

It was Bess who then saw the commercial potentialities of the outboard and persuaded her husband to start manufacturing them.

Ole, it seems, was a brilliant inventor but almost abnormally .shy.

But Bess was an extrovert and an extremely shrewd business woman with a flair for marketing.

In the summer of 1909, she coined the new company's first advertising slogan—"Throw the oars away! Use an Evinrude Motor!"

The Evinrude Co. flourished until 1913, when Bess' health failed and Ole sold out.

The next seven years were a long vacation for the Evinrudes. They explored the Florida waterways, the Great Lakes and the Mississippi in a 42-ft. cruiser of Ole's own design.

In 1920, the Evinrudes went home to Milwaukee with a new design for a lightweight, two-cylinder outboard motor.

Bess named it Elto (Evinrude Light Twin Outboard), and the Elto Co. went into business the next year.

By the late '20s, the outboard motor industry was thriving, and Elto had plenty of competitors, including the old Evinrude Co.

In 1929, Elto and Evinrude merged with a third company, Lockwood-Ash, forming Outboard Motor Corp.

It was in the same year that Bess Evinrude finally retired, although Ole remained president.

Bess died in 1933, and Ole 14 months later.

But Outboard Motor, with S. F. Briggs as chairman and young Ralph Evinrude as president, kept growing.

In 1935, it purchased Johnson Motors, a major competitor, and became Outboard Marine Mfg. Co.

Today, Outboard Marine Co. (it dropped the "Manufacturing" in 1956) has about 70% of the market.

It also manufactures utility vehicles, lawn and garden equipment and chain saws, but its Evinrude, Johnson and Gale motors are its major source of revenue.

OMC's outboard sales have risen from $26.4 million in 1950 to $140 million by 1960, when total net sales were $171.4 million.

Its two major competitors, who share most of the remaining 30% of the market, are Mercury Outboard Motor and Scott Div. of McCullough Corp.

Today's outboards can power anything from a small canoe to a 30-foot cruiser. Electric-starting, quiet and streamlined, up to 75 horsepower and capable of speeds to 100 miles an hour, they are a far cry from Ole Evinrude's original five-mile-an-hour rowboat pusher.

But Ole still deserves the credit for setting the U.S. afloat.

WATER SKIING GROWTH IS LARGELY DUE TO OUTBOARDS, WHICH CAN TOW SKIERS 30 MPH

HOUSEHOLD HORSEPOWER

Earl Richardson and George Hughes, designers of first successful irons and and stoves, were fathers of today's $6 billion household appliance industry

WHAT RICHARDSON AND HUGHES STARTED

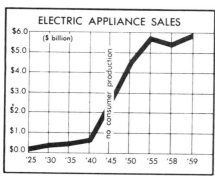

ELECTRIC APPLIANCE SALES

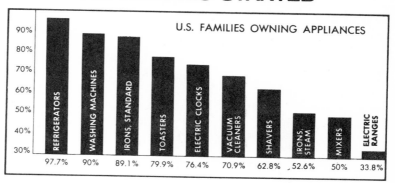

U.S. FAMILIES OWNING APPLIANCES

Figures—Electrical Merchandising

ROUND the turn of the century, two young men, one in Ontario, Calif., the other in Fargo, N.D., both began worrying about a problem of inconspicuous waste—and laid the foundations of today's $6 billion electric appliance industry.

In the early 1900s, the newly harnassed energy of electricity was being used almost exclusively for lighting. Most local power companies operated only at night, and rates were consequently very high.

It occurred to each of the two young men that electrical equipment for daytime use would mean cheaper power—and profit both for the power companies and for the manufacturers of the equipment.

And each was sure enough that he was right to throw over a secure power company job and start his own appliance manufacturing business on the thinnest of shoestrings.

The two were Earl H. Richardson, designer of the first successful electric iron, and George A. Hughes, "father" of the electric range.

Richardson began working on his iron in 1903, while he was employed as a meter reader by the Ontario Power Co.

Practically nothing is known about his early life—not even the date of his birth.

He was born in Kilbourne City,

175

Wis., probably in the mid-1870's, and, at "an early age," according to one of the few faded newspaper clippings about him that can be found, went to work for a power company in Tomah, Wis.

In 1895, he moved on to Pomona, Calif., where his father was in the grocery business.

He got his job in neighboring Ontario, according to one of the few Richardson legends, in the best Horratio Alger tradition.

Water from a burst pipe in the power company's headquarters had torn through a wall and flooded the generator. It looked as if the generator would have to be shipped to Schenectady, 3000 miles away, for repairs, when young Mr. Richardson, who, one imagines, had been sitting in the outer office waiting for an interview, stepped in and saved the day.

Richardson's electric iron was not the first on the market—one had been patented, by Henry Steele, as early as 1882.

But in 1903, most housewives were still heating their irons on the kitchen stove—even in the million homes that were already wired for electricity.

Richardson appears to have been the first to reason that electric appliance sales could be boosted only, with the cooperation of local power companies—and that encouraging use of appliances was the best way for power companies to boost *their* sales.

In the comfortably organized domestic world of 1903, Tuesday was ironing day. So, after Richardson had distributed a few dozen free irons to Ontario Power Co. customers, he persuaded his employers to generate electricity all day on Tuesday so that the irons could be used.

A year later, he left the power company and set up the Pacific Electric Heating Co. to manufacture irons. His first factory had four employes.

Before the year was out, the new company was enjoying moderate success. However, customers were complaining that the irons got too hot

in the middle.

Mrs. Richardson told her husband that what housewives really needed was an iron that got hottest at the point, for getting around buttonholes, ruffles and pleats.

In the next Pacific Electric model, the heating elements converged at the tip—and the future trademark, "Hotpoint," was born.

Between 1905 and 1908, the small company grew fast. A new factory, with 55 employes, opened in Ontario. A sales and shipping office was established in Chicago, and a Chicago manufacturing plant came next.

Richardson's merchandising campaign began with door-to-door selling and two-week "free home trials." In 1908 and 1909, Pacific Electric Heating became the first appliance company to advertise in national magazines, buying space in *Colliers* and in the old *Life*.

In 1911, the company changed its name to Hotpoint Electric Heating Co., and "Hotpoint," already a household word, became a registered trademark in 1914.

During the same years, another small company—the Hughes Electric Heating Co.—was thriving, too. Its president, George A. Hughes, was doing for the electric range what Earl Richardson was doing for the iron.

Hughes was born in Monticello, Iowa, in 1871, and grew up in Bismarck, N.D., a rough and tumble frontier town on the edge of what was still Indian country.

His father was a lawyer, and sent him "back East" to the University of Minnesota, where he studied in the school of journalism.

He went into newspaper work, and by all accounts was as good at it as he was to be at selling electric ranges in years to come. He was city editor of the Bismarck *Daily Tribune* at 23.

In 1896, when he was 25, he moved on to a Fargo, N.D., paper.

Shortly thereafter, he began—like many newspapermen before and since

—to think about getting into a better-paying field.

He decided on the fast-growing electric power business, and, with a grub stake from his father (who was then North Dakota's attorney general), went into competition with Fargo's only power company.

The young editor-turned-businessman proved to be a shrewd manager, and was able to wage and win a price war against his company's established competitor.

By the turn of the century, Hughes Electric Company was serving 10 towns in the Dakotas and Montana.

Like Richardson in California— and at just about the same time— Hughes began to think about getting more business for his company by finding more jobs for electricity.

And in 1904, he came up with an experimental electric range.

A few electric ranges had already been designed—one had been shown at the World's Columbian Exposition in 1893. But most existing models were crude, and none was practical.

Hughes became so convinced—in spite of a barrage of discouragement from electrical engineers—that a practical electric range could be designed and marketed that, in 1908, he sold out his utilities business, moved to Chicago, and founded the Hughes Electric Heating Co.

He started out with a basement workshop, a supply of second-hand coal stoves for conversion to electricity, and six employes whose payroll he could barely meet week to week.

In the summer of 1910, he took one of his strange-looking black stoves to the National Electric Light Association convention in St. Louis, Missouri.

He rented a booth, set up the stove, and began baking apples and frying bacon while crowds gathered. Several utility men were convinced enough to give him orders for a few ranges to take back to Chicago.

During the next few years, he traveled from coast to coast, giving sales talks and cooking demonstrations—

ORIGINAL HOTPOINT CO. MANUFACTURED FULL LINE OF SMALL APPLIANCES, SHOWN IN 1912 SATURDAY EVENING POST AD. THEIR LOOKS WOULD AMUSE TODAY'S CONSUMER AS MUCH AS THEIR NAMES — ELECTRIC EGG COOKER WAS "EL EGGO," COFFEE MAKER "EL PERCO."

and taking orders.

By 1915, his company was solidly in the black.

Three years later, Hughes Electric Heating, Hotpoint Electric Heating and the heating device section of General Electric Co. merged.

George Hughes became president of the new company, which was called the Edison Electric Appliance Co., but retained the Hotpoint trademark.

Earl Richardson, however, disappeared completely from the business scene. Although he could hardly have been much over 45, he apparently sold his interest and retired.

Hughes remained with Edison Electric, became chairman of the board in 1940, and died in 1944, one of the grand old men of the appliance industry.

In 1952, the company became Hotpoint Co., a General Electric division.

Today, electric appliances are part of the American way of life—to the tune of close to $6 billion in sales for 1960 and an anticipated $10 billion by 1970.

High-speed electronic ovens and ranges, ultrasonic washing machines, and even — eventually—dishwashers with mobile units for carting dishes to and from the table and sinks that will spout hot coffee or dry martinis—are looming on the horizon.

Hughes and Richardson, who were among the first to realize how many jobs electricity can do in the home, would probably not be surprised.

THE MEN WHO MADE THE MOVIES

Furrier Loew, scrap dealer Mayer, made movies mass medium, Hollywood world film capital

IN THE FIRST three decades of this century, movie-making traveled from the shabby lofts of Manhattan and Brooklyn to the newly built studios of Hollywood to become the glamor girl of U.S. industry.

And in Hollywood, for the first time in history, entertainment became really big business.

Behind the scenes in those early days—and sometimes right out on the sets—was a remarkable group of showmen-businessmen who had been quick to see the potentialities of the motion picture as a mass entertainment medium. And within this group, the names of Louis B. Mayer, producer, and Marcus Loew, theater man, stand out as sharply as do the names of Garbo and Valentino among the stars of that era.

The movies were born in 1896, when a capacity audience gathered in a New York vaudeville house to see a strange new attraction billed as "Thomas A. Edison's Latest Marvel, the Vitascope."

The Vitascope, which consisted of a series of jerky moving slides flashed upon a screen, bore about as much resemblance to today's wide screen epics as did the Wright Brothers' first flying machine to a modern jet.

Nevertheless, it drew cheers from the audience—and by the summer of 1896, every major vaudeville house in the U.S. was offering moving slides on machines turned out by any one of a dozen enterprising manufacturers.

By 1900, vaudeville audiences had grown tired of the novelty, and slides were being shown as "chasers"—the last act on the program, designed to send the customers home.

However, just three years later, Edwin S. Porter made a new kind of movie for Edison—*The Great Train Robbery*, which actually told a story.

Dozens of small producers began crowding into the field, turning out short and crude, but lively, comedies and melodramas.

And popular interest in the moving pictures soared again.

In 1905, "nickelodeons" began to open. These were usually tiny, shabby stores, equipped with a projector, a piano for musical accompaniment to the silent films, and all the folding chairs the proprietor could pack in. For the price of a nickel, customers were treated to perhaps half an hour's worth of cinematic odds and ends.

Between 1905 and 1907, 3000 of these establishments went into business.

They offered entertainment—that practically anybody could afford—to a mass audience which was being swelled, during the first decade of the new century, by the arrival of 9 million immigrants from Europe.

Recently arrived immigrants were, in fact, among the nickelodeons' best customers. The price was right for them, and so were the simple, heavily pantomimed stories which could be enjoyed without knowledge of English.

And virtually all of the new industry's business leaders were first and

LOUIS B. MAYER

MARCUS LOEW

178

second generation Americans—men who used their exceptional talents for salesmanship and showmanship to escape from the immigrant ghettos.

Marcus Loew, a Manhattan furrier, was one of the first of these nickelodeon entrepreneurs.

Loew had been born of immigrant parents in 1870, into the grinding poverty of New York's Lower East Side.

He had begun peddling newspapers at six, gone to work in a map-coloring plant for 35 cents a day at 10, and spent his teens in a garment district sweat shop.

Somehow, out of his $4.50 wage for a six day, 69-hour week, he managed to save $63 and go into business on his own as a fur broker at 19.

Although this first venture ended in bankruptcy, young Loew managed to hang on in the fur trade. By the early 1900s, he was prospering enough to be able to branch out into real estate.

On a selling trip to Chicago, he had made friends with two other fur merchants, Adolph Zukor and Morris Kohn, and through them, he became interested in penny arcades—then, as now, little amusement parlors that offered peep hole movies, slot machines, and other entertainment.

In 1905, he saw his first nickelodeon in Covington, Ky., and promptly decided to try the same thing in a penny arcade he had acquired across the river in Cincinnati.

The show attracted 5000 customers on its opening day, and 10,000 the following Sunday.

That was enough for Marcus Loew, and he hurried back to New York to begin converting the penny arcades he owned there.

By 1909, the nickelodeons—Loew's among them—were beginning to come up in the world. They were bigger and more elegant, offered vaudeville acts as well as movies, and charged admissions as high as a quarter.

In that year, Loew took over two theaters of the Shubert chain—a giant step forward into the big-time entertainment world.

A year later, in partnership with Zukor and another nickelodeon man, Nicholas Schenk, he formed Loew's Consolidated Enterprises.

And by 1911, his theater chain was prospering so mightily that he was able to reorganize the company, as

Loew's Theatrical Enterprises, with a capital of $5 million.

In the meantime, a young man up in Boston was getting out of the scrap metal business, in which he had not been notably successful, and into the nickelodeon business.

He was Louis B. Mayer, born in Russia early in the 1880s and raised in St. John, New Brunswick, where his father was a junk dealer.

He came to Boston in 1904, and spent the next three years trying to ply his father's trade.

In 1907, when he had decided that the junk business was not for him and was casting around for a way to get out of it, he had a chance to buy a nickelodeon cheap.

Located in nearby Haverhill, the establishment had been named the Gem, but was popularly called the Germ.

Mayer bought it, cleaned it up and renamed it the Orpheum.

And, a few months later, he brought off his first stroke of daring showman-

Bijou Dream, lavish Rochester, N.Y., nickelodeon, took up entire floor of business building, proudly flaunted "Admission 5¢."

"The Great Train Robbery," produced in 1903, was the first true feature film. It developed continuous, complete story.

179

Two merged their talents to form MGM empire

ship. As his Christmas attraction, he billed a film called *Passion Play*, the "life of Jesus Christ in 27 beautiful scenes."

It had been attacked from pulpits across the nation in such terms as "disgraceful sacrilege, horribly commercializing the sacred life of Our Lord."

But the public liked Biblical dramatizations just as much in 1907 as it does in 1961, and Louis B. Mayer had his first hit on his hands.

He was soon doing well enough to buy a second theater in Haverhill, and, shortly thereafter, to enter the film distribution end of the fast-growing new industry.

In 1915, the year when the first feature-length film, *Birth of a Nation*, electrified the country as *The Great Train Robbery* had done 12 years before, Mayer joined with other small distributors in a new production-distribution firm, Metro Pictures Corp.

A year later, having cleaned up a quarter of a million dollars on the New England distribution rights to *Birth of a Nation*, he became an independent producer.

He stole a star, Anita Stewart, from Vitagraph, one of the larger New York studios, and, after production of his first hit film, *Virtuous Wives*, left the East for Hollywood, which was just beginning to rival New York as a movie-making center.

Mayer was a volatile, sentimental little man who wept at his own movies and had fainting fits during office crises.

But by the early 1920s, he was a Hollywood power to be reckoned with.

He learned movie-making by haunting the lots and driving his directors to distraction with questions.

He attracted top talent—during the first 10 years of his career, producers like the brilliant young Irving Thalberg, directors like Fred Niblo, Reginald Barker and Erich von Stroheim

and actors and actresses like Norma Shearer, John Gilbert, Greta Garbo, Lon Chaney and Joan Crawford came to work for him.

He had a gift for giving the public exactly the kind of movies it would pack theaters to see.

And above all, perhaps, he was vastly ambitious both for himself and for the movie industry.

He was actually so shy that he often sat crying at his desk before important interviews—but he managed to exude an air of confidence.

When he was preparing to make his first Hollywood film, and his financial resources were far from limitless, he wired his director:

"My unchanging policy will be great star, great director, great play, great cast. You are authorized to get these without stint or limit. Spare nothing, neither expense, time nor effort. Simply send me the bills and I will OK them."

While Mayer was laying the foundations for his Hollywood empire, Marcus Loew, back East, was thinking about buying a studio.

As the movie industry became more complex and competitive, owners of huge theater chains like Loew's were virtually forced to buy into production facilities to guarantee their source of supply.

Classic "Birth of a Nation," directed by David Wark Griffith, packed theaters everywhere, made small fortune for Mayer.

Francis X. Bushman is obvious villain, Ramon Navarro obvious hero, in 1924 version of famous Wallace novel, "Ben Hur."

"Four Horsemen of Apocalypse," in 1921, made Rudolph Valentino international idol, intensified craze for Argentine tango.

And production-distribution firms like Metro Pictures, which Mayer had abandoned to strike out on his own, needed tie-ins with theater chains to guarantee a market for their products.

So, in 1920, Loew bought Metro. And, four years later, he merged his company with Goldwyn Pictures Corp., a production firm better known for the artistic quality of its films than for its ability to make money.

The manager chosen to head the new firm was none other than Louis B. Mayer — and Metro-Goldwyn-Mayer was born.

Its first major production was the original *Ben Hur*, which cost a record-breaking $4 million, grossed close to $10 million, and was the first of a long line of MGM extravaganzas.

Loew and Mayer were never particularly close associates.

Loew was as cheerfully even-tempered and conservative as Mayer was volative and flamboyant; he ran his theaters from New York and never moved to Hollywood.

He died in 1927, leaving a $30 million estate; Mayer lived the life of a Hollywood mogul with huge enjoyment until 1957, and left a mere $7.5 million.

But the merger of their talents marked the beginning of the movie industry's long golden age.

181

THE BIG BUSINESS OF BEAUTY

The feminine struggle for equal rights early in the 20th century
set the stage for Elizabeth Arden's blossoming career in beauty

AMERICAN WOMEN enthusiastically lavish over $2.5 billion annually on themselves for the sake of beauty.

The booming cosmetics industry, whose products and services ceased long ago to be luxuries, will soon be ready with a cornucopia of surprises for the fashion-conscious female. The stylish woman will be able to cover her face with a colorless beige foundation, brush on a youthful,

maidenly blush with a subtle rouge and coat her lips with pink or beige lipstick.

She will also be able to emulate the elegant looks of Hollywood's glamour goddesses with "lash lengtheners" and change the color of her hair to any of 50 different shades. The desired effect: a natural unmadeup look.

Newest addition to the long list of available beauty products is a

wrinkle remover, made of cow's blood, which camouflages creases in a woman's face up to eight hours at a time. Dewrinklers are expensive ($5 for 20 applications) and occasionally risky (a heavy rain can turn Cinderella back into a Plain Jane). Nevertheless, the industry expects the product to be worth $9 million a year in sales.

Fifty years ago the expression "She paints" was the most damning

The early 20th century saw a change in basic U.S. values which helped spawn today's booming beauty business.

ELIZABETH ARDEN

thing that could be said about a woman. Young girls were advised that the best cosmetic for healthy good looks was plenty of outdoor exercise, a balanced diet and kind thoughts that would insure pleasing expressions.

The woman largely responsible for the American Beauty Revolution was a far-sighted Canadian girl who went into business for herself in 1910, a time when most women considered working for a living as highly improper and unbecoming to the fair sex.

Elizabeth Arden, confident of success, made femininity into a science and started the beauty industry along the road to its present multi-billion dollar status.

Although sales of Elizabeth Arden products today are small compared to those of her arch-competitor, Helena Rubinstein, and microscopic next to the door-to-door operation of Avon Products, the firm is still considered the Tiffany of the industry.

The business of beauty is currently in its hey-day but widespread use of cosmetics is not solely a 20th century phenomenon.

American Indians were adept at extracting and mixing dyes and used paint extensively as ceremonial decoration.

Even the Colonial Era was full of opulence and glitter. Both men and women spent long hours at their toilette and, until the French Revolution, it was fashionable to copy the French who were known for their overindulgence in use of cosmetics. (Ladies often took so long to complete their beauty treatments that many turned the chore into a social event.)

During this period a considerable number of preparations were known and used openly: cold cream, bleaches, hair dye, eye shadow, rouge, pomade and face powder.

Early U.S. colonists depended upon cosmetics imported from England or upon their own ingenuity. A popular beauty treatment involved applying strips of bacon to the face before retiring to keep skin soft and to prevent wrinkles.

Face powder was made at home with powdered egg shells and toilet water. A lemon carried in the hand and sucked from time to time was considered helpful for keeping the lips red.

Most homemade products were harmless but some commercial cosmetics were injurious and a few were actually poisonous. No laws existed to regulate the use of toxic substances and cosmetics earned a dangerous reputation.

This fear was prevalent as late as 1890. An advertisement for Mme. Rowley's Toilet Wash emphasized, "it is recommended by eminent physicians as a substitute for injurious cosmetics" and added that it is "harmless and saves dollars uselessly expended for cosmetics, powders and lotions."

While makeup staged a brief comeback during the Civil War, the U.S. cosmetic industry fared poorly in the 19th century. Although the eminent style-setter Dolly Madison used rouge while she was First Lady, it was generally considered *de rigueur* not to paint.

Cosmetics use hit its lowest ebb in the late 1800s. Staid Victorian society tolerated little frivolity and flashiness. The only makeup a "lady" might use was a dab of cologne on her handkerchief and a subtle touch of face powder. Even actresses applied cosmetics sparingly.

The complexion was usually cared for with soap and steaming water, although such companies as Harriet Hubbard Ayer and Daggett & Ramsdell were beginning to establish a reputation with their cold creams.

The early years of the 20th century saw the start of a new age for women. The first salvos in a revolution which was destined to change many of the basic values in American society were fired by the suffragettes.

"Sensible and responsible women do not want to vote," wrote Grover Cleveland in the *Ladies' Home Journal* in 1905. "The relative positions to be assumed by men and women in the working out of our civilization were assigned long ago by a higher intelligence than ours."

President Cleveland notwithstanding, women all over the country were beginning to break out of the old, confining molds.

In 1901, a 160-pound schoolteacher shot Niagara Falls in a barrel. Carrie Nation began smashing

183

Men now dominate multi-billion-dollar cosmetics industry

saloons, the last undisputed refuge of the American male. Jane Addams began to establish settlement houses, demonstrating that the stronger sex had no monopoly on good works.

A Canadian girl, barely out of her teens, arrived in New York during these turbulent times. Florence Nightingale Graham came from Woodbridge, a small town near Toronto. The youngest of five children, she was born around 1890 although the exact year is not certain.

Her Scottish father had eloped with a Cornish bride and emigrated to Canada.

Florence left school before she was 18 and, following her namesake, entered nurses' training. She tired of it after a few weeks and later said she not only wanted to make people well but also "to make them beautiful."

She tried a variety of jobs — working for a bank, a truss manufacturer, a dentist and a real estate company (where she was fired because she couldn't type well enough).

Inheriting some of her father's roving spirit, she decided to come to New York in 1906. She first worked as a stenographer at the E. R. Squibb Company but soon found a line of work more to her liking.

She took a secretarial job in the Fifth Avenue offices of a London cosmetics firm, Eleanor Adair. But the Adair company was not a cosmetic house by today's standards. Cosmetics were definitely not in vogue and a woman's beauty equipment was limited to a bottle of glycerin and rose water and a box of rice powder.

The Adair salon's business was mainly beauty treatments — facial workouts and manicures. Its specialty was called "muscle strapping," a process which involved bandaging the face and throat and patting vigorously to bring the blood to the surface.

Here Florence discovered that she had "wonderfully magnetic hands for massage" and could give expert facial treatments. She found the work exciting and soon learned the basic formulas for making creams and lotions.

More important, she came to recognize that tremendous possibilities lay ahead in the field. She also realized that beauty had to be sold to American women.

In 1909, Florence went into partnership with a friend, Elizabeth Hubbard. They opened a shop on Fifth Avenue but the two girls were temperamently incompatible and parted company within a year.

The following year Florence struck out on her own, borrowed $6000 from a cousin and opened a salon at 509 Fifth Avenue. Most of the loan, repaid in six months, was spent on elegant interior decoration.

Her own name didn't seem quite right for a salon of beauty. Two of her favorite literary works were "Elizabeth and Her Garden" and Tennyson's long poem "Enoch Arden." She took one name from each and addressed an envelope to herself as "Elizabeth Arden." When the letter arrived in the mail, the name looked as good as it sounded.

The first Elizabeth Arden salon consisted of three treatment rooms and a laboratory. She emphasized massage treatments but soon began to formulate products. Her initial product was a light, fluffy cleansing cream called Amoretta (unusual because most creams at that time resembled lard), followed by Ardena Skin Tonic and a line of rouges and eyeshadows.

"The beginning of all beauty is cleansing," she said but noted that beauty cannot be applied entirely from the outside. She concentrated on physical fitness and body culture as well as skin care. Diets, exercise and relaxing treatments figured strongly in her beauty programs.

Business grew so steadily that she moved to a bigger shop and expanded her line of products.

Elizabeth Arden's success was due in part to her sales strategy. She aimed at two huge, but virtually un-

An 1889 magazine ad for Madame Rowley's Toilet Mask advocated removal of face wrinkles "recommended by eminent physicians and scientific men."

184

tapped, markets: middle-aged women who were losing the bloom of youth; women who were not born beautiful but wished to improve on what they had.

The greatest spur, however, came from the times in which she lived. Volatile young businesswomen were quick to sense that the old mores were being swept away and Elizabeth Arden capitalized on the phenomenon.

World War I marked the beginning of a revolt in manners and morals. Unspoken motto of the Jazz Age was "eat, drink and be merry." The older generation was shocked at young couples doing the fox trot, a dance which prompted unprecedented closeness. Supposely "nice" girls smoked and drank openly. The hipflask became the symbol of the decade.

ACCENT ON FEMININITY

The Roaring Twenties also brought an immense change in women's clothes and appearance. By 1921, flappers wore thin, short-sleeved dresses, rolled their stockings below their knees (often rouged), discarded corsets, bras and petticoats. The slender, boyish figure was every woman's ideal while bobbed hair signified the irresistible feminine urge for freedom.

However, the flappers were very different from their serious-minded and sensibly-shod suffragette sisters of the previous decade. Young women in the Twenties cherished their new-found freedom but they wanted to be alluring to men. The accent was on femininity.

Use of cosmetics was no longer a stigma associated with fast women. The entire female world became make-up conscious and there was no attempt to disguise the practice.

Beauty shops, where operators gave facials, plucked eyebrows and marceled hair, sprang up on every corner. They sold lipsticks in cartridge containers, eyebrow pencils and compact rouges. Gone were the bulky jars which had to be left at home on the dressing table. The new products, thanks to convenient packaging, could be carried in a lady's handbag.

Surviving statistics reveal that only two persons in the beauty culture business paid income tax in 1917. (One undoubtedly was Elizabeth Arden.) By 1927, 18,000 beauty and cosmetics companies were on Internal Revenue rolls.

Advertising reflected the great change in public attitude. The June 1919 issue of the *Ladies' Home Journal* carried only four ads which mentioned rouge. One stressed the product was "imperceptible if applied properly."

Ten years later the magazine carried the following ad: "It's comforting to know that the alluring note of scarlet will stay with you for hours."

In 1915, Elizabeth Arden married Thomas J. Lewis and became a U.S. citizen. She supervised the salon while her husband, as general manager, conducted the wholesale operation, supplying beauty products to department stores.

In 1922, the first overseas branch opened in Paris. The business boom of the Twenties sent Arden sales soaring. Her wholesale volume alone reached $2 million in 1925 and by 1929 it had doubled.

Elizabeth Arden was not only rich but famous. She had 14 stores in the U.S., 150 salons abroad and her products sold in 25 countries.

She appealed to women at both ends of the social scale. To those of limited means she offered do-it-yourself home treatments. For those able to afford $500 a week, she opened two beauty farms, both called Maine Chance, one in the state of Maine and the other, recently popularized by Mamie Eisenhower, in Arizona.

Her most passionate interest, aside from her business which she supervises to the closest detail even today, is race horses.

"A beautiful horse is like a beautiful woman," she once remarked. It is said that at one time she rubbed down a favorite horse with Ardena Skin Tonic because the horse liniment smelled so badly.

Despite the formidable female presence of Arden and Rubinstein, the U.S. cosmetic industry today is dominated by males. In some companies which today still bear the names of their founders (Dorothy Gray, Mary Chess), the ladies retired long ago.

The fashion fate of millions of women each year is decided by such men as Max Factor, Revlon's Charles Revson, Jacqueline Cochran's Andrew Lynn and Charles of the Ritz' Richard Salomon.

Although beauty is still a woman's business, the cosmetic industry is not.

Cover of a 1927 edition of The New Yorker *magazine lampooned current permanent wave mania sweeping U.S.*

Outlandish flapper fashions of the Twenties epitomized the new era of female freedom and individuality.

185

FLYING THE MAILS

**Early air mail routes blazed trail for today's commercial airlines;
first private air mail contractor was William Boeing,
aircraft manufacturer and airline magnate-to-be**

Late in 1919, the U.S. Post Office Department awarded its first air mail route to private contractors.

The route was a hazardous run over 48 miles of water from Seattle, Wash., to Victoria, British Columbia; the contractors were pilot Edward Hubbard and aircraft manufacturer William Boeing.

Ten years later, Boeing's United Air Transport and other fledgling airlines were flying the mails — and a few thousand adventurous passengers — from coast to coast.

The era of commercial aviation had begun, and the story of its beginnings is a remarkable one in which private enterprise, government initiative, and personal heroism all play their parts.

Bill Boeing deserves to be singled out as a pioneer of air transport because of his leadership in the development of the airlines and aircraft manufacture.

But few industries have so many pioneers.

There were manufacturers like Glen Curtiss and Glenn L. Martin, both of whom were in business before World War I, and Donald Douglas, who built the great DC-3, probably the plane in which most

First contract air mail route was flown by Eddie Hubbard (l.) and Bill Boeing in converted Navy plane

of today's jet passengers first rode.

There were the Post Office Department officials who staked their careers on the success of a new way of carrying the mails. And there were the pioneer pilots who risked — and very often lost -- their lives flying primitive aircraft over uncharted routes.

It is safe to say that the airlines probably would never have gotten off the ground without the financial support of the Post Office; large scale commercial air transport was simply too costly a venture for private business to undertake unaided.

And the Post Office's interest in air mail goes all the way back to the years before World War I, when planes were awkward, unreliable, and slow (60 mph was a spectacular speed), and the very idea of flying still fantastic to most people.

Air mail appropriations were introduced in Congress from 1910 on, usually to the sound of laughter from the House floor as one representative or another suggested that the Post Office Department should "get down to earth."

A few trial mail runs — by both balloon and heavier-than-air craft —were actually made in the pre-war years. (The first regular passenger run was also a pre-war venture — for a single Florida tourist season in 1914, the Tampa Air Boat Line shuttled back and forth between Tampa and St. Petersburg.)

But the first air mail appropriation did not come through until 1916, and then, when the Post Office asked for bids on a route in Alaska and one between New Bedford and Nantucket, it had no takers. The infant aircraft industry was too busy with war production.

Amateur Pilot

It was in the same year the 35-year-old William E. Boeing entered the industry.

Born in Detroit in 1881, he had studied engineering at Yale and Washington State College, and then settled in Seattle to go into the family lumber business.

In 1915, he learned to fly from Glenn Martin in Los Angeles, and bought a Martin plane for pleasure.

Like most of the amateur pilots of his day, he didn't have long to wait for his first accident. It was only a hard landing on Puget Sound, but the new plane was greatly damaged.

Plans for air mail service in the U.S. are described by Major R. H. Van Fleet to Pres. Wilson at first Washington-New York run.

Pioneer passenger service, Tampa Air Boat line, drew crowd for its first flight in 1914 (below), but was a commercial failure.

Aviation's early days
take high toll in human lives

In the course of a do-it-yourself repair job, Boeing decided that he could build a plane just as good as the one he had cracked up—and that building planes was what he was going to do.

He drew plans, set up shop in his hangar, and turned out two aircraft, which sold with such encouraging speed that he promptly incorporated his company and moved to a larger site -- a shipyard south of Seattle. A few months later, in the fall of 1916, the Boeing Airplane Company was in full swing — just in time for the World War I boom.

Fighter and reconnaissance planes had begun proving their worth in the earliest days of the war in Europe, and U.S. aircraft manufacturers, whose business had been growing steadily but very slowly before 1914, were suddenly swamped with orders.

Then, when the U.S. itself entered the conflict, they were completely overwhelmed. An industry that had built only about 200 aircraft in its entire history was asked to turn out no less than 29,000 practically overnight.

Only a few thousand of the

planes had been built before the war ended. But wartime research and development had produced aircraft — notably, the Curtis "Jenny" — far faster and better than those of the prewar years; thousands of young men had learned to fly; the public, dazzled by the valor of the airmen in the skies over France, was beginning to take aviation seriously; and last but not least, mail was traveling by air.

The first regular airmail service was inaugurated in 1918, by the Post Office and the Army in cooperation, to give Army air trainees some flying practice.

Its routes linked Boston, New York, Philadelphia, and Washington.

Then, shortly before the end of the war, in August, 1918, the Post Office took over the mail routes from the Army. It was to keep them —with the single exception of the

For Air Express attempt to fly nonstop to Chicago, Handley Page WW I bomber is loaded at Mitchell Field, N. Y., Nov. 1919. Engine trouble forced completion of delivery by train. Regular AE started in 1927.

experimental Seattle-Victoria franchise awarded to Hubbard and Boeing in 1919 — until the mid-1920s.

The wartime trial run was not a financial success; patriotic business men who had applauded the venture found the rates too high (24 cents for half an ounce) and the service not as good as advertised. (Overoptimistically, the Post Office and the Army had promised same-day delivery between New York and Washington — a feat that has yet to be accomplished.)

Perilous Venture

It did prove — at least, to the satisfaction of air-minded Postmaster General Albert Sidney Burlson and Assistant Postmaster Otto C. Praeger — that air mail could be a practical proposition.

But the real value of air mail obviously would lie in long runs, not short ones.

And long runs, with the aircraft and equipment of 1918, were easier to talk about than to fly. Of the first 40 pilots hired by the Post Office, 31 were to die in service.

The first air mail from New York reached Chicago in 1919, Omaha and then San Francisco in 1920.

At first, transcontinental air mail was flown only by day and transferred to trains at night, taking almost as long for the trip as did the mail on the fast, through trains.

Night flying — with no navigation aids, poor maps, no ground lighting to mark the airways, and few and inadequate airfields — was almost incredibly dangerous.

But Burlson and Praeger believed that it had to be tried — and so did their war veteran pilots.

Coast-to-Coast Service

The first coast-to-coast day-and-night flight was attempted in February, 1921. Of the four planes that took off, two from New York and two from San Francisco, two were grounded by weather, and one crashed.

That the fourth got through was largely due to the nerve and stamina of one pilot, Jack Knight, who later flew with United Airlines until 1941.

Knight had the third leg of the flight, from North Platte, Nebraska, to Omaha; but when he reached Omaha, he found that the westbound plane which was to have met him there, turned around and taken the mail back east, was grounded

Among the pioneer pilots of air mail's first years were Army Lt. Torrey H. Webb (below, r., with wife, before takeoff with first official load of air mail ever flown) and Jack Knight (below, l.) hero of Post Office Department's first transcontinental mail run. Start of regular New York-Chicago night flights (above) came in 1925.

in Chicago. He flew on to Chicago himself, with only a Rand McNally road map to guide him. And in two more relays, the plane reached New York. It had taken a total of five pilots 33 hours and 20 minutes to make the trip.

This kind of thing couldn't be done every day; it was not until 1925 that regular cross-country night flights began.

By then, the Post Office in cooperation with General Electric and American Gas Accumulator Co., had designed, developed, and in-

stalled a system of lighted airways, with emergency landing fields every 25 miles along the transcontinental route and powerful, revolving electric or acetylene beacons every ten miles — a giant step forward in aviation safety.

It was also in 1925 that the Post Office, now headed by Postmaster General Harry S. New, began turning the mail routes over to private contractors — a move that marked the end of seven lean postwar years for the aviation industry, and the beginning of the growth of the airlines.

Cmdr. Richard E. Byrd, who led the first flight to the North Pole in 1926, made important contributions to air safety by navigational aids.

Early manufacturer Claude L. Ryan (r.) supplied mail planes to Pacific Air Transport whose owner Vern Gorst is shown with Ryan after record flight from Frisco to Seattle.

Boston-New York mail route of the Colonial Air Transport opened in 1926. Gen. mgr. Juan Trippe (r.) later founded Pan American Airways.

Gen. Billy Mitchell (r.), here with humorist Will Rogers, was court-martialed for his outspoken criticism of armed forces for their failure to recognize military value of plane.

Christening of a Ford Trimotor by Amelia Earhart and Grover Whalen on July 7, 1929 launched the first coast-to-coast air line in the U.S.

Charles Lindbergh got New York's traditional hero's welcome on return from epoch-making transatlantic flight in 1927. His feat made millions of Americans air-minded, gave overnight boost to infant U.S. industry.

FLYING THE MAILS Part 2
Commercial air transport began to grow when Post Office gave mail routes to private contractors; Boeing's United was first major line

On February 2, 1925, Congress passed the Kelly Bill — "An act to encourage commercial aviation and to authorize the Postmaster General to contract for the air service."

Commercial aviation in the mid-1920s needed all the encouragement it could get. And the Post Office, which had at its disposal the chain of potentially lucrative air mail routes that it had been developing — and flying with its own planes and pilots — ever since 1918, was in the best position to provide the needed shot in the arm.

"Lindy" with ace pilots Al Williams, Jimmy Doolittle; with wife; with official of Guggenheim Fund (l. to r.)

Air mail contracts ended aviation's postwar slump

The aircraft industry had plunged into the doldrums at the end of World War I.

Out in Seattle, William Boeing had been reduced to turning out furniture to stay in business when the wartime contracts stopped coming in — and other manufacturers had been no less hard-pressed.

Most of their business, in the early '20s, still came from the armed forces, whose peacetime needs were small.

The Post Office Department's air mail appropriations were not large enough to allow for purchases of many new aircraft — most of the early mail routes were flown in converted World War I reconnaissance planes.

And the commercial market was practically nonexistent. Opportunities in the air for private enterprise were very limited before 1925.

Hundreds of tiny airfields had sprung up across the country; there were plenty of war surplus planes around, and plenty of ex-military pilots who wanted to go on flying. But the best that most of these young men could hope for was to earn a precarious living from teaching, exhibition stunt flying, or taking up joyriders on Sunday afternoons, or from such aerial odd jobs as crop dusting and photography.

Many small-scale passenger operations were launched, but at best, they were no bigger than today's air taxi services, and most of them were short-lived.

The business community was keeping an eye on the skies, but the cost of large-scale development of air transportation was too huge and the risks too great -- until the Kelly Bill came along.

Industry interested

Within two months of the act's passage, the Post Office was flooded with inquiries from prospective bidders for airmail routes — over 5000 of them.

And among the bidders were some of the best-known names in U. S. industry.

The directors of one newly formed company, National Air Transport

Air travel in the '20s was dangerous and uncomfortable, but hardy passengers like these (ready for takeoff in Pacific Air Transport Boeing 40B-4, above, and Colonial Airlines Fokker, below) kept coming back.

(NAT), included Philip Wrigley, Lester Armour, William A. Rockefeller and C. F. Kettering; another bid came in from Henry Ford, who had been interested in aviation ever since 1923 and had backed designer W. B. Stout in the development of a transport plane called the Ford Tri-Motor. (Ford's career in air transport was to be short; he found the field too unprofitable and sold out to Boeing's United Airlines in 1929. It was important, though — the fact that the manufacturer of the beloved Model T was willing to take to the air did a great deal to increase public acceptance of aviation.)

Coming of age

By the end of 1926, airmail routes had been assigned to 12 companies, NAT and Ford Air Transport among them, all with solid financial backing. The routes were short, and only one of the 12 lines (Western Air Express) showed a profit in its first year — but it was clear that air transportation was coming of age.

Another boost from Washington came during 1926, with the passage of the Air Commerce Act. This piece of legislation made the government responsible for licensing of interstate operators, investigation of accidents, extension and maintenance of the lighted airways that the Post Office had begun developing in 1924. It also gave the new Aeronautical Division of the Department of Commerce the job of making aerial maps and running a weather service to provide meteorological reports.

All these provisions made air transport — though still a hazardous business — a sounder investment for industry and a safer bet for the public.

Most people still considered flying the least likely way to get from one place to another; but more and more passengers were beginning to climb aboard the now privately-run mail planes.

Boeing bid

Then, in 1927, the Post Office took the next step — calling for bids on two longer routes, from the West Coast to Chicago and Chicago to New York.

When the bids were opened, the Post Office — and the industry — received a staggering surprise.

William Boeing of Seattle was offering to fly the mail east to Chicago for just $2.85 a pound — twice as low as any competing bid.

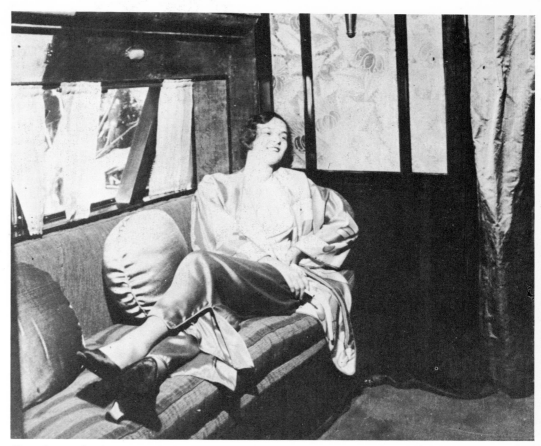

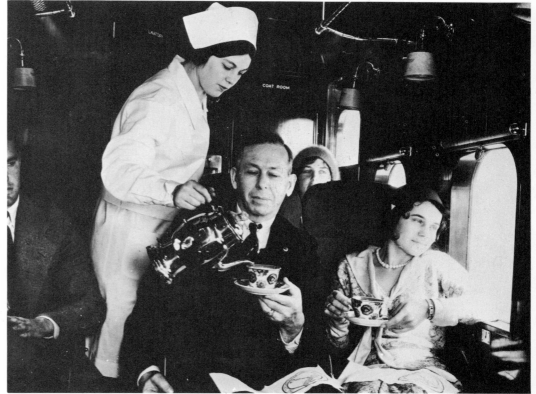

By the end of the '20s, fast-growing airlines were luring passengers with deluxe accommodations (lavishly appointed Western Airlines cabin, above) and personal service (below, stewardess serves coffee in flight).

Franklin Delano Roosevelt brought the airlines to the brink of disaster in 1934; but F. D. R. was the first President to make campaign flights.

AIR-MINDED AMERICANS

Year	Civil Aircraft Production	Passengers Carried (Thousands)	Passenger Revenues ($ Millions)
1926	654	6	.2
1930	2690	385	7.1
1935	1251	679	16.0
1940	6785	2803	53.3
1945	2047	6541	116.3
1950	3520	17468	446.7
1955	4820	38211	1064.7
1960	8181	56352	1860.4

Data: Federal Aviation Agency, Civil Aeronautics Board

These eight stewardesses — all of them registered nurses — were hired by Boeing Air Transport in 1930 for the San Francisco-Chicago flights.

Airlines indispensable by mid-1930s

Boeing had not been among the original bidders in 1925; but he had bought out one of them, Pacific Air Transport, less than a month after the routes were assigned. Although not a profit-maker, Pacific had had a fairly successful first year, carrying 1000 passengers along with the mail bags.

His low bid for the Chicago route was a gamble; but it must have seemed to him that a bet on the development of commercial air transport was the shrewdest one an aircraft manufacturer could place.

And the next few years, in which Boeing Air Transport, as his new company was named, grew into the first of the great airlines, United, were to prove him right.

Naturally, Boeing's bid was accepted. He had the experience and the equipment that the Post Office wanted, and Boeing Airplane was as stable a firm as any in the industry. If the $2.85 rate seemed ridiculous, that was his worry — and that of his disgruntled competitors.

Boeing always maintained that he designed and built the Boeing 40 mail plane between February, 1927, when the airmail contract came through, and July, when service started. It's hard to believe that the planes were not even on the drawing board before February — but in any event, they were flying only five months after the contract award.

The Boeing 40s were single-engine craft, with an enclosed cabin for two passengers and an open cockpit for the pilot. They were the first planes to be equipped with two-way, short-wave aircraft radio, perfected and installed in the Boeing plant and a major contribution to air safety.

In its first year, Boeing Air Transport carried 230,000 pounds of mail and 525 passengers. (The first was a Chicago newspaper woman named Jane Eads, who was taken along for a publicity ride and was ecstatic over her flight to the coast.)

The Model 40 had flown 2 million miles in two years before it was retired by the Boeing 80, which, for 1929, was a positively luxurious passenger plane.

The tri-motor 80 had a cabin for

12, with upholstered seats, reading lights, and cabin instruments to show the travelers their altitude and airspeed. It even had a lavatory (until then, planes had grounded for "comfort stops"), with hot and cold running water. And—another "first" — box lunches were served by a male steward. (In 1930, the first girl hostesses appeared on the San Francisco-Chicago run).

At the end of 1928, Boeing Airplane merged with Frederick B. Rentschler's Pratt & Whitney Aircraft to form the nucleus of United Aircraft & Transport Corp., the most powerful corporation the industry had yet seen. Chance Vought, a builder of military planes, and two propeller manufacturers, Hamilton and Standard Steel, soon joined up with Boeing and P&WA.

United Airlines, the transport arm of UA&T, was born in mid-1929, when Boeing won a bitter struggle with NAT (which had been flying the mail from Chicago to New York since 1927) for control of the coast-to-coast air route.

Boeing and Rentschler set the pattern for the rapidly developing industry.

Curtiss Airplane and Wright Aeronautical also merged in 1929, and began buying up smaller manufacturing firms to form North American Aviation. NAA too had its airline — Transcontinental Air Transport. (TAT surmounted the hazards and discomfort of night flying, which were still considerable, by transferring its passengers to trains at night. It got them from coast to coast in 48 hours, with red carpet service all the way).

The third of the corporate giants — and probably the most complex in structure, with dozens of manufacturing and transportation affiliates— was Aviation Corp., or AVCO.

Nowhere but up

As the 20s drew to a close, it appeared that the aviation industry had nowhere to go but up. Public enthusiasm for flying had soared after Charles A. Lindbergh's history-making Atlantic flight; so had aircraft and air transport stocks. In 1929, the U.S. airlines outstripped those of Europe for the first time, flying more air miles than the French, English, German and Italian lines combined.

But serious trouble lay ahead. Like so many other industries, avia-

tion was dealt a stunning blow by the depression. It was given a new lease on life in April, 1930, by the Mc-Nary-Watres Bill, which gave airmail carriers a flat per-mile subsidy, regardless of the amount of mail they carried. At the same time, the bill gave the Postmaster General the authority to consolidate lines and assign routes in the public interest.

Postmaster General Walter Folger Brown lost no time in making his new authority felt. Under his direction, the mergers proceeded at a faster clip than ever, and more and more of the smaller lines were pushed to the wall.

A number of AVCO's airline subsidiaries were forged into a new transcontinental line, American Airways (later American Airlines). And a merger negotiated by Brown between TAT and Western Express created another of today's great lines, TWA.

By the end of 1931, the Brown reorganization was complete. Three major lines, United, American, and TWA, were flying coast to coast; their parent companies, UA&T, AVCO, and NAA, dominated the industry.

Then, in 1933, Congressional investigation of the "spoils confer-

ences" between Postmaster Brown and industry leaders began; charges of graft, collusion, and excessive profit-taking by the manufacturing branches of the three great corporations were hurled. And on Feb. 9, 1934, President Franklin D. Roosevelt cancelled all commercial airmail contracts and turned the mail routes over to the Army.

The McNary-Watres Bill had, in effect, pushed the airlines out of the frying pan into the fire.

But the Roosevelt experiment didn't work. The Army pilots were totally inexperienced in night and distance flying, and 12 of them were killed in crashes before the month was up.

The airlines got the mail contracts back in May. However, the industry was completely reorganized, with the strict separation of manufacturing and transportation interests that still prevails today.

As for William Boeing, he retired from the presidency of UA&T in 1933, with a Guggenheim medal for "successful pioneering in aircraft manufacture and air transportation." He returned to Boeing Airplane Co. during World War II, and lived until 1956—long enough to see the dawn of the jet age.

The modern era of air transport dawned when Douglas DC-3 hit airport runways in the mid '30s. One of the all-time great aircraft, the Douglas DC-3 made flying a habit for a new generation of travelers.

BARON OF BROADCASTING

Lee De Forest's invention of the audion brought millions within reach of the very best in entertainment, education

ON ELECTION NIGHT, 1920, thousands of Americans throughout the nation gathered in front of local newspaper offices to read the returns of the Harding-Cox election.

Meanwhile, in East Pittsburgh, Pennsylvania, history of another kind was in the making. As officials of the Westinghouse Works sat in a small shack atop a factory building, they read the latest election bulletins into a primitive microphone. Their voices, transmitted to an antenna on the roof, wafted out on the night air.

No more than 500 amateur "ham" operators heard this initial broadcast over station KDKA. Yet the next morning news of the sensational feat was splashed across front pages from coast to coast. For weeks afterward, people marveled at the new miracle which could bring up-to-the-minute news into their living rooms.

Behind the birth of broadcasting lay 20 years of frustration for Lee De Forest, the father of radio. Without his invention of the audion tube, neither radio nor television would have been possible. For that matter, we would not have radar, loudspeaker systems, sound movies or photographic transmission.

One of the most important uses of De Forest's vacuum tube was to amplify the feeble current produced by radio waves.

No ivory tower engineer, De Forest not only perfected the technical means to make broadcasting possible but he also gave his invention a social conscience. In 1910, he envisioned radio as "a medium for bringing into each home the very best in entertainment, education, and information."

He accurately gauged the cultural impact of radio a decade before it came into being. He saw it as a means of widening the intellectual horizons of people who had no direct access to music, culture and news. He believed it would create new ties of understanding between people all over the U.S. and even throughout the world. "A new world cement," he termed radio.

All these goals—and more—broadcasting achieved during De Forest's lifetime.

As far back as 1865 an English physicist, James C. Maxwell, predicted the existence of electromagnetic waves, but it was not until 1884 that Heinrich Hertz of Germany actually proved such waves existed.

Then Guglielmo Marconi, the Italian inventor, produced a wireless

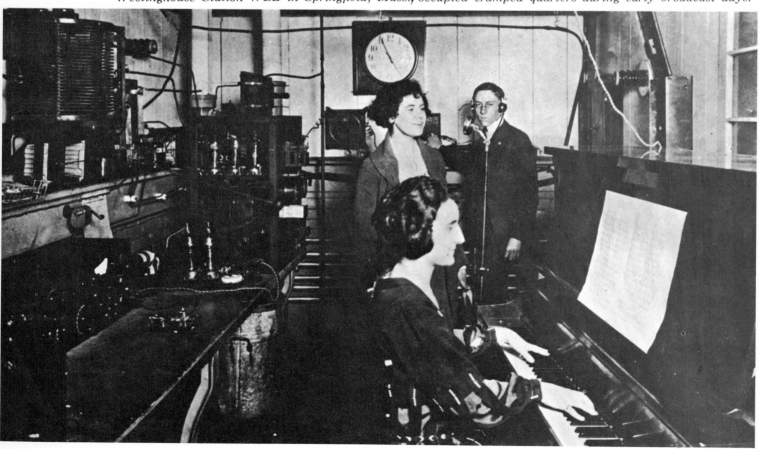

Westinghouse Station WBZ in Springfield, Mass., occupied cramped quarters during early broadcast days.

telegraph in 1896. The device was first used on ships, but its messages were confined to dots and dashes. The idea of transmitting speech evidently did not occur to Marconi.

The next step toward radio was made by an enterprising American engineer, Reginald Fessenden, who came up with the improbable idea of replacing the clatter of telegraph keys with music and speech.

Fessenden is credited with making the first radio broadcast in history from Brant Rock, Mass. On Christmas Eve, 1906, Morse code operators on ships along the Atlantic coast were mystified to hear singing and violin music instead of the familiar dots and dashes.

Constantly plagued by financial troubles, Fessenden became convinced that wireless telephony would not be possible or profitable for many years and, instead, he turned his attention to telegraphy.

It was left to Lee De Forest to develop the audion, a tiny glass and wire gridiron which could both detect and generate radio waves. The audion was perfected in 1906 but De Forest did not apply for a patent until 1907 because he could not afford the $15 fee required by the Patent Office.

Born in Council Bluffs, Iowa, in 1873, Lee De Forest was the son of a Congregational minister who soon moved to Talladega, Alabama, to head a school for Negroes.

The boy's childhood was a lonely one. Northerners were not particularly welcome in the small Southern community after the Civil War. Also, his father's position did not add to the boy's popularity.

Reared in genteel poverty, he dreamed of great riches and fame. He grew up in an era of spectacular new inventions: the gas engine, telephone, electric light. Science fascinated him and De Forest was determined to become an inventor.

He entered Yale University where he was encouraged by his professors to study electrical engineering and to do post-graduate research in the field of wireless communication. In 1898, he received a doctorate but the best job he could get was in the Chicago plant of Western Electric Company at the munificent salary of $8 a week.

One advantage of his routine, tedious job was that it left his mind free to work on wireless experiments at night.

Eight years and a score of preliminary inventions later, his diligence paid off with the audion.

During the summer of 1907, he made a test broadcast in New York City with a Swedish concert singer, Madame Eugenia Farrar. She had scarcely launched into a rendition of "I Love You Truly" when a wireless operator at the Brooklyn Navy Yard sprang from his chair and relayed the phenomenon to the officer in charge.

The earphones were passed from one astonished officer to another. Finally, someone reported the incident to the *New York Herald*. It duly appeared the next morning on page 5; a short paragraph accorded no more importance than a street fight.

De Forest's flair for publicity and his ambition to create a market for the audion led to further feats. In 1908, he broadcast from the Eiffel Tower in Paris. The program of phonograph music, heard as far away as Marseilles, caused a brief sensation.

Two years later, he broadcast a performance of "Cavalleria Rusticana" from the stage of the Metropolitan Opera House in New York. This was the first "live" broadcast of an opera. Unfortunately, the audience was limited to 50 listeners in the New York metropolitan area and one music-loving wireless operator on the *S.S. Avon* at sea.

But success of the audion also brought many troubles for De Forest. He had become an easy target for promoters. Frenzied stock selling had already landed him, and the companies to which he loaned his name, in considerable hot water. He had been involved in a patent infringement suit with Fessenden; had heard his audion derided in a courtroom as a hoax; been told by an eminent judge to "get a common, garden variety of job and stick to it," and had narrowly escaped criminal conviction for stock fraud.

During his lifetime, in which he was continuously entangled in patent litigation, he made and lost four fortunes.

Further misfortune came in 1911. The American Marconi Co. instituted a suit against him for infringement, while dissatisfied stockholders in his radio company complained they had been swindled. The bad publicity of the trial, in which De Forest was exonerated but his associates convicted, ruined his company beyond repair.

Meanwhile, he had succeeded in increasing the capacity of the audion to amplify signals up to 27 times. In 1913, he was able to sell the wire-telephone right of the audion to the American Telephone and Telegraph Co. for $50,000, retaining the right to manufacture audion tubes for sale to hams.

LEE DE FOREST

Early programming
was chaotic,
sporadic, unimaginative

When the U.S. entered World War I, the government ordered all amateur wireless equipment dismantled and De Forest began making equipment for military use. In 1917, he sold his remaining rights in the audion to AT&T.

After the war, leadership soon passed from his hands. He retired from radio and concentrated on other areas of electronics.

If De Forest is the father of radio, David Sarnoff was surely his prophet. Born in Russia in 1891, Sarnoff came to the U.S. at the age of 9, taught himself the Morse Code, and became an operator with the Marconi Co. By 1916, when he was 25, he had become assistant traffic manager at Marconi. In that year he submitted to his boss a memo which became the Magna Carta of radio:

"I have in mind a plan of development which would make radio a household utility in the same sense as the piano or phonograph. The idea is to bring music into the home by wireless."

He went on to predict almost every phase of radio programming: music, entertainment, sports, news and special events.

Sarnoff suggested the radio music box could be sold to the public for about $75 and he thought one million sets might be sold within three years. In this respect his vision was short-sighted. The Radio Corporation of America, set up in 1919 with Sarnoff as commercial manager, reported sales of $84 million during the two year period from 1922 to 1924.

After World War I, there were about 10,000 hams in the U.S. Their interest became a major factor in the development of radio because they made up the first audience.

Dr. Frank Conrad, an engineer at Westinghouse, began to broadcast from his garage in Pittsburgh in 1919. Ham audiences soon complained about his dull monologues and asked him to play phonograph records. As time went on, his fans became critical and he began to receive mail saying, "Play something lively" or "How about playing 'My Old Kentucky Home'?"

Thus began the career of Station KDKA, the first commercial station in the U.S. Others followed shortly: WBL (Detroit); WJZ and WOR (Newark); KYW (Chicago) and WEAF (New York). Within a few years the number of stations approached 1000.

By 1929, the price of a set remained as high as $135, but there were over 12 million owners.

In those early days one epoch-making broadcast followed another. Listeners heard the Dempsey-Carpentier fight, the first World Series broadcast in 1921, messages from Presidents Harding and Wilson, and the Republican and Democratic national conventions in 1924.

In between the special treats were long hours of dull talks — "The Art of Billiards," "How to Raise Bees" — screechy songs and ear-splitting instrumental numbers.

Musical performers, most of whom were unpaid, left a great deal to be desired. Most frequent was the studio pianist who filled in dead air time and appeared under different names a half dozen times a day.

Almost every singer was flamboyantly billed — "Princess Waukomis, contralto, full-blooded Indian princess" or "Solos by B. Paladino, mandolin player, recently arrived from Russia."

There was no such thing as regular programming. Stations went silent during lunch and dinner hours, so that its staff might eat. No broadcasting was done on Sundays or holidays.

Early reception was chaotic, requiring dedication on the part of the listener. A multitude of stations, particularly in metropolitan areas, operated on the same wave band, jumbling and blanketing each other's signals. It was common to hear two or three programs at once.

Secretary of Commerce Herbert Hoover urged all stations to abide by a gentlemen's agreement but his words went unheeded and even brought a telegram from the broadcasting evangelist, Aimee Semple McPherson. It called on him to tell his "minions of Satan to leave my stations alone."

Order arrived in 1926 when Congress created the Federal Radio Commission. It was superseded by the Federal Communications Commission in 1934.

Commercials have been a part of broadcasting almost from the beginning. The question of how to pay for the new medium brought a variety of suggestions. Initially, David Sarnoff thought costs should be met by a levy on set manufacturers and, later on, he hoped to find a billionaire philanthropist to subsidize the

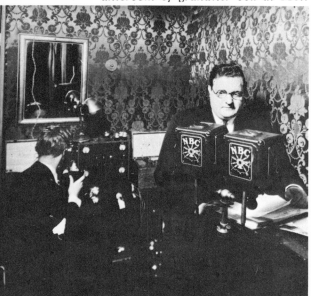

In early 1930s Milton Cross hosted Metropolitan Opera broadcasts from anteroom of grandtier box at Met.

Sports events always attracted wide radio audiences. Babe Ruth, Graham McNamee in '27 over NBC Radio.

operation. Secretary Hoover didn't have anything as specific in mind but he was sure the American public would never permit the medium "to be drowned in advertising chatter."

Nevertheless, on August 28, 1922, AT&T's Station WEAF broadcast the first commercial. It was a stodgy, 10-minute talk extolling Hawthorne Hall, a new cooperative apartment house in Jackson Heights, N.Y. The talk brought complaints from listeners and the press, but AT&T continued to build its roster of sponsors. Four months later it had 16, including a department store, an advertising agency and the YMCA.

At first each station broadcast only its own programs, but soon they began to link together for specials. AT&T was in the most favorable position for network programming because it had the advantage of its telephone lines. By 1925 it owned 26 stations, as far west as Kansas City, which were regularly hooked up. AT&T refused others use of the company's lines.

As a result, RCA's stations were forced to use telegraph lines which were not constructed to carry voice. Quality was poor and RCA fared badly.

In 1926, AT&T withdrew from radio, selling its stations to RCA which immediately set up the National Broadcasting Company. Since it then owned two stations in many cities, RCA opened a second

In April, 1939, NBC televised the formal dedication of RCA pavilion by David Sarnoff at World's Fair.

chain which it called the Blue Network. The original chain was dubbed Red Network.

In January, 1927, a rival, United Independent Broadcasters, Inc., appeared. When the Columbia Phonograph Company assumed control, it became known as the Columbia Broadcasting System.

Mutual Broadcasting Company came on the scene in 1931 and, in 1943 when the government ruled that a company could not operate more than one network, NBC's Blue Network was sold and re-named the American Broadcasting Company.

The Amalgamated Broadcasting System, organized by comedian Ed Wynn in 1933, has long been forgotten. Wynn went to Hollywood, leaving the details to others. The opening night appeared to have been arranged by the Marx Brothers.

Five thousand New Yorkers, selected at random from the phone book, tried to squeeze into a studio seating 200. Pastrami sandwiches and beer were *sold* to the guests. The master of ceremonies challenged an irate newspaper reporter to a duel, and a Federal radio commissioner got stuck between floors in an elevator. ABS forgot to pay its employees and the operation expired a month later.

If radio didn't upgrade the cultural and intellectual life of its listeners, it wasn't for lack of trying. Arturo Toscanini presided over the NBC Orchestra and the Metropolitan Opera was available every Saturday. Such news commentators as Lowell Thomas, Elmer Davis and William Shirer analyzed current events.

NBC and CBS conducted schools of the air. Discussion programs like Town Meeting of the Air and documentaries such as March of Time were plentiful.

On the other side of the coin, of course, were Gang Busters and its ilk, as well as that vast afternoon wasteland of soap operas.

Aside from elections, prize fights and President Roosevelt's Fireside Chats, the most popular programs were variety shows.

In 1929, Rudy Vallee pioneered the first variety program, a tabloid edition of vaudeville with music, comedy and light drama. His Fleischmann's Yeast Hour and his theme song, "A Vagabond Lover," ushered in the Great Depression.

In the world of variety shows there were no soup lines, no goose-

stepping dictators, no budget deficits. Only Jack Benny, Kate Smith, Burns and Allen, Fred Allen, Edgar Bergen and Charlie McCarthy, and Fibber McGee and Molly.

A startling event in 1938 called widespread attention to a fact that many in the industry were already aware of: radio was a dangerous and powerful weapon.

On a quiet Sunday evening, several million citizens heard a series of news bulletins and listened to eye witness accounts describing an invasion by Martians armed with death rays. Orson Welles and his Mercury Theater had prefaced the program by announcing it was a dramatic performance of H. G. Wells' "War of the Worlds."

New Jersey highways were flooded with people fleeing the nonexistent invaders and hospitals treated patients for shock.

A week after NBC made its debut in 1926, David Sarnoff announced that "television is just around the corner." In 1930, RCA began experimental television in New York and, a year later, CBS inaugurated the first regular TV programs.

At the beginning of World War II, there were 7500 TV sets in New York City. Four years after the war, there were 1½ million sets and 64 TV stations in the U.S.

The change in American life was obvious: increased consumption of cigarettes and liquor, re-arrangement of living room furniture, and tray dinners. The home enjoyed a revival as the center of family life but nobody talked much.

Radio listening declined abruptly. The industry feared it had nourished a parricide and predicted that radio was doomed.

On the 40th anniversary of his invention of the audion, Lee De Forest bitterly assailed the broadcasters. "What have you done with my child?" he asked. He had conceived of it as an instrument to upgrade the mass intelligence but he said it had become "a stench in the nostrils of the gods of the ionosphere."

Despite De Forest's indictment, much of his vision had come true. Radio brought within the reach of everyone an immense range of experience. It was available every day, whether one lived in Manhattan or on a snow-bound farm. Most important, by shattering regional and cultural barriers, it transformed the U.S. into a cohesive community for the first time.

COMPUTERS COME OF AGE

Electronic data processing, miracle of modern technology, was spawned in basement of University of Pennsylvania's Moore School of Engineering

WHEN ALDOUS HUXLEY wrote *Brave New World* in 1931, he envisioned a Utopia of the future with test tube babies; rockets hurtling passengers around the globe and happy people tranquilized by mass hypnosis.

It is interesting that Huxley's classic was not able to foresee two achievements for which the 20th Century will probably be best remembered: the harnessing of atomic energy and the development of the electronic computer. Both had been scientific goals for many years. Both became practical realities with the scientific spurt triggered by World War II.

The age of the computer began only two decades ago in the basement of the Moore School of Engineering at the University of Pennsylvania where the first electronic computer was built. Today, the worldwide market for electronic computers and data processing equipment is estimated at about $3 billion annually.

Computers have been a natural target for fanciful names — robots, giant brains, thinking machines. Whether or not computers can think is a matter of semantics, but there is little debate about their ability to solve problems infinitely faster and more accurately than the human brain.

Computers are now vital tools in space exploration, business, government, transportation, medicine, education and industry.

On an everyday level computers affect most people's lives by writing bills, calculating pay checks and unsnarling traffic jams. Computers have their lighter sides, too, and have been known to write poetry, compose music and play a wily game of chess.

In 1942, members of the Moore School of Engineering were busy computing artillery firing tables for the Army Ordnance Dept. Dr. John W. Mauchly, an associate professor of electrical engineering, found his methods of calculation frustratingly slow. The Johns Hopkins-educated professor began to wonder if the new science of electronics could be applied to the ancient science of mathematics.

Mauchly conducted a few experiments but because his fields were physics and electrical engineering, he had limited success. He needed an electronics expert.

Among his co-workers he found 24-year old research associate John Presper Eckert, who had recently received his bachelor's degree. Eckert, too, was dissatisfied with their hand calculations, although they were supplemented by an analog computer. They complained late into the evenings over coffee about the slowness and inaccuracy of their equipment.

The two men agreed that electronics, used primarily in radio and rudimentary television at that time, deserved broader application than just in the entertainment field. Mauchly knew more about numerical calculations and their mechanization than Eckert did. On the other hand, Eckert knew more about circuit design. Together they outlined plans for an electronic computer

JOHN P. ECKERT

JOHN W. MAUCHLY

ENIAC, world's first all-electronic digital computer, weighed 30 tons and contained 18,000 vacuum tubes.

which they hoped could perform at fantastic speeds.

They submitted their ideas to the Army in April, 1943. Since World War II had begun, any means for speeding work was welcomed and the Army gave the University funds to work on the computer. By July, 1943, the project got underway with Eckert as project engineer and Mauchly as consultant together with a team of twelve scientists.

Three years and 200,000 man-hours later, the first all-electronic digital computer was finished. It was officially christened Electronic Numerical Integrator and Calculator, a mouthful which they quickly shortened to ENIAC.

The 30-ton giant looked awesome. So large that it filled the entire basement of the engineering building, it contained 500,000 hand-soldered connections which linked 18,000 vacuum tubes. It consumed as much electricity as a large broadcasting station. A great deal of the wiring had to be changed each time it was given a new problem.

But, it was 1000 times faster than any previous numerical calculator. It could solve a problem in two hours which would normally take 100 engineers a full year to compute.

It differed from all previous calculators because it used vacuum tubes instead of electromechanical switches. Secondly, it possessed enough logic to solve problems by making decisions or choices as it went along.

ENIAC was put to work at the Aberdeen Proving Ground in Maryland in August, 1947. It solved many of the trajectory problems of 280 mm. atomic cannon, computed ballistics tables and eventually worked with weather prediction, the hydrogen bomb, cosmic rays and wind tunnel design.

Meanwhile a group of scientists under Dr. Howard Aiken were constructing a semi-electronic computer at Harvard University. International Business Machines helped build the Harvard Mark I, a general purpose digital computer. It was almost entirely controlled by mechanical switches. Most of the components were standard IBM parts.

As early as 1936, before he joined the Harvard faculty to teach math, Dr. Aiken had dreamed of building a large-scale computer but found it difficult to interest anyone else. He learned from reading *Passages from the Life of a Philosopher* by the 19th Century mathematician Charles Babbage that his idea had been thought of at least a century before.

In 1937, IBM came to his rescue and, with the help of IBM engineers, he started to build a computer. The project lasted over six years and cost $250,000. When finally assembled in 1944, Mark I weighed 35 tons and contained 500 miles of wire. It performed with great accuracy but its mechanical parts limited its speed and flexibility. IBM presented the machine to Harvard, whereupon it was immediately comandeered by the Navy for gunnery and ballistics design.

Although the electronic computer is a recent development, the history of computers stretches far back in time. The first computer must have been a nameless Neolithic man who learned to count up to ten on his

Business firms comprise 45% of U.S. market
for data processing systems;
military uses include missile tracking, logistics and ballistics

fingers. Then came such devices as pebbles laid on the ground and beads strung on wire. The abacus was the standard calculating device of all antique civilizations. It is still used in the Far East and in some Chinese laundries in the U.S.

In 1642, 19-year old Blaise Pascal tired of adding long columns of figures at his father's office in Rouen, France. He invented the first adding machine, a gear-driven apparatus the size of a shoebox, which counted numbers on a series of notched wheels.

In 1812, Charles Babbage, a mathematics professor at Oxford, designed a "difference engine" capable

of carrying out series of arithmetic operations without an operator instead of doing just one calculation at a time.

He spent his own fortune and the British government's money in a vain effort to construct the engine, but his concept was too far ahead of the technology of that day. He is generally acknowledged as the first to envision a modern computing machine.

Part of the embittered Babbage's problem was that he was notoriously incoherent when he spoke about his beloved engine. His most loyal supporter was Lady Lovelace, daughter of Lord Byron and a competent

mathematician in her own right. She served as interpreter and popularized his theories. The two became rather chummy and tried to develop an infallible system for betting on horse races. Their mathematics were sound but the horses were not.

The U.S. Bureau of the Census did much to advance calculating systems. In 1872, Charles Seaton, a chief clerk, invented the first mechanical tabulator which simultaneously registered horizontal and vertical sums. Another bureau official, Dr. Herman Hollerith, came up with the first punch-card tabulator in 1887.

An important step took place in

Babbage's Difference Engine could carry out series of arithmetic calculations without human operator. Model (right) was prototype of today's mechanical calculator.

Oxford mathematics professor Charles Babbage ushered in era of the computer. His Analytical Engine (below) was the first practical working model of a computer.

UNIVAC project engineer examines microminiaturized computer model which weighs less than 17 pounds.

1919 when W. H. Eccles and F. W. Jordan discovered an electronic trigger circuit. It is the basis of the "flip flop" mechanism in electronic computers and is the device which enables them to count.

In 1925, Dr. Vannevar Bush, then professor of electrical engineering at the Massachusetts Institute of Technology, designed and built a successful differential analyzer. This first large - scale computing machine solved lengthy and intricate differential equations in a few minutes. Although the M.I.T. computer permitted faster solutions than ever before, it was handicapped by levels and wheels which slowed down its speed.

New strides in the early 1940s made it possible to perform electronically computations the differential analyzer did mechanically. With the completion of Mark I in 1944 and ENIAC in 1946, a new family of high-speed digital computers came into existence.

By the time ENIAC had been built, it was almost obsolete. During its construction Eckert and Mauchly discovered new and better methods and a second ENIAC was never constructed. However, the original machine served well at Aberdeen until 1955 when it was donated to the Smithsonian Institution.

In the meantime the two pioneers set up their own company, Eckert-Mauchly Computer Corp. and, by 1950, produced a second computer. BINAC was faster and cheaper to operate than ENIAC. It handled magnetic tape instead of punched cards and featured an internal self-checking system.

BINAC introduced two elements which were to make future models more efficient. It used magnetic tape to store information and it replaced vacuum tubes with crystal diodes, enabling a reduction in size and an increase in speed.

With BINAC the computer began to shape up as a development which might have commercial applications. (The original reason for computers had been to solve mathematical problems.)

Soon it became evident that other information might be processed as well. Since BINAC had enormous speed and ability to follow extensive lines of logical reasoning, it was ideally suited to handle large quantities of routine business information.

Remington Rand, Inc. (now Sperry Rand) acquired the Eckert-Mauchly Corp. in 1950 and both men went to work for Rand. Today, Eckert is vice president of UNIVAC Division of Sperry Rand Corp. Mauchly is president of Mauchly Associates, a firm which develops special-purpose computers and functions as a management consultant.

Shortly after BINAC, Eckert and Mauchly started to build UNIVAC (Universal Automatic Computer), the first computer designed to handle business data. Its ability to deal equally well with numbers and descriptive material made it specially attractive for commercial use.

The first UNIVAC was delivered to the U.S. Bureau of the Census in 1951 where it was used to process statistics. In 1954, a business concern bought a UNIVAC.

The machine came into the public spotlight on election night 1952 when it predicted a landslide victory for General Eisenhower. Despite hasty apologies by the TV commentators, UNIVAC turned out to be unerringly correct.

Electronic data processing came of age with UNIVAC. Computers teetered on the brink of becoming a big business but, as late as 1950, many believed the market would be small. It was estimated that perhaps a few dozen would take care of all scientific and business needs. (Over 17,000 computers are now in use.)

This miscalculation was accepted by many at that time, including IBM. After two or three years of indecision, IBM, under Thomas Watson, Jr., plunged into the field. Today, IBM reportedly has 75% of the computer market, far outstripping competition from Sperry Rand, RCA, Control Data, GE, NCR, Burroughs and Honeywell.

Business data processing systems also account for more than 45% of the present market. Initially, the machines were given routine functions — payroll, inventory, billing, record-keeping. Marketing, research and production were next.

Now computers help companies predict the future by calculating the effects of changing forces on a complex situation. In this way they influence such decisions as whether or not to invest in a new plant.

The second largest chunk of the market (40%) is represented by the U.S. Government. The military uses computers for rocket and submarine tracking, in logistics and ballistics, and in early warning systems for guarding against surprise attack.

The amount of information processed by the various government departments has increased several hundred-fold since the first UNIVAC was installed at the Census Bureau 13 years ago. Computers have provided the chief means of coping with it.

In the field of science and engineering (15% of the market), computers are used to control industrial processes; as a tool in atomic physics, chemistry and medicine; and as a vital partner in satellite checking and space flight communications.

Perhaps a harbinger of things to come is a talking political candidate named ELPSAC. The Thermodynamic Computer Corp. describes it as a solid-state humanoid, using magnetic memory components, high-speed recall relays, political environment sensors and instantaneous reactance circuits.

ELPSAC's magnetic drum can pre-store characteristics of 25,000 faces. When it meets a voter, it comes up with his name, number of children, how his grandfather voted in 1888, and a myriad of other uncanny facts. It also shakes hands, kisses babies (with sanitary disposable lips) and makes luncheon speeches.

So far, ELPSAC is still a pilot model, but there's no telling what might happen if it decided to run for office.

BIRTH OF THE ATOMIC AGE

Italian-born physicist Enrico Fermi unleashed the
atom's mighty fury and discovered the world's newest energy source

ON THE CAMPUS of the University of Chicago stands a medieval-looking wall, complete with ancient battlements and turrets. Its facade conceals the west stands of Stagg Field, a football stadium unused since the sport was outlawed at the school 25 years ago.

A plaque — the birth certificate of the atomic age — has been erected on the sooty wall:

ON DECEMBER 2, 1942 MAN
ACHIEVED HERE THE
FIRST SELF-SUSTAINED
CHAIN REACTION AND
THEREBY INITIATED THE
CONTROLLED RELEASE OF
NUCLEAR ENERGY

On that afternoon, Dr. Arthur Compton of the University of Chicago made a cryptic, unrehearsed telephone call to Dr. James Bryant Conant, president of Harvard and head of the U.S. Office of Scientific Research and Development. James Bond could have done no better.

"The Italian navigator has reached the New World," said Dr. Compton.

"And how did he find the natives?"

"Very friendly."

The navigator was Enrico Fermi, Italian-born physicist who had emigrated to the U.S. in 1939 a few weeks after winning the Nobel Prize.

On that historic day in 1942 he succeeded in releasing the inexhaustible energy locked in the atom. Since man first rubbed two sticks together thousands of years ago, every form of energy on earth had been created by the sun whether it came from wood, coal, oil or water.

Fermi and the team of men and women working under him were the first to tap a new source of energy,

one that did not originate in the sun. The actual amount of energy released that day was scarcely enough to power a flashlight, but its implications were tremendous.

Just three years before Fermi himself had predicted it might take 25 years before the splitting of the atom could have practical application. But the necessities of war decreed otherwise.

On August 6, 1945, President Truman announced to a stunned world that the U.S. had dropped an atomic bomb equal to the power of 20,000 tons of TNT on Hiroshima.

But in peace time equally sinister implications soon became evident.

In January, 1946, the political columnists Joseph and Stewart Alsop wrote: "Even now . . . no one has grasped the fullness of the change in world power relationships wrought by scientists of World War II."

Atomic energy held out to mankind the greatest choice in history: to obliterate civilization or to create a paradise on earth. Peacefully used, nuclear energy can supply the world with limitless energy for more than a billion years; create water supplies; develop the earth's mineral wealth; control the weather; and revolutionize industry, medicine, and agriculture.

Fermi's feat was the culmination

DR. ENRICO FERMI

of a half-century of endeavor by many scientists in many lands.

It began in 1905 in Bern, Switzerland, with an obscure clerk in the Swiss Patent Office who propounded a theory of relativity. Albert Einstein was the first to realize that mass and energy are interchangeable; an enormous amount of energy is locked up in a minute quantity of matter.

Knowledge of this cosmic treasure house was accepted for several decades. But all the most brilliant scientists, Einstein included, believed that the smashing of an atom and the subsequent release of its energy was beyond the reach of man.

So it was only logical that, in 1934, when Enrico Fermi first split the atom at the University of Rome, he failed to realize what he had done.

In January, 1934, Fermi received news that the famous French husband and wife team of physicists, the Joliot-Curies, had discovered artificial radioactivity by bombarding aluminum with fast alpha particles. He decided to try the experiment himself, except that he used recently-discovered neutrons as projectiles.

Always a systematic man, he planned to test every one of the 92 elements starting with hydrogen. By summer Fermi reached element 92, uranium. He discovered that the uranium became radioactive and at least one of the radioactive products was none of the existing elements close to uranium. Fermi decided he had discovered a new element with the atomic number 93, an element which does not exist on earth because it is too unstable.

For more than five years scientists repeated Fermi's uranium experiments thousands of times and came up with the same answer, so great was the power of pre-conceived ideas.

Had Fermi been aware that he had split the atom, possibilities of an atomic bomb would have been obvious back in 1934. This could have given Hitler an arsenal with which to rule the world.

After the war *New York Times* reporter William L. Laurence asked Fermi how he had missed.

"It was a thin piece of aluminum foil, 3 mils thick, that stopped us all from seeing what actually took place," he answered.

In 1936, two Swiss physicists who were repeating Fermi's experiment left out the foil. The incredible reac-

University of Chicago's Stagg Field was birthplace of the atomic age. Nuclear reactor built by Fermi (below) was dismantled in 1943, then reassembled at Argonne National Laboratory where it is still operating.

tion which followed caused them to agree "the damned instrument is sparking" and they hastily replaced the foil.

Enrico Fermi was born in Rome in 1901. His father, a man without formal education, worked for the railroad. His mother had been a school teacher.

As a child he was shy, untidy, and not especially outstanding in school. He wrote poorly and recited miserably. Both his mother and teachers thought he wasn't very intelligent.

When he was 14 his older brother, to whom he was very close, died suddenly of a throat infection. His interest in science dates back from this period when he found solace in his studies, especially mathematics and physics.

Aside from his love for outdoor sports, he devoted most of his time to reading and experiments. With crude apparatus he and a friend worked out a theory of the gyroscope from the spinning motion of a top.

At 17 he wrote an impressive

paper on vibrating strings and won a scholarship to a college for outstanding students in Pisa.

Fermi received a degree of Doctor of Physics in 1922 and returned to Rome a few months before Mussolini and his Black Shirts took over. Perhaps he had an intimation of what the fascist regime would mean, for he announced to his family:

"Young people like me will have to emigrate."

Shortly afterwards he accepted a fellowship to study in Germany. Although he learned to speak German and had no financial worries, he felt uncomfortable among the Germans and returned to Italy within a year.

For several years he taught math and mechanics in Rome and Florence. Then, at the age of 25, he was named full Professor of Physics at the University of Rome. By this time he had achieved a considerable reputation in Italy and abroad. He had already published some 30 papers on theoretical physics, dealing

To have practical importance, Fermi had
to produce self-sustaining reaction

mainly with the behavior of molecules, atoms, and electrons.

Three years later honors began to come his way. He was elected to the Royal Academy of Italy and given the title of His Excellency, a designation which irritated him. Once, while on a skiing trip, he registered at a small hotel and the manager asked:

"Are you any relation to His Excellency Fermi?"

"A distant relative," Fermi replied.

"His Excellency often comes to this hotel," the manager informed him.

Fermi made several trips to the U.S. and South America where he had been invited to lecture. However, his main energies centered on his laboratory where he had gathered a brilliant group of young colleagues and where he conducted his experiments with neutrons.

First atomic bomb was detonated in 1945 over lonely desert terrain 50 miles from Alamogordo, N. Mex.

By 1938, the political situation in Italy had become unbearable to Fermi. Mussolini had invaded Ethiopia and Hitler was marching on the Rhineland. The alliance of the two dictators resulted in a new manifesto: Jews do not belong to the Italian race.

Since Fermi's wife Laura was Jewish the Fermis decided to leave Italy. Fermi wrote to four American universities for a position. To avoid suspicion and censorship, he mailed them in four different villages outside Rome. If their intentions to emigrate had been discovered, they feared passports would be withheld.

All four colleges extended jobs and Fermi accepted an offer from Columbia University.

But an unexpected development a few weeks later provided a perfect solution for an unobtrusive exit. Fermi won the Nobel Prize in physics for his work with slow neutrons.

With his wife, two children and a nursemaid, Fermi set out for Stockholm to receive his award in December, 1938. It was just as well he had no intention of returning, for the Italian press castigated him for two unforgivable crimes. He failed to give the Fascist salute to the King of Sweden and he wore bourgeois tails instead of a uniform.

A few weeks later Fermi stood on the deck of the S.S. Franconia and looked at the New York skyline.

"We have founded the American branch of the Fermi family," he said to his wife.

He eagerly assumed the duties of his new position at Columbia, continuing his basic studies on the nucleus of the atom. But less than three weeks after Fermi arrived in the U.S. a bombshell exploded in the international scientific community.

Two scientists at the Kaiser Wilhelm Institute in Berlin cautiously announced they had split the uranium atom and they christened the new process "nuclear fission."

Their announcement was cautious for two reasons: Otto Hahn and Strassmann were chemists and they knew that according to all the accepted concepts of physics their feat was impossible. Second, as chemists,

they were reluctant to challenge such illustrious physicists as Einstein, Bohr and Fermi.

Their experiments were essentially the same as Fermi's except they used new techniques of radiochemistry. When Fermi had bombarded element 92, uranium, he thought he had created a new element, 93.

When the Germans did the same, they realized they had produced elements 56, 57, and 58 — barium, lanthanum, and cerium. At first they did not believe what they saw, but repeated tests made them fairly positive they had split the uranium atom.

Fermi had not been able to see the woods for the trees in 1934. Now everything became clear. Yet he realized that splitting the atom did not necessarily mean that nuclear fission would be a practical source of energy. He knew that if it were to have any importance there would have to be a self-sustaining reaction — chain reaction.

Fission must produce further fission, like a chain of firecrackers, until energy was built up. He immediately set out to find out how.

Ironically, it was the physicists, usually thought of as ivy-towered and absent-minded, who first made the U.S. government aware of the possibilities of atomic energy for war. Most of them were exiles from Nazi oppression: Alfred Einstein from Germany, Fermi from Italy, and Edward Teller and Leo Szilard from Hungary. They were the first to sound the alarm.

The frightening rise of the Third Reich and the fact that fission had been discovered in Germany led them to believe Hitler's scientists were working on atomic energy for military weapons.

Actually, it was found out after the war, the Germans were years behind.

Rousing the government and the Army was not easy. In March, 1939, a bare three months after the fission announcement, Fermi met with the Navy Department. In halting English he briefed the military men on the implications. The Navy brass listened politely and said, in effect, "Don't call us, we'll call you."

A more high-level approach was thought necessary. In August of the same year a letter to President Roosevelt was drawn up. Albert Einstein was chosen to sign it. It said, in part:

"... it may become possible to set up a nuclear chain reaction in a large mass of uranium, by which vast amounts of power ... would be generated. Now it appears almost certain that this could be achieved in the immediate future.

"This new phenomenon would also lead to the construction of bombs ..."

President Roosevelt immediately set up an Advisory Committee on Uranium and appropriated $6000 for Fermi's research.

The scientists voluntarily imposed a cloak of secrecy over their work and retired to Pupin Hall at Columbia. For the next two years Fermi used his meager $6000 bankroll to build an atomic furnace made of layers of graphite interspersed with chunks of uranium oxide.

His object: to prove that a slow and controlled chain reaction would light an atomic fire or an uncontrolled reaction explode a bomb.

The decision to make an all-out effort in atomic energy was not reached until the day before Pearl Harbor. The next day the U.S. was at war and Fermi became an enemy alien. Nevertheless he was judged trustworthy and allowed to continue his work.

1942 saw the beginning of the race against time. Early in the year Fermi's project was moved to the University of Chicago and he set up shop in an abandoned squash court under the stadium. Round-the-clock construction of the reactor or "pile" started in November and, by December 2, it became evident the reactor was ready for the ultimate test.

The squash court that day was a combination of the ridiculous and the sublime. Although it was unlikely that the fire would get out of control, every precaution had been taken. The pile was encased in an absurd-looking square balloon. Two physicists stood on a platform over the furnace holding buckets of cadmium solution in case of an accident. They were called the suicide squad.

At 9:45 A.M. Fermi ordered the first of the electrically-operated rods withdrawn from the pile a few inches at a time. By mid-afternoon, when the last rod was pulled out, he closed his slide rule and announced:

"The reaction is self-sustaining."

His tense face broke into a smile. For 28 minutes the atomic fire was allowed to burn and then Fermi gave the signal for it to be shut off. He had succeeded in releasing the energy of the atom and controlling it at his will.

One of the physicists produced a bottle of Chianti and the group drank a silent toast from paper cups.

At a party in the Fermi home that evening Mrs. Fermi was mystified to hear each of her husband's co-workers shake his hand and offer congratulations. Her repeated inquiries brought no answers. Finally Leona Woods, the only woman physicist in Fermi's group, whispered:

"He has sunk a Japanese admiral."

In the following days she made futile attempts to clear up the mystery.

"Enrico, did you really sink a Japanese admiral?"

"Did I?" he would say with a poker face.

Mrs. Fermi found her answers after Hiroshima.

Meanwhile President Roosevelt had established a special Army Engineer organization to assume responsibilty for construction of an atomic bomb. It was called Manhattan Engineer District and Major General Leslie Groves was named its head.

The wheels started to turn quickly. Du Pont began producing plutonium at Hanford, Washington, while separation of fissionable uranium got underway at Oak Ridge, Tennessee.

A secluded spot was needed to build a laboratory where the design and construction of the bomb would be carried out. This was the most secret aspect of the project. Dr. J. Robert Oppenheimer, who was in charge of this work, suggested an area near his parents' home in New Mexico.

On a lonely mesa 65 miles from Santa Fe, the town of Los Alamos was born. The town was not marked on any map; it had no official status; its residents could not vote. It did not exist.

By 1944, scientists from every part of the U.S. and England, Fermi included, had disappeared to Los Alamos.

It is said that when General Groves summoned his officers for instructions on how to deal with the extraordinary galaxy of scientific stars at Los Alamos, he began his speech with an affectionate introduction:

"At great expense we have gathered on this mesa the largest collection of crackpots ever seen."

All prominent scientists were assigned aliases. Enrico Fermi became Eugene Farmer. He also acquired a body-guard, an Illinois-born Italian named John Baudino who was a lawyer by profession. Baudino displayed a fine aptitude for physics and soon learned how to operate the original Stagg Field reactor, which led Fermi to remark:

"Soon Baudino will need a body-guard. He knows too much!"

A few minutes before dawn on July 16, 1945, an unearthly purple and orange ball of fire erupted from the sands 50 miles from Alamogordo, New Mexico. The giant column took the shape of an immense mushroom. Thunder roared and reverbrated through the desert. The bomb worked.

Three weeks later a B-29 named Enola Gay took off from Tinian Island in the Marianas. Destination: Hiroshima.

The goals of the Manhattan District Project had been reached. Never before had such a colossal task been completed in such a short time.

On New Year's Eve 1946, Fermi returned to Chicago. Now an American citizen, he became Professor of Physics at the University of Chicago and plunged into a completely new field of research, investigation of the meson. He also took time out from his work to teach physics to freshmen students.

In 1946, he received the Congressional Medal of Merit for his help in developing the atomic bomb.

Late in 1954, the Atomic Energy Commission set up a special award of $25,000 for contributions to the controlled release of nuclear energy. Enrico Fermi was named the first recipient. Unknown to the public, Fermi was already in an advanced stage of cancer. Twelve days after he received the award he died at the age of 53.

To honor his memory and to reward others for advancing atomic science, the AEC then created the annual Enrico Fermi Award: a gold medal, a citation, and $50,000 tax-free. Seven men since Fermi had won this prize, including Edward Teller and J. Robert Oppenheimer.

For better or for worse, the Italian navigator had unlocked the door to the Atomic Age.